JOHN KENNETH GALBRAITH

CONTEMPORARY ECONOMISTS

General Editor: John Pheby, Professor of Political Economy,
De Montfort University, Leicester, England

The *Contemporary Economists* series is designed to present the key ideas of the most important economists of this century. After an opening biographical chapter, the books in this series focus on the most interesting aspects of their subject's contribution to economics, thus providing original insights into their work. Students and academics alike will be fascinated by the wealth of these economists' contributions and will be able to look with fresh eyes on their discipline.

John Kenneth Galbraith

James Ronald Stanfield
Professor of Economics
Colorado State University
Fort Collins, Colorado

St. Martin's Press
New York

JOHN KENNETH GALBRAITH
Copyright © 1996 by James Ronald Stanfield
All rights reserved. No part of this book may be used or reproduced
in any manner whatsoever without written permission except in the
case of brief quotations embodied in critical articles or reviews.
For information, address:

St. Martin's Press, Scholarly and Reference Division,
175 Fifth Avenue, New York, N.Y. 10010

First published in the United States of America in 1996

Printed in Great Britain

ISBN 0–312–16151–4

Library of Congress Cataloging-in-Publication Data
Stanfield, J. Ron, 1945–
John Kenneth Galbraith / James Ronald Stanfield.
p.   cm.— (Contemporary economists)
Includes bibliographical references and index.
ISBN 0–312–16151–4
1. Galbraith, John Kenneth, 1908–   .   2. Economics—United
States—History—20th century.   I. Title.   II. Series.
HB119.G33S73   1996
330'.092—dc20   96–10527
                                                                CIP

To the Spring of 1967

Contents

Contents

Preface

The scope of this book is standard. The aim is to provide an intellectual portrait of John Kenneth Galbraith. The first chapter offers a brief biographical sketch of Galbraith and some selections from his prose to exhibit his celebrated wit. Chapter 2 surveys his work prior to the first installment of his central trilogy in 1958. Chapter 3 examines *The Affluent Society* and Chapters 4 and 5 are devoted to his magnum opus, *The New Industrial State*. Chapter 6 discusses the final book of his trilogy, *Economics and the Public Purpose*. Chapter 7 provides a summary of the policy recommendations of the Galbraithian System and Chapter 8 places Galbraith's work in the context of intellectual history.

Galbraith may well be the most famous economist of the last half century. Yet there is no doubt that he also represents a very obscure American institutionalist tradition. This paradox I cannot resolve for the reader. Perhaps it is merely a by-product of Galbraith's desire to augment his sales by avoiding academic notation or by exaggerating the originality of his work. Perhaps his success speaks to a desire of the public for literate, relevant economics in an age of intense formalism in the profession. As noted, I cannot say. The Galbraithian Paradox puzzles me.

J Ron S

Acknowledgments

I appreciate the confidence that John Pheby and Giovanna Davitti accorded me in commissioning this book, and their forbearance at my missing the deadline for submitting it.

I dedicate this book to the Spring of 1967. In that youthful season, I encountered the influences that once and for all set my life course.

The book is offered as partial repayment for one of my great intellectual debts. The work of Ken Galbraith has fundamentally shaped my career. Either he rescued me from entrée into the comfortable complacency of the neoclassical fold or, more likely given my own constitution, from egress to another walk of life. I also very much appreciate Ken's generous permission to quote freely from his many books and essays.

But as Galbraith came from a flow of events and interpretations so also I had been prepared to be his receptive reader. I cannot imagine anyone having a better basic education than I received in the Tarrant County Texas public school system. I especially remember Anna Ruth Leach, Billy Tyler, Joan Dyer, and Derema McCulley.

I benefitted from a truly outstanding economics faculty at the University of Texas at Arlington. Tom Committee provided me a thorough and lively grounding in the microeconomic analysis of choice and markets. Ted Whitesell introduced me to the issues of the state's economic role and made me memorize the classic treatise of Richard Musgrave. Though I did not develop the basis they provided in mathematical economics and the quantitative investigation of regional economics, I appreciated the skill and friendship with which Paul Hayashi and Walt Mullendore offered them to me. I never fully recovered from the excitement that John McCall brought to the Keynesian model nor from the thoroughness with which Ghazi Duwaji insisted that I learn it.

Most specifically in regard to the present book, I am indebted as well to two other professors whose classes I had the privilege of taking in the Spring of 1967. In a class in the history of economic thought, Joe Ashby introduced me not only to the field that became my major interest but also to *The Affluent Society*. Dick Shuttee made me aware of Richard Lester, Betty Friedan, and the statistical abstract in a labor economics course. From the two of them I came to respect the evolution of ideas and culture, to mistrust complacency, to value descriptive statistics, to appreciate the task of anticipating social change and its attendant problems, and to see this task exemplified by the ferment in gender and family relationships in my lifetime. In retrospect, the principles of the institutional approach to economic analysis could scarcely have been conveyed with more wit, charm, and assiduity.

Thus occupied with what became an obdurate interest in economic institutions and their bearing on the political economic performance which is so fundamental to the quality of our lives, I eagerly awaited the June 1967 publication of *The New Industrial State*. I abused my position as flunky in the Arlington Texas public library and took the book out for personal edification before I catalogued it and made it accessible to the general taxpaying public. No doubt I cut myself in line ahead of a substantial wait list. No doubt also I malingered in my duties, hiding in the stacks while I worked through the book.

I cannot overemphasize the excitement with which I read the book, nor thus to the pivotal Spring of 1967. I was elated and transformed. To that point I had been a rather indifferent student, far more devoted to table tennis, bridge and gin card games, and the sensations of mind-altering substances, than to my studies. Whatever I may have accomplished in my academic career thereafter, and be it for the better or the worse, I owe to the awakening I experienced in the remarkable spring of 1967.

Finally, and most important of all, in that momentous spring of 1967, I became engaged to Jacqueline Bloom Stanfield, with whom I have since celebrated more than a quarter of a century of very earthly matrimony. Together we have withstood the test of time and all the challenges laid down for us by one of the most tumultuous eras in human history in so far as family and gender relationships are concerned. Bent but not broken, wounded but not vanquished, we march on together toward a future which is in some degree of our own making. For my part, I do so with infinite gratitude that since that beautiful season of 1967, I have never walked alone.

1 The Useful Economist

Ken Galbraith, like Thorstein Veblen, will be remembered and read when most of us Nobel Laureates will be buried in footnotes down in dusty library stacks.

(P.A. Samuelson, 1991)

This exemplary intellect has been the conscience of the economics profession (and sometimes its unhappy conscience) for more than a generation.

(S. Bowles, R. Edwards and W.G. Shepherd, 1989)

John Kenneth Galbraith, a leading scholar of the American institutionalist school, is the world's most famous economist in the second half of the twentieth century. Among American economists of any era, he is rivalled only by Thorstein Veblen for the introduction of phrases that take on a life of their own in the literate idiom. Countervailing power, the conventional wisdom, the affluent society, the new industrial state, and the technostructure have become familiar even beyond Galbraith's remarkably very wide readership. In the present century no other economist, excepting perhaps John Maynard Keynes, can claim so secure a place in the belles-lettres of the English-speaking world. This introductory chapter provides a brief biographical sketch of the man and his times, including an overview of his major works. It also offers a few tidbits to exemplify his fabled wit.

A MOST UNCONVENTIONAL ECONOMIST

Kenneth Galbraith was born in 1908 to a Scotch-Canadian family in a rural area of southern Ontario (see Galbraith, 1964b and 1981, the basis for this section). He was the second of four children born to William and Catherine Galbraith. The Galbraiths, like most of their neighbors, seem to have been sternly religious and staunchly dedicated to practical knowledge. William Galbraith was a farmer but at various times also ran an insurance agency and taught school; he was also actively engaged in Liberal Party politics at the local level.

Kenneth Galbraith recalls having had a happy childhood but there were some bleaker aspects (Lamson, 1991). His mother died when he was fourteen and the family struggled for some time adjusting to the trauma.

Galbraith found farm labor boring in large part and no doubt there was much of it to do. He was a gangly youth, without talent in schoolboy athletics, and somewhat isolated from his classmates. There are indications that he was prone to sudden mood swings and difficulties with a strict teacher/principal that suggest behavioral adjustment problems. No doubt these are early indications of the 'cloud' of depression for which Galbraith sought psychotherapy in the early 1950s. The experience of therapy revealed a longstanding pattern of cyclical 'euphoria and depression.' The insights gained left Galbraith with an abiding appreciation for the services of psychiatrists (Galbraith, 1981, pp. 304–5).

His academic struggles in high school behind him, Galbraith in the fall of 1926 enrolled at the Ontario Agricultural College which was then a part of the University of Toronto and is now the University of Guelph. For his bachelor's degree (1931, with distinction) he studied agricultural economics. Apparently to the chagrin of his Guelph faculty, this enabled him to secure funding at the University of California. There he studied agricultural economics, receiving his PhD in 1934, upon submission of a dissertation on public expenditures in California counties.

Berkeley was then a citadel of left-wing economics, housing the likes of Robert Brady, Leo Rogin, and others who supported migrant workers, small farmers, and trade unions (1981, ch. 2 and Galbraith 1971a, pp. 344– 60). In his studies Galbraith recalls studying Marshall, with whose legacy he has since staunchly dissented, and Thorstein Veblen, with whose legacy he is readily associated. In 1934 Galbraith left Berkeley and began his long – though frequently interrupted – tenure at Harvard University, where he is now an emeritus professor.

Galbraith, ever a man of his times, had his intellect forged in the midst of the tremulous eras of the first half of the century. He would have been aware of the First World War but the great American celebration that followed probably exerted greater force on his developing intellect. The exuberance of a business culture which had, not for the first nor the last time, forgotten all the lessons history made available surely caught his eye. The second of the great merger waves swept through industrial structure as the financial markets soared to enormously lofty heights. The inevitable crash and the catastrophe of the 1930s left an indelible imprint of just how unregulated the putatively self-regulating market really was.

Galbraith would have duly noted that the red scare was a serious obstacle to intelligent thought and action with regard to the reforms needed to widen, balance, and preserve the 1920s prosperity. Then and beyond, the fear of anytning remotely suggestive of socialism was enervating to political and intellectual discourse; the S-word itself became a cudgel with which one could silence one's adversaries.

The Second World War powerfully displayed the truth of Keynes's contentions about fiscal policy and the aggregate level of employment, output, and income. But Galbraith also came away convinced of the asymmetric and inflationary implications of utilizing aggregate demand policy without complementary attention to structural considerations. Such deeper concerns about the post-war prospect were lost in yet another great American celebration in the 1950s. This time the festivities were attended by an even more virulent red scare, the scourge of McCarthyism, abetted by a considerable number of ambitious politicians who never paid the price for condoning this rabid anti-communism.

The celebration spread to the economics profession and by the 1960s, the new economics was proclaimed to be virtually invincible in so far as its battle with the business cycle was concerned. This complacency among conventional economists was remarkable in light of the alarms sounded by dissenting economists, the grave problems of the international system, festering ecological destruction, and a political economic establishment that daily grew more out of touch with reality. Galbraith's outlook was much affected by the long political stagnation that began with the debacle in Vietnam and the tragi-comedy of Watergate. At the same time the stagflated 1970s brought home his message about the importance of economic structure.

Spurred considerably by vanity as well as the need to comment upon his times and reflect upon the possibilities of improvement, Galbraith became a very prolific author. In addition to his major trilogy, to be adumbrated momentarily, he has published more than two dozen books, including two novels, a co-authored book on Indian painting, memoirs, travelogues, political tracts, and several books on economic and intellectual history. He also collaborated on and narrated a Public Broadcasting System television series, 'The Age of Uncertainty'.

For his ability to actually sell copies of his books, the wags have intoned that Galbraith likely wrote *The Affluent Society* principally in order to join it. At any rate, for an academic economist to sell so many books to the wider intelligentsia is very unusual. On this count alone Galbraith would have to be regarded as truly a most unconventional economist.

But he is so in other respects, including his penchant for setting aside his academic career to devote large amounts of time to public service. Galbraith worked in the Department of Agriculture during the New Deal and in the Office of Price Administration (OPA) and Civilian Supply during the war. From his wartime work emerged a monograph, *A Theory of Price Control* (1952a), which, though not widely influential, contained some of the seminal ideas of his major works. With the cessation of hostilities in Europe, he worked with the Office of Strategic Services, directing research on the effectiveness of the Allies's strategic bombing of Germany.

In 1947, Galbraith was one of the liberal founders of the Americans for Democratic Action, an organization he later chaired. After working prominently in the presidential campaigns of Senator Adlai Stevenson and President John F. Kennedy, Galbraith served as US Ambassador to India in the early 1960s. A very outspoken critic of US involvement in Vietnam, he campaigned on behalf of the presidential ambitions of Senators Eugene McCarthy (1968) and George McGovern (1972). Later he was to work in the campaigns of Congressman Morris Udall (1976) and Senator Edward Kennedy (1980).

Galbraith's ardent partisanship is quite unusual. To be sure, political activity is not uncommon among economists. There are highly visible advisers to candidates and administrations and frequent testimony to congressional committees. There are popular essays that convey the author's political slant. Economists at least tend to know each other as inclined to one political persuasion or another. But Galbraith's uninhibited partisanship coupled with his refusal to neatly separate his politics from his economics sets him well apart from his more conventional colleagues.

Galbraith's lack of conventionality is not entirely personal eccentricity in that he represents the pragmatist tradition in American economic thought. As a matter of principle, institutional economics is less interested in being a universal science of economic behavior than in being a useful component of present society. The instrumental philosophy developed from the seminal contributions of Thorstein Veblen and John Dewey regards economics and all social science as the process of bringing systematic knowledge to bear upon the social problems of the day. Institutional economics offers not only a radically different conception of the role of the economist as social scientist but a fundamentally different vision of the nature of the economic process in and of itself. On this much more will be said herein.

Not least is Galbraith useful because of his unconventional approach to economics. He passionately advocates that we come to think of the economic process in a manner that is fundamentally different from the normal view. His major argument in this regard unfolds in the trilogy, *The Affluent Society* (1958), *The New Industrial State* (1967), and *Economics and the Public Purpose* (1973b).

Other than this trilogy, and perhaps *A Theory of Price Control*, Galbraith's *American Capitalism: The Concept of Countervailing Power* (1952b) stands out in importance. The central argument of the book is that the growth of economic power in one economic sector tends to induce *countervailing power* from those who must bargain with the powerful. Hence, unionized labor and politically organized farmers rose in response to powerful manufacturers. The government is often involved in supporting the rise of this countervailing power and, in Galbraith's view, should be. With its characteristic emphasis on the reality of economic concentration and on the microeconomic foundations of stabilization issues, this book solidified Galbraith's position as a continuing spokesperson for the New Deal perspective in economics.

Galbraith coupled the new economics of J.M. Keynes with the New Deal corporatist view, as did other institutionalists of the time, notably C.E. Ayres and Allan G. Gruchy. Indeed, as shall be argued in the next chapter, *American Capitalism* continues the institutionalist explanation of the Great Depression that began with Veblen and was continued by Rexford Tugwell, with whom Galbraith worked in the New Deal. This theory is also continued in the Monopoly Capital School literature based on the seminal work of Baran and Sweezy, that exerted a powerful influence on the 1960s counterculture in economics.

With *American Capitalism*, Galbraith's interest in power and his strong dissent from the neoclassical synthesis which was maturing at that time were set. The competitive model so often used in economics textbooks, which had then been resurrected in the neoclassical synthesis which combined neoclassical microeconomics with Keynesian macroeconomics, maintains that good results follow from certain assumptions about the structure of the economy. Galbraith argued that such assumptions are not met in the actual economy, are unlikely to ever be met, and probably should not be met. He recognized power as an essential element of economic life and argued that only by examining the power of corporations, unions, and others can economists address the vital issues of social control and economic policy.

The first book of Galbraith's central trilogy, *The Affluent Society*, examines the continuing urgency attached to higher consumption and production despite apparent opulence. The institutionalist explanation for this paradox, very familiar to students of Veblen, is that obsolete ideas are held over from one historical period to another. These ideas persist not by inertia alone but also because they are convenient to powerful vested interests. *The Affluent Society* argues that the outmoded mentality of more-is-better impedes the further economic progress that would be possible if contemporary affluence were put to more reasonable use. Advertising and related salesmanship activities create artificially high demand for the commodities produced by private businesses, and lead to a concomitant neglect of public sector goods and services that would contribute far more to the quality of life.

The Affluent Society was Galbraith's breakthrough as a best-selling author and guaranteed some, albeit reluctant, hearing of his dissenting ideas in the economics profession. Indeed, he was eventually honored with the American Economic Association's prestigious presidency over the objections of some of the Association's more conventional members. With its emphasis on the role of culture and history in economic life, and especially its review of the debilitating effects of an invidious pecuniary culture which seemingly has no higher social purpose than expanding pecuniary one-upmanship, *The Affluent Society* gave a much needed shot in the arm to the American Institutionalist School of economics.

The book also influenced both the Great Society program and the rise of the American counterculture in the 1960s, though many self-styled radicals of the period were critical of Galbraith's refusal to adopt revolutionary rhetoric and Marxian verbiage. They no doubt also shared with Robert Heilbroner (1970, p. 235) the view that Galbraith would rather make a joke than push a point to its ethical implication. Although the present author agrees with this lamentation, he will argue that radicals generally fail to appreciate the fundamentally radical character of the Galbraithian, and institutionalist, paradigm. Indeed, this paradigm is the basis of 1960s radical economics much more directly than the classical Marxist perspective, notwithstanding the radical chic use of the terminology of the latter.

In *The New Industrial State*, Galbraith expanded his analysis of the role of power in economic life. A central concept of the book is the *revised sequence*. The conventional wisdom in economic thought portrays economic life as a set of competitive markets governed ultimately by the decisions of sovereign consumers. In this original sequence, the control of the production process flows from consumers of commodities to the organizations that produce those commodities. In the revised sequence, this flow is reversed and businesses exercise control over consumers by advertising and related salesmanship activities.

The revised sequence concept applies only to the administered sector, i.e., the manufacturing core of the economy in which each industry contains only a handful of very powerful corporations. It does not apply to the market sector in the Galbraithian dual economy. In the market sector, comprised of the vast majority of business organizations, price competition remains the dominant form of social control. In the administered sector, however, comprised of the one thousand or so largest corporations, competitive price theory serves mostly to obscure the relation to the price system of these large and powerful corporations. In Galbraith's view, the principal function of market relations in this industrial system is not to constrain the power of the corporate behemoths but to serve as instruments for the implementation of their power.

Moreover, the power of these corporations extends into commercial culture and politics, allowing them to exercise considerable influence upon popular social attitudes and value judgments. That this power is exercised in the shortsighted interest of expanding commodity production and the status of the few is both inconsistent with democratic and liberal canons and a barrier to achieving the quality of life which the affluent new industrial state could provide.

The New Industrial State not only provided Galbraith with another best-selling book, it also extended once again the currency of institutionalist economic thought. A new generation of institutionalists was born of this book and the Baran and Sweezy classic, *Monopoly Capital* (1966), that preceded it by a bit more than a year. This new generation may be in some sense more radical, or at least less patient, than the generation before it (Dugger (ed.), 1989 and Stanfield, 1995a).

The book also filled a very pressing need in the late 1960s for a comprehensive re-examination of the role of the large corporation in social life. The conventional theory of monopoly power in economic life maintains that the monopolist will attempt to restrict supply in order to maintain price above its competitive level. This was the starting point of Veblen's classic treatment of the financial consolidation of industry and its sabotage of the production process in the name of profit. The social cost of this monopoly power is a decrease in both allocative efficiency and the equity of income distribution.

In the 1960s, this conventional economic analysis of the role of monopoly power did not adequately address contemporaneous popular concern about the large corporation. This growing concern focused on the role of the corporation in politics, the damage done to the natural environment by an obsessive commitment to economic growth, and the perversion of culture by advertising and other pecuniary considerations.

The New Industrial State gave a plausible explanation of the power structure involved in generating these problems and thus found a very receptive audience among the rising American counterculture. Galbraith's work also updated the work of Veblen to emphasize the macroeconomic and cultural effects of the financially concentrated control of society's industrial capacity. Here again Galbraith's work is a competing and companion essay to that of Baran and Sweezy, which likewise contributed to the fuller development of the Veblenian, and the closely related Marxist, models (Papandreou, 1972).

Economics and the Public Purpose, the last work in Galbraith's major trilogy, continues the characteristic insistence on the role of power in economic life and the inability of conventional economic thought to deal adequately with this power. Conventional economic thought, with its competitive model and presumptions of scarcity and consumer sovereignty, what Galbraith called the *imagery of choice*, serves to hide the power structure that actually governs the American economy. This obscurantism prevents economists from coming to grips with this governing structure and its untoward effects on the quality of life.

Galbraith argued that economic ideas should be evaluated by the *test of anxiety*, i.e., by their ability to relate to popular concern about the economic system and to resolve or allay this anxiety. He contended that conventional economic thought fails this test and again offers his basic model from *The New Industrial State* as an alternative approach to understanding the contemporary economy.

Later books, and the stream continues, restate, amend slightly, and elaborate aspects of the trilogy, but they do not enlarge thereon in any major respect. *The Anatomy of Power* (1983) is a curious admixture of an essay on power with a sweeping overview of economic history. *The Culture of Contentment* (1992) offers acerbic commentary on the convoluted political economic logic of recent decades. It examines the declining political representation of the less fortunate in America, expanding upon lectures Galbraith began giving in the late 1970s (1979a and 1979b). Two other books, the curiously titled *Money* (1975) and *Economics in Perspective* (1987) combine economic history and the history of economic thought. In the latter, at least, Galbraith achieves characteristically readable edification. And the stream continues with the recent historical overview of economic policy in modern times (Galbraith, 1994).

Formally educated in agricultural economics, committed to the institutionalist perspective (if not altogether explicitly so), possessed of a highly literate and completely non-mathematical writing style (thus enabled to become an enormously successful author), an openly partisan Democrat, a public servant and a public gadfly (ever apt to set aside academic life for political sojourns), Galbraith is a most unconventional economist. He is as well a most *useful economist*.

IN HIS OWN WORDS

Galbraith's title as a useful economist, and his ability to sell his books, owes much to his ability to entertain as he tries to inform. One can hope to capture the thrust of his work sufficiently to convey the Galbraithian System to the reader with reasonable accuracy. But it would be folly to aspire to present the legendary prose style and mordant wit in any but his own words. Hence, to complete this introductory chapter, the author shares with the reader a few of the his favorite Galbraithisms with minimal surrounding explanation of context.

Galbraith is ever a critic of the conservative and business thrust of American popular culture. Plus, as noted, he has long argued that American society could make better use of its considerable affluence. On the reluctance to expand the range of options available to individuals in balancing their financial need to work with their self-realization needs for leisure, he observed that those 'who speak much of liberty should allow and even encourage it' (Galbraith, 1967, p. 373).

Nor has Galbraith ever suffered agreeably the views of those who would blame the victims of the industrial disease of unemployment: 'When jobs are unavailable, no useful distinction can be made between those who are voluntarily and those who are involuntarily unemployed. Neither can find work' (Galbraith, 1958, p. 299).

Galbraith regards the consciousness of American business figure thusly: 'The American business psyche is an acutely vulnerable thing; it associates all change with perverse ideological intent' (Galbraith, 1979c, p. 24).

In 1953, under the behest of the university's governing administration, the Harvard economics department was examined by an external committee for its zeal in supporting the ideas of Keynes. 'Clarence Randall, then the unduly articulate head of the Inland Steel Company' was a leading figure in the investigation. Galbraith noted that the examination was handicapped because 'the investigators, with one or two possible exceptions, had not read the book and were thus uncertain as to what they attacked' (Galbraith, 1971a, pp. 55–6).

Galbraith was critical of the American military and strategic establishment as well as the conservative American mind. On the conservative propensity to blame communist rabble-rousers for unrest in poor nations, he observed: 'It is the Communists. There is a fine, simple, hard-boiled quality about this explanation which economizes thought and for this and other reasons appeals to the American conservative . . . It is an elementary mark of sophistication always to mistrust the man who blames on revolutionaries what should be attributed to deprivation' (1971a, p. 223).

That this economy of thought led to a related propensity for the USA to supply arms even to overtly reactionary regimes so long as they were perceived to be anti-communist was not lost on Galbraith. He noted that these guns often wind up in the hands of anti-American forces one way or another and puzzled over the thinking of 'those who believe that wherever there is a soldier he should be given an American gun' (1971a, p. 250).

Galbraith was an early convert to the ideas of J.M. Keynes, if not to the great English economist's literary skills. In introducing his essay on 'How Keynes Came to America' he noted that this voyage of ideas required a small army of translators and propagators, due in large part to 'the almost unique unreadability of *The General Theory*. . . . As Messiahs go, Keynes was deeply dependent on his prophets' (Galbraith, 1971a, p. 44). Galbraith went on to observe that Keynes 'was regarded as too candid and inconvenient to be trusted. Public officials are not always admiring of men who say what the right policy should be. Their frequent need, especially in foreign affairs, is for men who will find persuasive reasons for the wrong policy'. Galbraith has never been very tolerant of those who resisted the Keynesian message about the superiority of fiscal policy to monetary policy. He used the case of Marriner Eccles, who headed the Federal Reserve Board in the 1930s, and Laughlin Currie, who administered research at that organization at the same time, to make the point. Both men were exponents of the use of fiscal policy to boost aggregate demand. Galbraith was bemused, for 'not often have important new ideas on economics entered a government by way of its central bank. Nor should anyone be disturbed. There is not the slightest indication that it will ever happen again' (Galbraith, 1971a, p. 48). Currie had apparently not been afforded tenure at Harvard. This, in Galbraith's view, was due in part to the fact that Currie's 'ideas, brilliantly anticipating Keynes, were considered to reflect deficient scholarship until Keynes made them respectable. Economics is very complicated' (1971a, p. 48n).

Galbraith was a major architect of the price control system of the Second World War. Decades after the fact, in speaking of his initial design for controls, he acknowledged abject error; he did so with wit and good humor, and indeed, claimed to have benefitted from the experience: 'The experience of being disastrously wrong is salutary; no economist should be denied it, and not many are' (Galbraith, 1981, p. 163).

Galbraith has often reminisced about the hiring of Richard Nixon by the OPA while Galbraith was its director. Galbraith will take no blame from his liberal friends for thus starting Nixon's career: 'in line with a notable Nixon tradition, I must plead that I didn't know what was going on. I didn't meet Mr. Nixon' (Galbraith, 1979c, p. 347). Nixon in retrospect claimed to have worked for the Office of Emergency Preparedness, the overall bureaucratic situs of OPA and much more besides. Of Nixon's reticent memory, Galbraith remarked that 'it was much as though a Marine had said he worked in the public sector' (Galbraith, 1981, p. 157).

Galbraith apparently does not share the common view that Nixon's White House machinations brought the great democracy to the threshold of annihilation. Noting that Nixon's years as president marked a high tide of popular protest, he questioned whether Nixon was competent enough to effect anything so drastic and claims to be firmly of the belief 'that anyone who spoke out under Nixon had little to fear, anyone shut up by Richard Nixon had nothing to say' (Galbraith, 1979c, p. 350).

The economists who advised Nixon and his ilk have been frequent subjects of Galbraith's pointed barbs. Of the experience of economic policy designs in the administrations of Presidents Nixon, Carter, and Ford: 'In modern times the standards by which economists in public office are judged have become very relaxed; . . . [administration] economists have all presided over grave misfortune and emerged from public service with enhanced reputations . . . all have gone on to distinguished and better-paying jobs' (Galbraith, 1981, p. 158).

In the rich vein of Republican economists, Galbraith mined other gems. President Kennedy's successful campaign 'was helped by Eisenhower's economists. . . . Ike's advisers were showing that economists cannot be outdone even by Cold Warriors in winning defeat for the politicians of their party' (1981, p. 387). Arthur F. Burns, who chaired the Council of Economic Advisers under Eisenhower, in Galbraith's view, 'always associated respectability with mild obsolescence' (1971a, p. 57).

Of Alan Greenspan, later to become Chairman of the Federal Reserve Board, and with William Simon, a principal economic adviser to President Gerald Ford, Galbraith purred, 'we are a friendly people. We listen respectfully even to established architects of political disaster' (Galbraith, 1979c, p. 29). Of William Simon in the same regard, 'he has warm praise for the way Gerald Ford followed his advice and that of Alan Greenspan . . . although he is more reserved in taking credit for Ford's defeat' (Galbraith, 1979c, p. 105).

Galbraith has been a persistent advocate of the need to apply wage and price controls to control inflation. But he did not think much could be accomplished with rhetoric and moral suasion alone, and therefore did not think that President Ford's WIN (Whip Inflation Now) buttons would be very effective. Nor did the concurrent Council on Wage and Price Stability impress him; he thought that it lacked the authority and organizational presence necessary to be effective. Indeed he viewed these innocuous nostrums to be so feeble that the agencies established to apply them were authorized to 'exploit only the right of free assembly' and 'denied all power except that of free speech' (Galbraith, 1979b, p. 33).

Public figures other than economists were also the objects of Galbraith's pointed humor. He referred to Congressman John Taber of New York, with whom he had disagreements of some sort in the 1950s, as 'an articulate fossil' (1979c, p. 161). Earlier Taber had been a critic of the wartime effort to control prices. Galbraith later reminisced that Taber 'strongly opposed all of our activities, as he opposed all of the twentieth century' (Galbraith, 1981, p. 182).

In the middle of the 1970s Galbraith found that much of the sentiment supporting the notion of an emerging conservative majority had a curiously circular genealogy. Galbraith observed that a senator would indicate the specter of the ruin that would surely ensue were prospective legislative action approved, that the unhappy scenario would be relayed to Michael Evans and Robert Novak for mention in their column, then find its way back to the Senate as proof of widespread popular concern. Galbraith thought this to be 'the only completely successful closed-circuit system for recycling garbage that has yet been devised' (Galbraith, 1979c, p. 49).

Speaking of environmental concerns, in closing a discussion of how the citizenry may know if environmental protection is finally being taken seriously, Galbraith adumbrated a number of sensible items, such as recognition that environmental protection will require tax dollars and changes in what is produced and consumed. He then identified his 'own personal test . . . the gasoline service station. This without rival, is the most repellent piece of architecture of the past two thousand years' (Galbraith, 1971a, pp. 286–7). Service stations are not only too numerous, invariably filthy, and prone to offering 'hideously packaged and garishly displayed merchandise' they are also 'uncontrollably addicted to great strings of ragged little flags' (1971a, pp. 286–7).

During the 1972 party conventions Galbraith appeared along with William Buckley on the *Today* television program to share their views upon the events that had unfolded the evening before (Lamson, 1991, p. 205). In answer to the question of whether or not he enjoyed the televised debates with Buckley, Galbraith maintained that 'Bill Buckley is the ideal opponent – pleasant, quick in response, invulnerable to insult and invariably wrong' (Galbraith, 1973c, p. 7).

Galbraith has found ample opportunity to deploy his clever humor more gently in bringing attention to those economists with whom he feels significant affinity. On the penchant of Thorstein Veblen to seek the censure of his audience, 'when faced with a choice between strict accuracy and what would outrage his audience, he rarely hesitated' (Galbraith,

1979c, p. 124). Very similarly, he cited Joseph Schumpeter's half-century old remark to an impecunious graduate student that no gentleman could live well on less than $50,000 a year. 'Given the choice between being right and being memorable, Schumpeter never hesitated' (Galbraith, 1981, p. 49).

While directing the post-war bombing survey Galbraith employed Paul Baran, or rather was entrusted with his 'care and management'. Baran 'was . . . ever in pursuit of the most unpopular political position available'. Having witnessed the comportment of another friend and Baran, Galbraith commented that although they shared similarly socialist views, because 'neither could brook agreement, they clashed bitterly' (Galbraith, 1981, p. 327).

About the same time, in England, Galbraith arranged American military transportation for Piero Sraffa to return to his native Italy. Sraffa was convinced a revolution was imminent and, having convictions favoring such political action, he did not want to miss it. Had such a revolution occurred and Sraffa's role been prominent, Galbraith no doubt would have had some explaining to do. But knowing Sraffa, he concluded there was no cause to worry, for 'he was one of the most leisured men who ever lived; a Communist revolution led by him would have shown no perceptible movement' (1981, p. 74).

Not surprisingly Galbraith reserved some of his most invective wit for those among his professional peers with whom he disagreed. Of his fellow economists, too many of whom tend to prefer 'their free market faith to practical achievement' (1981, p. 356), he observed: 'an economist without a price system is a priest without a divine being' (1981, p. 134). Much of the time Galbraith's humorous castigation of his peers was designed to contrast the instruction of experience and policy relevance against the conventionally upheld doctrine that he considered woefully obsolete and dangerously out of touch with the texture of the day's problems. Alas, 'economics, especially as it is taught, has an enduring commitment to the past' (Galbraith, 1985, p. xxxv).

Galbraith once noted that the economists who took the lead in the New Deal era, though their views came to be rather widely held at a later date, nonetheless were denied the trappings of professional academic success. 'The honors went to men who, in general, urged wrong but reputable policies' (1971a, p. 13n).

In Galbraith's view, too many economists were misguided by the persistent commitment to the competitive model. Attachment to the highly satisfactory results of this theoretical model tends to induce neglect of the serious breaches that separate the actual economy from the model.

Of course, when such breaches are noted, the conventionally mandated endeavor is to restore and maintain competition. 'Liturgically this remains the response. The paper sword of neoclassical economists in the United States . . . remains the antitrust laws. They are the ultimate triumph of hope over experience' (Galbraith, 1981, p. 282). Galbraith considered the suggestion that more vigorous enforcement of the antitrust laws could be an effective antidote to inflation to be an especially egregious example of wishful thinking. The 'call for enforcement of the antitrust laws as an inflation remedy . . . is the last resort of the bankrupt mind' (Galbraith, 1979c, p. 33).

The *neoclassical synthesis* is the term coined by Paul Samuelson to refer to the dominant paradigm of the period after the Second World War (Samuelson, 1964; Stanfield, 1995a, ch. 3). It invokes the reunification of the discipline around both the Keynesian macroeconomic concern for inadequate aggregate demand and the 'verities' upheld in the neoclassical microeconomic appraisal. Galbraith was a dedicated critic of the neoclassical synthesis and its theoretical neglect of the structural factors that induce the simultaneous occurrence of inflation and unemployment. 'Modern medicine would not be more out of touch with its world if it could not embrace the existence of the common cold' (Galbraith, 1979c, p. 358). Galbraith is convinced that the economists' theoretical disregard of the juxtaposition of unemployment and inflation, and also of the related problems of power and inequality, 'is unconvincing to the average citizen who, unlike the more acquiescent economist, is untrained in illusion' (1979c, p. 19).

Galbraith's mordant mien was very evident in the paper he gave at the 1969 meeting of the American Economic Association in which he portrayed economics as a faith. No doubt there were a few neophytes in the audience, their curiosity of the celebrity having gotten the better of their professional propriety and disdain. Galbraith expressed the hope that the younger generation of economists would reject the sterile elegance of the conventional model and choose instead to address the evident issues of the dualized and administered political economy. He turned to the young with some reluctance, it appeared, having concluded that in their midlife comfort their older peers lacked the vinegar for the contentious atmosphere that would obtain if the issue of power were accorded the centrality in economic theory that it occupies in reality. For comfort he continued is not yet the milieu of the young and perhaps their desire to make a mark for themselves can be turned to the creation of a more relevant economics. Galbraith delivered this hope with an acerbic touch that perhaps signified that his optimism was slight. He warned the younger economists in his audience that 'while one can exist decently in obsolescent maturity, the world rightly makes fun of the *young* fogy' (Galbraith, 1971a, p. 87).

Economists of the Austrian School have been the most tenacious adherents to the precepts of classical liberalism. They labored in obscurity for a quarter of a century after the Second World War but eventually emerged and came to be widely regarded as not altogether uninteresting and perhaps as even to comprise a viable alternative analysis to the highly formal models of conventional economics. Of course Galbraith would consider as effusive praise anything short of pointing out their abject commitment to the last century, and to be sure they do often seem to be waiting for the twentieth century to blow over.

One such economist was Gottfried Haberler, who was for a time Galbraith's departmental senior at Harvard. Haberler, like so many others, had migrated to the USA in flight from fascism in the inter-war period. Galbraith gleefully juxtaposed the prominent expatriates to the success of economic policy in their birthplace. 'In the decades following World War II, Austrian economic policy has been a model of successful, undogmatic pragmatism. None can doubt that it benefitted greatly from the emigration of these distinguished scholars to the United States' (Galbraith, 1981, p. 273). The most prominent modern member of the Austrian School was the Nobel laureate Friedrich A. Hayek, whose views are more complex and more incisive than those of modern liberal faith are ever likely to admit (Kern, 1982). Galbraith condescends that Hayek is 'a gentle man of comprehensively archaic views' (Galbraith, 1981, p. 78).

No doubt Galbraith would be even less inclined toward kindness to another Nobel laureate, George Stigler. Among other economists, Stigler had scathingly reviewed *American Capitalism* at the 1953 gathering of the American Economic Association clan. Showing a caustic touch of his own, Stigler (1954) likened Galbraith's effort to playing with blocs. David McCord Wright, who less than deftly wielded Schumpeter's magnificent capitalist dynamics, also served on the panel. Of Stigler and Wright, Galbraith later remarked that 'neither approved new thought, however plausible' (Galbraith, 1981, p. 283).

The episode may have convinced Galbraith to eschew writing for a narrowly academic audience in future. There was no doubt also a residual bitterness that may have occasioned the increasingly acerbic tone of his comments on his more conventional peers in his subsequent works. Stigler later expressed 'shock' that so many more Americans read *The Affluent Society* than Adam Smith's classic *The Wealth of Nations*. Galbraith feigned, or so I imagine, a reluctance to respond lest he seem to be urging his own book rather than the universally acknowledged classic. He could have simply noted the contrast in content, style, and chronology of his book and Smith's classic – after all one should be shocked that Stigler was shocked, in what America did he reside? But Galbraith ruthlessly retorted that perhaps he had been 'missing the deeper cause of Stigler's sorrow which might have been not that so many read Galbraith and so few read Smith but that almost no one reads Stigler at all' (Galbraith, 1971a, p. 12n).

One should not come away from this introduction with the image that Galbraith was haughty and self-satisfied. He was unreservedly partisan to be sure and he delighted in needling those with whom he differed. He was capable perhaps, of mild anger at the prospect that the citizens he cared about would continue to suffer from the economic half-truths foisted upon them by those who were supposed to be in the know in such regards. But much of his superciliously contemptuous mien was carefully cultivated self-posturing. His infamous arrogance was often the object of self-deprecatory humor. He once recalled that he had experienced a problem in personal relations with his colleagues at all five of the universities with which he had been affiliated. He did not think that the problem was envy for his being more diligent and more able. Rather, the problem arose 'from my fear . . . that my superiority would not be recognized' (Galbraith, 1981, p. 18).

In 1946 Galbraith was given the State Department assignment of advising the occupation administration on economic affairs in Germany, Japan, and elsewhere. General Lucius Clay was head of operations in Germany and General Douglas MacArthur in Japan. Concerning the reactions of the generals to his advice, Galbraith commented that 'Clay . . . was not impressed with my guidance on economic affairs and . . . MacArthur may not have been aware of it' (Galbraith, 1979c, p. 161).

Galbraith took advantage of the Freedom of Information Act to access the file compiled about him by the FBI. The content of the file 'was not agreeable, but it must have been a grave disappointment' to the politicians who had asked the FBI to conduct it. The principal revelation was 'investigation favorable except conceited, egotistical and snobbish' (Galbraith, 1981, pp. 311–12). Looking back at the ignominious 1956 electoral defeat of his liberal cause, Galbraith avers that 'to win is to be affirmed in truth by the voters; to lose means only that one's convictions are being tested by adversity' (1981, p. 358).

Galbraith frequently adverted to his vanity about the sales of his books and about his literate prose. Noting that *The Age of Uncertainty* (1977) sold rather well in Japan, he noted also that his 'admiration for Japanese literary taste was unbounded' (1981, p. 534). Galbraith likes to tell of how he came to recognize the importance of the title one assigns to one's book. *The Great Crash* (1954a), he found upon inspection, is a difficult sell in the bookstores of airports. *The Great Crash* was cited for its literate style. 'Any writer who says that he is negligent of such praise is almost certainly lying' (Galbraith, 1981, p. 312).

High praise was accorded to *The Affluent Society*, prompting Galbraith to recall that 'only a strong character can resist such praise. I made no attempt' (1981, p. 354). Not all commentary was favorable of course. With regard to such criticism Galbraith seems to have approved of the advice given him by John Steinbeck: 'unless the bastards have the courage to give you unqualified praise, I say ignore them' (1981, p. 313). In his introductory remarks on the occasion of the publication of the fourth edition of the book, Galbraith gently mocked himself: 'Were I a . . . dispassionate reviewer devoid of all personal animus, as, needless to say, I so regard myself, I would have only slight objection to the early chapters' (1984, p. xiii).

But enough. It is time to proceed with the examination of the contours of the Galbraithian System. Chapter 2 surveys the development of Galbraith's thinking in the years before the advent of the first installment of the central trilogy in 1958. Thereafter, a more detailed examination is given to the trilogy, including an overview in Chapter 7 of the policy regime implicated by the Galbraithian System. The final chapter of the book examines Galbraith's place in intellectual history.

2 Economic Balance and Countervailing Power

> The theory of oligopoly has been aptly described as a ticket of admission to institutional economics.
>
> (E.S. Mason, 1939)

This chapter examines Galbraith's work in the early 1950s. The books in question are a far cry from the integrated model of late democratic capitalism, the Galbraithian System, which emerges in the trilogy *The Affluent Society*, *The New Industrial State*, and *Economics and the Public Purpose*. But the Galbraithian vision begins to take shape in these early books, in which we can detect the concerns for inflation and the bifurcated economic power structure.

Already present is the characteristic Galbraithian insistence upon the inadequacy of the modern liberal strategy of aggregate demand policy, moderate income redistribution, and intervention to correct market failures owing to externalities and public goods. The seeds are here sown for the now familiar Galbraithian case that a more directly interventionist strategy than the modern liberal scenario will be required for the attainment of macroeconomic stability, progress in the area of social justice, and a reasonably effective disposition of industrial society's bountiful wherewithal. Galbraith early on insisted that we need a political economy that integrates the behavior of the state into our theories of economic performance.

American Capitalism: The Concept of Countervailing Power (1952b) is the book which first propelled Galbraith to celebrity status within the profession. It was an uneasy fame in that the predominant economic opinion was decidedly antagonistic to the Galbraithian enterprise. A rather uncivil set-to ensued at a session devoted to the concept of countervailing power at the 1953 meeting of the American Economic Association. Before considering *American Capitalism*, it is necessary to examine two other books from the early 1950s which also introduce themes which become pivotal to the Galbraithian System, *The Great Crash* and *A Theory of Price Control*. After that attention can turn to the conventional model of economic behavior as Galbraith attends to it in *American Capitalism* and then to the theory of countervailing power.

THE GREAT DEPRESSION AND THE TASK OF PRICE CONTROL

Galbraith's analyses of the 1930s depression and his anticipation of the post-war macroeconomic predicament provide nuances of the issues that became the focus of his major works, the problems of economic power and macroeconomic instability.

The Great Crash, first published in 1954, examines the relation of the financial collapse to the wider economic mayhem of the 1930s. Several prominent institutionalist themes are interwoven in the appraisal, not the least of which is the necessity of treating the pecuniary power structure as bearing a critical relation to the real economy. Galbraith insisted that no Chinese Wall separates Wall Street from the wider economy because 'there is an essential unity in economic phenomena' (Galbraith, 1954a, p. 2). This is very reminiscent of Veblen's *The Theory of Business Enterprise* as is the sarcasm displayed in Galbraith's jibe at the financial elite whose 'sense of responsibility . . . for the community as a whole is not small. It is nearly nil' (1954a, p. xxi). Galbraith also reminds one of the Veblenian separation of making goods versus making money and the cultural criticism aimed at the pecuniary habit of mind in his observation that 'the values of a society totally preoccupied with making money are not altogether reassuring' (1954a, p. 81).

On a more fundamental level Galbraith's analysis of the Great Depression displayed the imprint of the institutionalist tradition. In *The Theory of Business Enterprise*, Veblen had dated the modern industrial depression from the era of comprehensive industrialization. He argued that the response to the overproduction peril posed by this advance in the industrial arts was financial consolidation. This was a temporary respite at best, however, and Veblen foresaw stagnation to be the normal tendency of corporate capitalism, a tendency that would beset society with a dramatic increase in salesmanship and other forms of institutionalized waste.

Tugwell perhaps more than anyone applied this framework to the Great Depression (Sternsher, 1964, ch. 2). A very similar analysis, right down to the psycho-cultural malaise emphasized by Veblen, is to be found in *Monopoly Capital* by Baran and Sweezy. Of course Baran and Sweezy are not generally regarded to be institutionalists, but rather as Marxists or neo-Marxists, yet careful reading of their classic uncovers a characteristic Veblenian slant.

Galbraith's analysis of the phenomena of speculation resembles the 'financial instability hypothesis' most prominently associated with Hyman Minsky (1986; *see also* Phillips, 1988; Kindleberger, 1978; and Galbraith, 1993). Speculation tends to grow and portfolios to weaken as the experience of prosperity is extended, pushing into the recesses of the mind memories of the last financial debacle. The easy money policy that accompanied the early speculative ascendancy was not the cause of the speculation. The tightening in the late 1920s did not reverse the speculation nor should it have been expected to do so. Higher interest rates may deter many from borrowing, but the last and least to be so effected are the speculators who have unbounded optimism in their pyramids in the sky. What is now known as adverse selection is surely at work in this regard (Wray, 1990, p. 180). Galbraith did seem inclined to believe that more stringent regulatory tools, had they been requested by the Federal Reserve Board and granted by Congress, coupled with a stern dose of moral suasion, may have stemmed the speculative tide because 'mood' is more important than the level of interest rates to the frenzy (Galbraith, 1954a, pp. 37–40 and 174; see also Wray, 1990).

But the frenzy does require a flow of saving to serve as the base for the loans to be devoted to speculative investment. In noting this and subsequently tying it into the relation between the industrial economy and the financial crash, Galbraith displayed the institutionalist model to which advert has been made above. The ample flow of saving that the era of prosperity generated is related to the very structural imbalance that concerned Tugwell. This saving came from the growing property incomes that derived from the relation between technical change and oligopolistic pricing. In the 1920s, 'output per worker in manufacturing industries increased by about 43%' (Galbraith, 1954a, p. 180). But wages and prices were comparatively stable, as we would expect given oligopolistic downward price rigidity and the immaturity of union organization. Also buttressing the profitability of manufacturing was the situation in agriculture, which Galbraith noted was weakening from the 1920–1 economic crisis as its prices fell but its costs – structured by purchases from oligopolistic manufacturers – were stable.

Not surprisingly profit margins widened in manufacturing industries and the proportion of income represented by profits, interest, and rent nearly doubled (Galbraith, 1954a, pp. 180–2). This increase fueled the saving of the well-to-do, supporting their personal spending and nurturing their confidence in the munificence of the American way. With cash and optimism they invested, fueling the investment boom in production capacity and the speculation-fed ascent in the nominal values of financial securities. In such swell times, other imbalances, overt corporate larceny, a weakening banking system, and a growing international debt service problem were all too easy to ignore, especially given the credulity of the conventional economic intelligence of the day.

Hence the subsequent extended economic pall must be viewed as the result of interacting forces of the industrial and pecuniary aspects of the modern economy. Rampantly speculating on the upward elasticity of their weakening portfolios, the true believers strode with indefatigable confidence toward inevitable tumble. But this financial pyramid-building in the sky was interlaced with economic structural changes. The perverse income and wealth dynamics of oligopolistic pricing and technological change both kindled the speculative mood and financed its application. So also this vicious circle undermined the prosperity by weakening the ability of the larger underlying population of workers, farmers, and small business operators to purchase the products from the rising industrial capacity. The massive imbalance between what the economy could produce and that which its people could buy was not finally overcome until the advent of the next world war. Apparently, as soldiers common people command much more real income than as civilians.

There is another sinister side to the structural changes at issue in the institutionalist examination of the Great Depression, a *structural inflationary bias*. In the 1920s inflation overall was very mild, but it was so because of weak agricultural prices and stable real wages in the face of hearty increases in the productivity of labor. Absent the weakness of labor and agriculture, so also would be absent the source of price restraint. Absent also a commitment to restraining price increase by stringent aggregate demand policies, and price restraint is absent altogether.

In fact, of course, the experience of the 1930s ushered in significant changes designed to strengthen the position of labor, agriculture, and small business in the economy. So also the 1920s financial consolidation and management centralization in many retail areas added balance to the income flows in the economy. Finally, World War Two virtually guaranteed the success of Keynesian recipes for combatting the specter of large scale unemployment.

Thus attuned to evolving economic structure, the ingrained inclination of institutionalists, Galbraith asserted with incredible prescience the incipient predicament of the postwar economic era. In *A Theory of Price Control*, which had its roots in a series of articles published shortly after the war (Galbraith, 1946, 1947, 1951), he observed that 'inflation, more than depression, I regard as the clear and present economic danger of our times and one that is potentially more destructive of the values and amenities of democratic life' (Galbraith, 1952a, p. 9). In this monograph, Galbraith began to link Keynesian aggregate demand policy to achieve high employment with a direct intervention mechanism to arrest the inflationary interaction of wages and prices. To make any headway in this regard, then and now, it would be necessary to break through the preconception that inflation is caused by excess aggregate demand and that controls necessarily impede efficiency by limiting relative price flexibility.

Galbraith insisted that in the contemporary *dual economy*, consisting of a more or less competitive market sector and an oligopolistic sector, the task of price control is greatly simplified. Price controls may imply rationing by some non-price means. If so, an oligopolistic industry presents an advantage to a price control authority. The small number of firms are familiar with their customers which will facilitate any necessary rationing.

Oligopolistic firms already administer relatively fixed prices and if necessary ration their output by close relations and contracting with customers. Prices are relatively fixed for a number of reasons, including tacit agreement among sellers, buyers and regulators who are accustomed to extant prices, menu costs, and administrative inconvenience. In the main Galbraith simply submitted that 'it is relatively easy to fix prices that are already fixed' (1952a, p. 17).

The cost and supply structure of oligopoly further simplifies the task of price control. The prevalence of excess capacity means that there will be a considerable lag between imposition of a controlled price and the shortage that is implied by price ceilings in conventional market theory. Moreover, the tendency toward constant or decreasing cost implies the possibility of increased output without corresponding cost increases.

Galbraith's argument here is related to the Keynesian insistence upon the predominance of output changes in response to aggregate demand changes, at least in situations of insufficient aggregate demand. But if chronic excess capacity is the normal state of late capitalism, this applies to situations much closer to macroeconomic balance than the severe recessions envisioned by neo-Keynesians. Sraffa's path-breaking article from the 1920s should always be viewed as antecedent not only to Robinson's imperfect competition but to the Keynesian breakthrough as well (Sraffa, 1926). The predominance of quantity adjustments is most relevant to a mature industrial economy. So also in such an economy, the very concept of cost becomes ambiguous (Baran and Sweezy, 1966; Minsky, 1986; Stanfield and Phillips, 1991).

Here then emerges the concept of the *dual economy* that is to become a central tenet of the Galbraithian System. The task of the price authority is manageable in some market structures but not in others. Most conveniently, the manageable sector is the one which requires control while the unmanageable one does not. Hence, 'one of the central tasks of price adminstration

is to distinguish between the two' (Galbraith, 1952a, p. 26). This observation was soon extended by Galbraith into a generalized treatment of
stabilization policy in the dual economy (Galbraith, 1957).

In discussing the nature of price control in a disequilibrium system, such
as results under circumstances of all-out mobilization, Galbraith made
interesting comments upon inflationary expectations and saving and upon
the necessity of very close discipline in wages and wage goods industries
(Galbraith, 1952a, pp. 39, 42). His main objective, however, was to contrast the task of price control in such a disequilibrium context to that in
more normal times, which he referred to as limited mobilization as in
the Korean Conflict but which would apply to Cold War circumstances or
even peacetime pursuit of high employment. The principal difference is
that the over-arching task of the war effort does not supersede individual
preferences and claims for equitable treatment. Moreover, this scenario is
not bounded by the certainty that cessation of hostilities will eventually
occur but must be viewed as more or less permanent. Hence appeals to the
population to save well above their long term desires to do so are not
applicable because there is no disequilibrating imbalance, no moral equivalent of war, and no bounded prospect for the return to normal living.

Galbraith insisted that the habitual inclination of economists is to ignore
the applicable case by focusing solely upon macroeconomic balance without controls or macroeconomic imbalance with controls. The relevant case
in his view is macroeconomic balance with controls. This follows of course
from the phenomena of the wage and price spiral in the vicinity of macroeconomic balance.

In discussing the wage and price interaction Galbraith not only stated
clearly the tradeoff later to be indelibly linked with the name of A.W.
Phillips but also grounded the matter in the culture of industrial relations
and the context of popular sentiment. Galbraith also noted that the wage
and price dynamic requires validation by private borrowing or public deficit spending, which again displays his affinity with Minsky's financial
instability hypothesis (Minsky, 1986; see also Galbraith, 1952b, p. 181).

Galbraith noted in passing that intensified competition would alter the
relatively pacific nature of industrial relations that then characterized the
American economy (Galbraith, 1952a, pp. 66–7). After 1970 such intensified competition, from abroad, was to usher in a new era of militancy on
the part of American management; for better or for worse, labor was slower
to respond to the altered circumstances that import penetration implied.

Here then Galbraith stated the basic stabilization perspective of institutionalism. Keynesian aggregate demand policy is not sufficient in and of
itself; it must be supplemented with a direct intervention process aimed at

the supply side of the economy. Galbraith was not alone in early advocacy of *structural policy*. Before him Tugwell and others had pointed in that direction and Allan Gruchy early on began to lament the short-run character of neo-Keynesian economics and the need for a longer run strategy focused upon supply side management. This strategy must be based upon the vital distinction made in the concept of the dual economy. Further there is no reason to expand aggregate demand beyond macroeconomic balance. The nineteenth-century debate between inflationists and deflationists should be ended and the goal of macroeconomic balance with structural policy adopted.

THE CONVENTIONAL ECONOMIC MODEL

As the above indicates, Galbraith was early on uncomfortable with the treatment of power and macroeconomic instability by his more orthodox peers. This concern culminated in his first widely noted book, in which he advanced the notion of *countervailing power* (Galbraith, 1952b). These are interrelated concerns. Power reduces the automaticity of the self-regulating market. Powerful economic agents are able to shelter themselves from the exigencies of competition.

This retards the myriad microeconomic adjustments upon which spontaneous macroeconomic balance is based. Macroeconomic intervention, if it leaves the powerful untouched to apply their discretion in the pursuit of their objectives, has serious undesirable social consequences. To address this predicament Galbraith insisted that the discipline must critically examine its habitual recourse to the conventional model of competitive markets. In a rather excessively sanguine mood he cast the matter in the book along the lines of the way in which the problem of power and macroeconomic instability were undermining confidence in the traditional model.

The Problem of Power

Much of the appeal of the competitive market model inheres in its handling of the problem of power. As goes the familiar story, the management of the business firm, empirically, is visibly engaged in making decisions about the allocation of society's resources and the distribution of its income. In the competitive model this naïve observation is cast aside in favor of the less evident but presumably more essential underlying reality of competition. The business managers are said to operate from a highly constrained position. Those with whom the manager deals – the firm's consumers, workers, and suppliers – have resort to the manager's competitors and therefore cannot be subjected to the manager's arbitrary discretion.

Antitrust supervision renders nugatory the collusion of the manager with his putative competitors. Consumers bid for products according to their tastes which result from the organic process of social life – the nexus of relationships of family, kinship, friendship, and religious organization. Preferences for the allocation of one's labor power or private property derive from the same source. Managers of other enterprises which supply inputs face their own competitors and, hence, effective constraint of their decision-making.

In the case of the corporate enterprise, so the conventional story continues, the manager becomes visibly distinct from the owner but remains subservient to the latter in a fiduciary, principal and agent relationship. The key factor is again the existence of competitors. Owners, in order to signal their dissatisfaction, can elect to hire competing managers from the available pool of talent or to sell their equity in the corporation and, in effect, hire a competitive firm in the market for capital.

The moral of the story is that any apparent power on the part of the manager is really exercized in the interest and at the behest of the consumers of the enterprise's products and the suppliers of its factors of production. All trails lead back to the household whose choices are the ultimate seats of sovereign influence. Thus through competition the decision-making that occurs in the business enterprise is legitimated because it is ultimately accountable to household sovereignty (Stanfield, 1995a, ch. 4). Such is the *imagery of choice*, as Galbraith was to put the matter of mystification in *Economics and the Public Purpose*.

For this imagery to be convincing to the inquiring mind, it must correspond to the observed conduct of business. The effectiveness of competition must be plausible and the performance of the economy must match the outcome predicted by the story told by the competitive model. The explanation of observed economic conduct must be comprehensive and efficient in its correspondence to the observed economy (Eichner, 1983).

Obviously, Galbraith was unconvinced and, in what proved to be a bout of ingenuous optimism, penned a chapter entitled 'The Abandonment of the Model', which appears to suggest pandemic doubt in the profession about the competitive model's empirical correspondence. He reviewed empirical work which emerged in the wake of the great financial consolidation at the turn of the century, which incidentally, was one of Veblen's preeminent concerns in *The Theory of Business Enterprise*. This empirical work clearly revealed the dominance of an essentially non-competitive market structure. The theoretical new departures associated with Edward Chamberlin and Joan Robinson added to the statistical basis for abandoning the competitive market model. Prices, and the costs they express or cover, could no longer be viewed as the result of impersonal or genetic forces if they were the result of the exercise of power.

Accordingly the presumption of static efficiency promised by the market model could not be sustained. Static efficiency revolves around the notions of consumer or household sovereignty and necessary supply price. It can be said to obtain when the goods produced and the structure of resource allocation match the structure of genetic household preferences for goods and for the supplies of the factors for producing these goods. Genetic preferences, of course, stem from the organic process of social interaction; they are, or should be, of interest to the economist as an economist only if their formation is observed not to be independent of the business enterprise whose behavior they validate.

The growing recognition of economic power could then be expected to bring increasing concern about the correspondence of observed production costs to their minimum level and about the independence or genetic character of the wants or purposes served by the commodities produced. Market power means that, with respect to price, the demand for firm's products and/or the supply of its inputs is less than perfectly elastic. Or, in less obscure jargon, the pressure of competition from substitute sellers of its products or buyers of its inputs is less than absolutely substitutable for its customers or its suppliers.

Thus possessed of market power to some degree, the corporate manager achieves to that degree the ability to administer prices and costs. Such administration implies a degree of discretion and calls into question the necessity of observed corporate costs and the market determination of the observed pattern of income distribution. Hence the legitimacy of the observed decision-making becomes suspect. The power to administer prices is tantamount to the power to tax and such has long been censured when not accountable to effective representation.

The problem becomes all the more sinister when the revenue thus collected is observed to be an arsenal for influencing the formation or articulation of the genetic preferences of the population. Advertising and sales effort expenditures to influence consumer opinion are easily observed to be prominent factors upon the late capitalist scene. Nor need one be especially susceptible to the muckraker's art to note that corporate interests seek to influence the direction of political discourse.

By such observation, the use of the competitive market model to render nugatory the apparent exercise of discretion by the corporate manager was called seriously into question; thereby was the problem of power to be released from its Pandora's box of the competitive model. One finds intimations here of the *dependence effect* or *revised sequence* as well of the symbiotic relation between the state and the administered sector to be found later in the mature Galbraithian System.

The Memory of the Great Slump

Galbraith argued that another blow to the competitive market model was dealt by the faltered economic performance of the 1930s. Here again no great effort was required to observe that the Great Depression signalled reason to doubt that the actual economy displayed the self-regulating features so prominently associated with the competitive market model. Indeed, more dramatic contraindication of empirical correspondence would be difficult to contrive. The prolonged slump necessitated abandonment either of the theoretical notion that a competitive economy is self-stabilizing or of the conviction that the actual economy is competitively organized. The economists' response in the form of the Keynesian Revolution is even now the subject of intense debate as to which of these alternatives comprises its basic message.

The policy associated with Keynes came to be widely based on the first notion – that a competitive economy is not necessarily stable in the aggregate but that the actual economy is reasonably competitive. This interpretation, known as the *neoclassical synthesis* at the suggestion of Paul Samuelson (1964; see also Stanfield, 1995a, ch. 3), tends to reduce the problem of aggregate control to the relatively indirect manipulation of aggregate demand. This is the weaker of the two interpretations in terms of its consequences for political economic philosophy. The notion that instability is the result of inevitable power embodied in the structure of modern industrial capitalism implicates a more direct role for the state in the regulation of the exercise of such power. Such is the thrust of the Galbraithian and institutionalist message, and thus a predominant concern of the present study.

But strong implications follow from either interpretation. The notion that competitive capitalism in its modern form chronically displays inadequate aggregate demand is fraught with consequential implications for the role of the state that eventually has microeconomic implications (Galbraith, 1952b, pp. 80–3). The state becomes a partner to the business enterprise in the successful operation of the economy to produce and deliver goods. In a culture so committed to the material side of life, there is much prestige to the administration of matters economic. It seemed to Galbraith that such respect henceforth in principle would be shared by business with the state.

So also does the specter of excessive saving call for the revision of venerable formulae for ordering the propriety of matters economic. The Keynesian paradox of thrift undermines the tenuous compromise by which Victorian England and its cultural offshoot in mainstream economics saved the world from the pagan enjoyment of life that the decline of the puritan ethos implied. The founders of the Cambridge School sought in the response to scarcity the functional equivalent of religion-based propriety. If lack of buyers for the output of existing productive capacity is seen to limit its profitable use, the urgency, indeed the wisdom, of delaying gratification so as to add to that capacity becomes, logically, suspect. So also is one led to question the blatant inequality that ineluctably generates such saving by the wealthy and such deferred gratification by the needy.

The private consumption of those who want or need more thereby seems to come about at little or no real cost. Resources otherwise unused do not appear to be of eminent value in terms of their alternative employment. The same impression of low or zero opportunity costs applies to government spending to attend to various collectively consumed goods and services.

Hence, the microeconomic implications of the weaker Keynesian interpretation, if government is to so provide, what shall it provide? To what purpose shall government aspire to effect the structure of output? That this issue has failed to take a wide hold upon the mind economic or the body politic led Joan Robinson (1972) to refer to the 'second crisis of economic theory'. Nor can one sensibly dodge the issue by resort to the tax side of fiscal policy: taxes are not routinely neutral in their effects on relative prices and incomes. Hence, their application or revocation inevitably effects the pattern of resource allocation and income distribution. The concept of tax expenditures thus renders a potentially valuable service in countering the obsession with the expenditure side of the fiscal impacts of government. The shift to the tax side in the application of fiscal policy is one sleight of hand manifested by the imagery of choice. Obscurantism need not be logical to be effective; it need only capture the minds of those entrusted with the public's confidence in matters of formulating the theory and practice of economic policy.

The increased role of the state, especially by way of deficit finance, and the suspicion that thrift was a less than uncomplicated social asset, cast a psycho-cultural pall of its own. The known verities of propriety and social conduct left no doubt as to the social virtue of thrift nor of the prestige and proper authority on matters moral and political of those wealthy enough to practice it. At stake was the legitimacy of the capitalist class – though not of course, to the same extent anyway, that of the interwoven managerial and entrepreneurial strata. Ineluctably, the social validation of wealth is bound up with the savings-centered theory of economic progress first handed down from the mount by Adam Smith (Ranson, 1987).

Also morally certain was the wasteful, even dangerous, foolishness of anything more than the minimally necessary level of government involvement in the organic process of social life and its articulation through market exchange. Hayek's (1944) classic warning about the destiny of those societies which abandon the classical liberal road to the good society provides a guide to the disquiet aroused by the specter of the post-war social contract. It also remains a supplementary and very useful counterpoint to many of the problems that Galbraith has endeavored to have addressed.

The Paradox of Success

Thus in the early post-war period, Galbraith detected a deep insecurity with respect to the issues of microeconomic structure and macroeconomic performance. It seems that his desire to focus this concern and the economics and politics guided by it motivated *American Capitalism*. He was concerned that the 'depression psychosis' would lead economic interest groups to gird up their relative price and income positions for the inevitable downturn and for policy makers to be preoccupied with heading off an insufficiency of aggregate demand. Consequently he feared that the social ill of inflation, which he regarded as the more likely insidious undertow on the body social, would be neglected.

At least for economists, a further source of uneasiness was the 'ogre of power' and the lack of reason to assume that the microeconomy would result in an efficient static outcome. The available models of conduct in situations of non-competitive market structure strongly guided expectations toward the view that oligopolists would tacitly reach outcomes very near the monopoly case. Quantity of output would be held down in order to maintain price at a level that maximized profit. This profit would be above the normal or accepted return of the competitive model.

Barriers to entry, associated with advertising budgets and brand name recognition, would discourage potential competitors who lacked the huge sums necessary to compete for public goodwill. Cost barriers that stem from the economies of large scale production already achieved by the established corporations operate to similar effect – no matter in this regard whether they are technological (rooted in the reduction of real social costs of production) or merely pecuniary (stemming from the exercise of power over prices or political discourse). Cost barriers blunt the cutting edge of the competitive sword since they impede new entrants in search of a share of the extraordinary profits.

In the conventional economics story, the profits or quasi-rents earned in less-than-competitive situations lack the defense of being competitively earned. Their distributive impact is defensible only by way of the negative: collective action in search of a remedy might lead to a worse outcome. Nor is equity the heart of the matter; inefficiency becomes endemic. Resources turned away from oligopolistic industries are underemployed elsewhere in the economy. Relative prices inaccurately inform decision-makers about the relative scarcity of the products. Thus they will be led to economize falsely in the use of the products and substitute reduced consumption or more costly or less appropriate, but more competitively priced, products. Such substitution reasserts a measure of competitive control of the oligopolist's price behavior, but it does so at the expense of a deadweight loss of welfare to society. The troubling implications of inefficiency and ill-begotten income remains.

Paradoxically, in contrast to this unsavory prospect, Galbraith found that the actual economy of the early post-war era was performing rather well – at least with respect to the concerns of depression, inefficiency, and obtrusive government. Microeconomic inefficiency, macroeconomic stagnation, and the disconcerting increase in the role of the state had not yet delivered on the promise of disaster they presented to those of conventional economic faith.

In his search for resolution of this paradox of gloom versus the reality of success, Galbraith unravelled the theory of countervailing power. He subsequently used this theory to anticipate inflation as the more serious threat to the post-war social contract, and to argue for a change of focus among economists and policy-makers.

The first part of the resolution of the paradox is suggested by Schumpeter's contrast of static and dynamic efficiency. As we have seen, static efficiency is concerned about the cost and accuracy of production in accordance with household preferences at a given time. Dynamic efficiency is concerned with the growth of production through time, most especially with the growth of factor productivity through time. Schumpeter argued that the essence of capitalism is to be found in Creative Destruction, the incessant process of innovation that simultaneously creates new economic opportunities as it renders obsolete prior constellations of economic value (Schumpeter, 1962).

For Schumpeter this raised the possibility that a non-competitive structure may be more dynamically efficient than a competitive structure. His *ship-steadying hypothesis* is that the quasi-rents collected by non-competitive firms provide a war chest to finance the outlays and risks of pursuing innovation. The further possibility then arises that the gain in social welfare from dynamic efficiency may more than offset the loss associated with static inefficiency. This was precisely Galbraith's argument concerning the apparent economic success in the face of grave doubt. Technological change which increased productivity of inputs offset the inefficiency of application of these inputs at any given time.

In advance of elaborating the theory of countervailing power, it is worth noting that the concern that Galbraith apparently thought to have been pandemic was not in the final analysis widespread. Neither his countervailing power concept nor any similar model of the administered or power economy came to be widely adopted to explain the paradox of the fear of failure in the face of the apparent systemic success. The adaptation to the seemingly improbable success occurred but it did not occur along the lines of a reconstructed theory of microeconomic foundations as Galbraith had hoped. Nor did the focus of concern shift to the inflationary bias that occupied his attention.

There were various dissident traditions – American institutionalists, a spattering of Marxist opinion, and perhaps the Austrians to a different intent – which eventually rose to relatively more prominent positions in the discipline. But they suffered marginalization and obscurity for twenty-five years after the Second World War as the economists of the neoclassical synthesis complacently celebrated an era of economic success that owed little to the correspondence of their models to reality.

The success that Galbraith hoped would lead to reexamination of the conventional economic model was somehow taken instead as its confirmation. The irritant presented to the conventional model by the expanded role of government and the existence of considerable private power was put by the by. These facts were elided apparently upon the conviction that the system's successful operation must be the result of a workably competitive economic structure since by definition such a structure was required for such an achievement. Times were good. Competition generated good. Hence the economy must be competitive. Or so the syllogism seems to have been in retrospect.

There were arguments concerning the more socially responsible demeanor of the large corporation. Operated by a professional managerial class these behemoths were said to be less ruthless, even less intent upon their bottom lines. More concerned with their public image they were said to have become 'soulful' and to practice considerable temperance in balancing the return of stockholders' equity against the other stakeholders in the corporate edifice. Galbraith no doubt saw more relevance in these assertions than his more orthodox brethren (Galbraith, 1961, pp. 174–6) and he, not they, sought to formulate a new microeconomic theory so as to incorporate these nuances into a new political economy.

The treatment of expanded role of the state is especially interesting. Those who supported this expansion did so in an *ad hoc* fashion, they did not develop a political economy that explained the new role of the state. The state thus lay in the shadow so long as the capitalist system performed reasonably well. In a crisis situation, the state's role could be conveniently rediscovered and made culpable for the stumble of capitalism. Those who opposed the new role of the state were ready to explain its insidious effects with monetarist and expectationist macroeconomic models and with public choice and rent-seeking microeconomic models. Thus did the agency of success become transmogrified into the seat of failure (Heilbroner, 1985). Thus did the state become a compliant subject for the invective of succeeding waves of ingenuous, or dishonest, politicians and economists from the Carter years beyond to the celebration of the absurd that was to follow in a world filled with the nativistic rhetoric of Thatcher, Reagan, and their clones.

THE CONCEPT OF COUNTERVAILING POWER

The roots of the oligopolistic market structures that were the source of Galbraith's concern lay in the financial consolidation to which Veblen (n.d.) sought to draw attention in *The Theory of Business Enterprise* (Galbraith, 1961, pp. 171–2). This 'age of consolidation' continued, albeit in significantly modified form, into the soaring financial era of the late 1920s (Galbraith, 1954a, p. 49). Galbraith, of course, sought not to allay but to redirect the foreboding he detected among his peers and the public at large. The concept of countervailing power was offered to resolve the paradox of apparent success in the wake of fear of failure but at the same time to sort out developing tendencies that imply the onset of problems to which attention should be directed, the sooner the better.

Galbraith (1952b, p. 110) referred to the 'paradox of the unexercised power of the large corporation'. The market structure seems to be non-competitive but the expected calamity of inefficiency has not materialized. He argued that the preoccupation with restraint of power, and hence the maintenance of efficiency, through the process of market competition is the source of myopia with respect to this paradox. He offered countervailing power to fill the breech.

The concept of market competition is focused upon rivalry between buyers with other buyers and sellers with other sellers. One faces constraint over one's actions that stems from the existence of rivals on one's side of the market. Thusly preoccupied, those who seek constraint find it lacking in the absence of traditional price competition in the core industries in which the 200 largest corporations operate. Consumers appear to lack protection from monopoly pricing when a handful of firms supply them products at administered prices generated by tacit collusion. Laborers appear to lack protection from monopsonistic buyers of their services. Farmers appear to lack protection when buying inputs and selling output to these oligopolistic industries. Yet no apparent disaster is revealed by experience in the early post-war era.

Countervailing power is Galbraith's term for a constraint on power that emerges from the opposite side of the market. Those threatened by exploitation in the absence of important choice among competitors seek to redress the balance of power by developing the ability to negotiate from positions of strength. They seek countervailing power. The strongest manifestation of this tendency in the private sector per se is the development of large retailers such as Sears, Roebuck & Company and the Great Atlantic & Pacific Tea Company.

In Galbraith's view, these powerful buyers of manufactured products spontaneously emerged from the profit ambitions of the retailers themselves. Faced with buying from oligopolistic manufacturers, these retailers retaliated by forming themselves into buying complexes capable of exercising oligopsonistic power of their own. Their threat to remove their patronage to another supplier proved difficult to ignore. In the extreme, they can offer the further threat, realistic in light of their size and access to a residual earnings flow, to vertically integrate by setting up their own production capacity so to supply their retail shelves. The force of this threat enabled them to countervail the original positions of market power filled by the manufacturers.

This countervailing power thus acts to protect consumers from the power of manufacturers of consumer goods. Galbraith apparently presumed that the gains of volume buying are passed on to the consumer because of competition in the retail market.

Support for the notion of countervailing power is found in the fact that the second great merger wave, that of the 1920s, in contrast to the first wave around the turn of the century, was remarkable for its inclusion of retail and distribution enterprises. This second merger wave also demonstrated a tendency toward vertical integration, in contrast to the largely horizontal character of the first merger wave. Chain stores in department goods and groceries, mail-order firms, and cooperative buying by independent or non-chain retailers quickly became familiar features of the American economic landscape.

The spontaneous generation of countervailing power in the private sector does not complete the task, however, and here Galbraith interjected a further bit of historical explanation. As noted, government had expanded greatly in the wake of the inter-war turbulence. This expansion is explained in part by the need of some interests to secure government dispensation in support of their efforts to develop countervailing power.

Farmers and workers are notable in this regard. Farmer cooperatives to deal with the two-sided disadvantages of the agricultural sector are common. Farmers have attempted to cooperate in buying inputs and in selling output to the urban centers. The latter, marketing cooperatives were not in the main successful because of the premium that any individual could earn by agreeing but reneging on the agreement. This is a well-known application of the prisoner's dilemma in which the gains of all cooperating are squandered because each individual is reluctant to act upon the assumption that all will indeed cooperate. Purchasing cooperatives enjoy greater success because the benefit of belonging is easier to convey to those who hold up the bargain. Not surprisingly, the main focus of agrarian policy was to control the production and marketing of agricultural output.

Labor, like the farmers, struggled for a long period against the superior power of its employers. The eventual entry of organized labor into the post-war establishment required the active intervention of the state to mandate good-faith industrial bargaining. The state also supported the labor interest indirectly with aggregate demand maintenance and income support programs. The power of any economic agent in selling a commodity is enhanced by the prevalence of a relatively tight market.

Galbraith argued that the concept of countervailing power necessitates a new view of the state's role in the economy. Its pivotal domestic function becomes assisting where necessary the development of countervailing power in relation to positions of original power. This he maintained should lead to a re-viewing of the role of the state. Support of labor and agricultural interests should be case-specific. The goal is not to sustain the rise of original power but to assist the development of countervailing power in the face of original power. Antitrust laws should be applied with care and with an eye to whether their object is countervailing or original power.

Here Galbraith in effect was insisting that policy be designed and applied with cognizance of a dualized economic structure. This is to become a major theme of the Galbraithian System. In a passage noteworthy for its prescience, he observed that 'we may expect domestic political differences to turn on the question of supporting or not supporting efforts to develop countervailing power' (Galbraith, 1952b, p. 151). In many ways the 'conservative' and 'liberal' positions on the American political spectrum came to divide roughly along this line.

At any rate Galbraith's concern with the political economy of distribution, like that of other institutionalists, was not solely one of humane concern for social justice. In the spirit of Keynes they sought enhanced macroeconomic performance by overcoming the endemic maldistribution problem of mature capitalism (Ayres, 1946 and 1962). Maldistribution is part of the microeconomic foundations of macroeconomic instability, as are structural imbalances generally. So also is the existence of market power a vastly significant element of these microeconomic foundations. On this too Galbraith has had much to say and in this regard also did much of the Galbraithian System begin to take shape in *American Capitalism.*

Countervailing power also leaves a considerable macroeconomic problem in its wake. The 'Keynesian formula', a.k.a. the *neoclassical synthesis,* consists in influencing the overall business climate via aggregate demand policy but leaving alone the details of business and consumer decision-making (Galbraith, 1952b, p. 178). Galbraith and other institutionalists, as already noted, were among the first to question the adequacy of this strategy. Galbraith found this strategy problematic with respect to its neglect of microeconomic structure and its neglect of the reality of business and political culture.

Galbraith (1952b, pp. 180–90) also mused about the difficulties posed to the neo-Keynesian scenario by the boom phenomenon. As time passes, the 'depression psychosis' ebbs and 'old-fashioned speculative boom' re-emerges. Confidence that government will avert any serious slump can erode business reluctance to build inventories and generate 'vigorous borrowing' for investment. The consuming public, its income already shored up by income protection schemes that balance the flow of income, may also become confident that no serious slump is likely and see no reason to build up the precautionary balances that Keynes introduced and may engage instead in debt-financed consumption.

Absent old fashioned ideology against unbalanced budgets, the populist pressure toward inflationism may be difficult to resist. In any event, what Galbraith was later to refer to as the *political asymmetry* of the Keynesian aggregate demand strategy involves the legislative bias toward combatting unemployment rather than inflation because increased public largesse and tax reductions are more palatable than spending cuts and tax increases (Galbraith, 1952b, pp. 194–5).

The eventual pricking of such a speculative bubble must necessarily consist of a sharp reduction in the level of economic activity. The policy makers are thus left with the choice of ratifying inflation or causing a sharp correction. Much of Galbraith's analysis here is comparable to the 'financial instability hypothesis' of Hyman Minsky who also detects a fundamental 'inflationary bias' in the economy under the guidance of the neoclassical synthesis (Minsky, 1986).

Galbraith added to the inflationary prospect a serious problem of microeconomic structure. A brisk or sellers' market shifts the power balance toward sellers. Manufacturers can pass on increased costs of higher wages and distributors of higher wholesale costs. The wage and price interaction sets in and adds a further boost to inflation that is dynamic and continuous so long as it is validated financially. Galbraith (1952b, p. 193n) seems to have come very near the concept of endogenous money in his expectation that barring a sharp reversal of the speculative boom, financing will likely be available.

Of course, the policy could be instead to attempt to maintain an economy of slack so that the force of countervailing power remains effective. Galbraith (1952b, pp. 197–9) seems here to have favored this option and to have considered wage and price controls to be warranted only if military considerations require maximal production. This is curious not only in relation to his subsequent work but also in relation to *The Theory of Price Control* published alongside *American Capitalism*, all the more so since the former preceded the latter in gestation.

INTIMATIONS OF THE GALBRAITHIAN SYSTEM

Nor is the confusion with regard to stabilization policy the only unsatisfying aspect of *American Capitalism*. Even sympathetic observers commented that Galbraith needed a more general and systematic theory of power (Schweitzer, 1954; Adams, 1953). Galbraith has since distanced himself from much of the argument of *American Capitalism* and greatly refined his treatment of power. In particular, the wider political problem to which Adams referred became very prominent in the mature Galbraithian System in which the *public cognizance* concept was formulated to refer to the entrenched political power of the administered sector.

The notion of countervailing power does point toward the formation of a post-Second World War political economic *establishment* in which both countervailing and original power are ensconced. There is much to recommend Ben Ward's characterization of the modern liberal attitude that much of the success of the affluent democracies is bound up with development of an establishment that confers a stake in the system upon a wide range of political economic interests (Ward, 1979).

This is not to deny that important groups have been persistently left out of the post-war social contract, nor that efforts to overcome this neglect ultimately placed considerable strain on the post-war social contract (Bowles, *et al.*, 1983; Clarke, 1989; Stanfield, 1990). The failure of the establishment to embrace the countervailing power logic and to strive to include more disenfranchised strata into its orbit was in many ways the subject of a later book by Galbraith, *The Culture of Contentment*. Lester Thurow (1992) has also commented upon the myopia of the American political economic establishment in that it lacks the confidence that it will participate in a successful long term strategy based upon temperance of its short term interests.

The seeds of *The Affluent Society* are found in the chapter entitled 'The Unseemly Economics of Opulence' (Galbraith, 1952b) in which Galbraith tacked on the theme of affluence and waste. He asserted that the American economy is wasteful and inefficient in a static sense, but that it can afford this waste because of its dynamic efficiency. The most spectacular waste is advertizing and related selling costs which are uniquely characteristic of affluent societies. 'No one would advertise the sound-effects of processed breakfast foods striking the milk to . . . [those] who have only the resources to buy oatmeal' (1952b, pp. 100–1).

That Galbraith confessed 'equanimity' with regard to this waste is puzzling not only in light of the stridently critical mood of his later works, but even with respect to the far from complacent thrust of his argument in the book under discussion. The discussion of the misplaced concern of economists with the expansion of private consumption is an obvious harbinger of the *theory of social balance*. Indeed the following passage rivals the more memorable indictments of the later book.

> The result is an inefficient deployment of the economist's own resources. He is excessively preoccupied with goods *qua* goods. . . . he has not paused to reflect on the relative unimportance of the goods with which he is preoccupied. He worries far too much about partially monopolized prices or excessive advertising and selling costs for tobacco, liquor, chocolates, automobiles and soap in a land which is already suffering from nicotine poisoning and alcoholism, which is nutritionally gorged with sugar, which is filling its hospitals and cemeteries with those who have been maimed or murdered on its highways and which is dangerously neurotic about normal body odors. (Galbraith, 1952b, p. 102)

This is not a complacent paragraph. Indeed one would rather say it contains a sense of urgency at the prospect of a social economy going mad without benefit of counsel from its relevant professional therapists, economists. Uniquely suffering Veblenian 'trained incapacity' by their indoctrination in the formal economics of ineluctable scarcity and the allegedly self-regulating process of market exchange, economists are here depicted as so out of touch with reality as to be the agents of the very dementia they are hired to remedy.

Moreover, Galbraith's use of phrase so forceful as 'dangerously neurotic' without explanation or elaboration must be questioned. He did anticipate much of his later concern with social imbalance and the persistence of poverty and inequality that is unnecessary in an affluent society. There are strong harbingers to his subsequent insistence in *The New Industrial State* upon the significance of the dual economic structure. There is even a hint at the exploitation and self-exploitation upon which success in the market sector is said to rest in *Economics and the Public Purpose*. But there is not anything approaching a psycho-cultural critical theoretic that would warrant the use of so potent a term as 'dangerously neurotic.' Galbraith, not for the last time, ducked the repercussions of his own model.

American Capitalism, as Galbraith has conceded, is a deeply flawed book. It lacks the clarity that has become Galbraith's trademark. The forceful presentation of economic structure that has come to characterize the Galbraithian System is diluted by the preoccupation with excessive aggregate demand and the psychology of the boom. Perhaps, along with the other two books from this time, it is best viewed as an energetic burst of vision in which an important pattern model is emerging of an economy in motion that is axially structured very differently from the way it is conventionally depicted.

Even here in its infancy the Galbraithian System is the unerring guide to the future at almost every remove in the postwar context. Galbraith's insistent anticipation of the chronic and decisive maladies of the post-war social order is virtually unmatched. It began with the theory of countervailing power and the prospect of an American capitalism beset by inflationary bias and a dubious preoccupation with private consumption in the face of an 'unseemly opulence'. It eventually substantiates the indictment suggested by the phrase 'dangerously neurotic.' The reader is advised to press on, for the story is portentous and stimulating.

3 Affluence and Social Imbalance

I know not why it should be a matter of congratulation that persons who are already richer than anyone needs to be, should have doubled their means of consuming things which give little or no pleasure except as representative of wealth.

(J.S. Mill, 1848 [1985])

Fired by an emotional faith in spontaneity, the common-sense attitude toward change was discarded in favor of a mystical readiness to accept the social consequences of economic improvement, whatever they might be.... Household truths of traditional statesmanship ... were ... erased by the corrosive of a crude utilitariansim combined with an uncritical reliance on the alleged self-healing virtues of unconscious growth.

(K. Polanyi, 1944)

John Kenneth Galbraith's *The Affluent Society* is one of the most famous books of the last twenty-five years. Its fame and, with the qualification that its basic message has gone unheeded, its influence, are indicated by its large sales; the adoption of its terminology; and the reviews, citations, and discussion given it (Sharpe, 1972; Hession, 1972; Gambs, 1975; Munro, 1977; Reisman, 1980).

Ironically, the book emerged from Galbraith's effort to write a different book, that was to be titled 'Why People Are Poor,' on 'the causes of the poverty that made economic improvement so urgent' (Galbraith, 1981, p. 305). Galbraith reckoned that an examination of the poverty that persisted in the United States was an appropriate preliminary step toward the investigation of poverty in the less-developed nations. *The Affluent Society* was the serendipitous result of this intended preliminary excursion: Galbraith (1981, pp. 335–7) came to see that affluence rather than poverty was novel and unexamined and that its understanding was the missing ingredient in the treatment of twentieth-century poverty.

The Affluent Society vaulted Galbraith from a well-known, if eccentric economist into an intellectual celebrity. Whatever his intent, as Robert Heilbroner has remarked about his own best seller, *The Worldly Philosophers* (1986), the book turned out to be an annuity. Its success sustained a varied career in public service and social commentary for Galbraith and

41

guaranteed wide attention, even among economists, to the later works (1967 and 1973b) in his major trilogy.

Many of the concerns of *The Affluent Society* showed up in the challenge to economic growth as the highest social purpose. For a decade and a half after the book's appearance, the most remarkable aspect of intellectual life and popular culture was the *counter-culture*. Throughout the 1960s social movements gained strength in their efforts to increase collective action to protect the environment, improve working conditions, beautify America, and generally to look beyond fetishistic attachment to commodities in pursuit of the good life. Given his stance in the tradition of evolutionary positivism, Galbraith would be the first to cite circumstance and fact over the academic scribbler; nonetheless his ideas played no small part in this challenge to the conventional wisdom that more commodities are better.

Nor did Galbraith emerge from a vacuum. John Stuart Mill (1985) had long before questioned the wisdom of endless accumulation and acquisition and looked forward to a time when the human urge for progress would be focused upon cultivating the art of living. Karl Marx, Thorstein Veblen, and Simon Nelson Patten had developed the notion of a thoroughgoing abundance that might eventually implicate a fundamental reordering of social priorities. John Maynard Keynes (1963) in his famous essay on the prospects for the grandchildren of his generation had divided wants in a manner very similar to Veblen and hypothesized the eventual solution of the economic problem of scarcity. In Galbraith's own time, the historian David Potter (1954) had further explored the theme of affluence and human character.

There were even others expressing similar ideas on private affluence and public squalor, notably Alvin Hansen and Arthur Schlesinger, Jr. But *The Affluent Society* seized the minds both of those who found its message palatable and those who did not, and became the lightning rod on the discourse about the habitual inclination to identify the good life with the goods life (Brown, 1988).

In this chapter, the argument of *The Affluent Society* is summarized by explication of the two major concepts of the book, the *dependence effect* and the *theory of social balance*. The first of these asserts that the habitual acceptance of the doctrine of consumer or household sovereignty fails to examine the tendency for the wants of consumers to be influenced by the powerful purveyors of the commodities said to be produced to satisfy these wants. Galbraith posits the pernicious results of this habitual or *conventional wisdom* with the notion of social balance by which he contrasts the copious abundance of commodities produced to serve private virtue and vice with the squalid results of the inveterate parsimony accorded to the supply of public goods. The chapter closes with a few remarks on the prophetic vision of the book and its relevance to the 1980s and 1990s.

THE DEPENDENCE EFFECT

The first of two major concerns in *The Affluent Society* is explaining the urgency attached to higher consumption and the paramount stature accorded to the growth of production that persist in the democratic industrial societies despite their unprecedented affluence. In general, as stressed by the American institutionalists, the explanation is that ideas are held over from one historical setting to another in which, whatever their validity in the historical furnace in which they were forged, they are obsolete and ill-suited to the new reality around them. These ideological holdovers persist not merely by inertia alone but because they are convenient to powerful vested interests.

This theme is familiar from Veblen's *Theory of the Leisure Class* (1953) in which the conservation of archaic traits is maliciously pilloried. Indeed this comprises a central aspect of Veblen's celebrated dichotomy between the forward thrust of knowledge and skill and the resistant tug of the ceremony and habituation of extant use and wont. It is similar in all important respects to Marx's aspirations to penetrate the illusions attendant to everyday life so as to demystify the seeming inevitability of capitalist economic institutions (Stanfield, 1995a, chs 11, 12). For Marx as well, something like *cultural lag* ensues and humanity is unable to realize the full potential of the forces of production it has created until and unless a fundamental reconstruction is accomplished with respect to the governing relations of the material process. For radical institutionalists, the envisioned reconstruction may be less abrupt than Marx's project but it comprises no less important place in their consideration of the human prospect (Stanfield, 1995a, ch. 8).

Galbraith's term for the habitual intellectual inclination that fetters the pursuit of human betterment is the unforgettable *conventional wisdom*. The main currents of the conventional wisdom in economic affairs were established in the eighteenth century, refined in the next century by the classical and neoclassical traditions, and amended by the Keynesian Revolution in the present century. After centuries of relatively slow permanent economic growth, the modern discipline of economics arose concomitant to the persistent and spectacular growth of output known as the Industrial Revolution. Given the long history of mass privation and the new history of economic insecurity due to industrial instability, the 'tradition of despair' developed. This preoccupation with the dismal aspects of economics discourse is central to the inveterate focus of economic thought upon scarcity and the interwoven issues of real income production, inequality, and insecurity.

Galbraith argues that by the middle of this century, economists had defused the issues of inequality and insecurity by subordinating them to the overriding objective of raising production. There had been an arrest of the tendency for inequality to worsen and a shift away from the extravagant embellishments of personal life that Veblen ridiculed in *The Theory of the Leisure Class*. Indeed for Galbraith it seemed clear that administration of the forces of production was surpassing personal ostentation as the mode by which to signify personal prowess (Galbraith, 1958, p. 94). But the major force in the uneasy truce on inequality was the solvent of economic growth. Growth in real income enables all classes to advance in absolute terms and averts the vastly more pithy and controversial problem of income and wealth redistribution. A modern liberal and classical liberal consensus on growth thus supplants the bitter controversy on inequality.

So too did the growth consensus submerge the issue of economic insecurity. So long as income is linked to productive performance, economic security is possible only through the high employment made possible by sustained growth. For good measure, national security is added to the side of expanding output because industrial supremacy is seen as a necessary ingredient to superior military preparedness. The primacy of securing growth of aggregate output becomes the Rosetta stone from which to decipher the apparent cacophony of modernity in which nothing is truly sacred save the doctrine of scarcity.

There are also strong vested interests behind the 'paramount position of production'. Those who in one way or another enjoy their income, prestige, and power because they can contribute to, guide, or understand the process of expanding production, have a vested interest in maintaining the top priority accorded to economic growth. Put negatively, any decline in the importance attached to expanding output would *pari passu* lead to a decline in their income, prestige, and power. Business executives and technical professionals who run the social machinery of production, wealthy people who have accumulated purchasing power, politicians whose platforms and constituencies are based on government fostering of growth, and academic economists whose central ideas are concerned with scarcity and growth all have varying degrees of vested interests in the continuing preoccupation with expanding production.

In short, the *growth lobby* had emerged. Strong ideological sentiment and powerful political economic interests became wedded to the central proposition that the more GNP, the better. Much else that concerned or should have concerned society was deposited beneath the growth rug. To challenge growth became a sure sign of immaturity if one could be so pardoned, insanity if not. 'It is an index of the prestige of production in our national attitudes that it is identified with the sensible and practical' (Galbraith, 1958, p. 122). Karl Polanyi's (1944) prose decrying the classical liberal faith in the crude corrosive of material progress may be more applicable to the post-war growth lobby than ever before. Certainly it is difficult to conjure a more crude and indiscriminant arbiter of social success than that promoted by GNP fetishism.

Nothing in *The Affluent Society* so activated controversy as the discussion which deals with the maintenance of popular emphasis on consuming more, i.e., with assuring that people continue to want more no matter how much they possess already. In discussing the process of want creation, Galbraith utilizes the concept of the *dependence effect* by which wants arise from what one sees others consuming, especially as portrayed in advertising. Emulation is the passive and probably innate aspect of the process of want creation. People emulate one another in an attempt to curry favor, display their modernity or good taste, or keep up with others in the incomes race. The active and crucial elements of the process are advertising and other salesmanship activities. These present a persistent cultural theme: BUY! The presence of such vast efforts to create wants leads Galbraith to doubt the case for the continuing urgency of expanding output to satisfy them.

Galbraith could have been more careful in stating the dependence effect. Consider a key sentence in his argument. 'If the individual's wants are to be urgent they must be original with himself. They cannot be urgent if they are contrived for him' (1958, p. 152). There is a vastly misleading phrase here as well as a profoundly important key word. The misleading phrase is 'original with himself'. This establishes a straw person that is altogether too easily assassinated. As Hayek (in Phelps (ed.), 1965, pp. 37–42) observed, all wants are culturally derived so it is a *non sequitur* to assert that wants which are learned rather than innate are relatively unimportant.

The word *contrived* is pivotal, and it deflects another point made by Hayek that the want-creating activities of producers are only a part of the cultural milieu. This pluralism argument is anticipated by Galbraith's emphasis upon wants being contrived to serve the needs of powerful purveyors of commodities. Excessive corporate power in the media may obstruct the sustenance of a genuine pluralism and its expression via a genuinely democratic process of decision-making on the basis of inquiry and reason (Stanfield, 1979, chs 3, 4; Tilman, 1987). A plurality of cost centers financing the expression of viewpoints does not guarantee genuine pluralism per se. Pluralism is not well-served if the various cost centers are only willing to pay for the same basic message, no matter that it is here wrapped in a promotion for nose spray and there in a commercial for diet soda.

Strong doubt must indeed attach to the urgency of wants so contrived. The specter thus arises of *self-justifying commodity production*, commodities produced to serve the pecuniary interests of the businesses selling them without having passed muster as to their value to any reasonable substantive purpose in the human life process. This perception raises troubling questions about legitimacy and value in the contemporary institutional configuration (Stanfield, 1995a ch. 4). There is an important difference between the general acquisition of tastes through acculturation and the systematic imposition of tastes to fit the needs of powerful vested interests. Life as a marionette earning and spending incomes is inconsistent with all known conceptions of the good society, so much more so if the marionette's behavior is cited as inveterate evidence against the feasibility of environmental protection, greater social equality, increased social amenities, and reduced economic insecurity. Further, as Galbraith indicates, the important aspect is the participation of the commodity producer in demand creation. The message of *The Affluent Society* is that democratic industrial society is wedded to an ideology of consumption and economic growth (Stanfield, 1995a, ch. 6); its central cultural context, the core of its idea and value systems, is that more-is-better. People are socialized to judge the system and its leaders by the economic cornucopia, to seek happiness via consumption, to solve problems by buying, and to relate to one another through possessions. The intent of advertising is to convert any and every human need to commodity terms; any feeling of impotence, lack of belonging or sense of purpose, or unhappiness is portrayed as a consumption problem. If one is not happy, s/he is systematically taught that the problem must rest with the selection of a deodorant, toothpaste, hairstyle, automobile, diet soft drink, or other consumer commodity. The ideology of consumption systematically indoctrinates people into a commoditized interpretation of their needs. All needs are reduced to needs for commodities and any perceived deficiency in one's life is seen necessarily to stem from inadequate consumption. No matter the problem at issue, the only answer is to consume more.

The intellectual bedrock of the continuing importance of more output is provided by the economic doctrine of insatiable consumer wants. For the conventional economist, human wants are *datum*; neither their formation nor their quality is appropriate subject matter for economic investigation. Further, the extent of wants is assumed to exceed the extent of the resources available to satisfy them. This effectively prohibits practitioners of the economic arts from examining, by any standard or to any effect, such questions as the influence exercised on popular wants by powerful economic agents or the validity of established wants with respect to social canons of legitimacy.

The habitual proclivity of economists deflects attention away from the issue of want formation, away from the generation and distribution of earnings capacity, and away from the collective structuring of the context within which individual preferences and capacities are applied (Stanfield, 1995a, ch. 1). Of course, economists do not dictate popular consciousness, but in an econocentric culture, they exercise important influence upon it.

Galbraith refines these issues in the later entries in his trilogy. He formulates the *revised sequence* concept in which producers rather than consumers are sovereign and the *imagery of choice* indictment of the neoclassical synthesis for its obscurantist service to the powers that be. However, even in the later works, it must be conceded that Galbraith rests his case on *a fortiori* evidence. The large corporations have an interest in manipulating consumer tastes and they expend prodigious sums of money in an effort to do so. The question nonetheless remains open as to their success in this regard (Schudson, 1984). At least one should attempt to explain the rising gullibility to manipulation. There would seen to be nothing inherent in affluence that would weaken the mental resistance to persuasion. A further step is necessary, namely, analyzing the content of these wants and constructively criticizing the learning process so as to indicate how it can be improved (Zebot, 1959).

Perhaps something along the lines of the Marxist concept of alienation would serve to close this lacuna in the Galbraithian System (Stanfield, 1995a, ch. 10); so also could the analysis be improved by explicitly linking it to the instrumental reasoning emphasized by institutionalists such as C.E. Ayres. The concept of alienation examines human estrangement from some fundamentally and characteristically human aspect. This in turn allows the postulation of some higher standard of efficiency such as that offered by the process of instrumental reasoning (Stanfield, 1995a, ch. 13). The analysis thereby suggests the critical scenario that, unable to secure fulfillment of their generic human needs in the commodity production society, people pursue gratification in the stultified outlets defined for them by the culture of commodity fetishism.

Perhaps the systemic effect of the ideology of consumption is less in doubt. In later works, Galbraith places renewed emphasis upon the overall, cumulative effect of sales activities. Although individual advertisements are competitive, buy product A rather than B, their aggregate message is 'buy,' period. Moreover, in a commercialized society, the messages of powerful producers exert a disproportionate influence on cultural programming and social attitudes, and ultimately on the conduct of the state.

SOCIAL IMBALANCE AND PUBLIC SQUALOR

The second major concern of *The Affluent Society* is to examine the implications and consequences of the tenacious devotion to economic growth. The general issue here is that the mentality of more-is-better is obstructionist and stands in the way of the further economic progress which would be possible if the tremendous wealth of democratic industrial societies were put to saner and more humane use. Galbraith foresaw grave consequences in relation to the preoccupation with economic growth. Economic security is threatened by the runaway growth in consumer debt that rises concomitantly to the preoccupation with consumer persuasion in business practice. Easier credit checks, lower down payments, longer repayment terms, and inducement for people to go further and further into debt are permanent and necessary fixtures in the landscape of the consumer society described in *The Affluent Society*. This increases uncertainty and economic instability, thereby threatening economic security. Witness the recent concern about a capital shortage, the falling propensity to save, and credit-fed inflationary buying.

Less convincingly, Galbraith argued that national security is threatened by the illusion that high growth per se is sufficient to preserve the peace. The incessant effort to convince people that they need to consume at ever higher levels, Galbraith surmised, might make it difficult to convince them to forego consumption for necessary defense.

Galbraith also argued that the paramount position of production makes persistent inflation all but inevitable. The economy must be operated near full capacity where excess demand and the market power of organized economic agents make inflation *normal* rather than exceptional. Policies which would contain inflation, most especially policy founded on the crude instruments of monetary and fiscal policy, would also damage production and are therefore inadmissable because of the paramount position of production (see also Minsky's discussion of inflationary bias, 1986; and Stanfield and Phillips, 1991). More effective policy measures, such as wage-price controls, incomes policy, national economic planning, and other structural and supply-side policies cannot be effectively applied until policy formulation is freed from the restrictive grip of the conventional wisdom.

Some of the most telling discussion in *The Affluent Society* is that which deals with the *theory of social (im)balance*. Galbraith maintained that the preoccupation with expanding production and the process of consumer want creation that sustains it would contribute toward a penurious public sector. Added to the traditional anti-government bias of market capitalist ideology, the incessant attention to private consumption obscures the need for collective action in areas critically important to the quality of life in contemporary society. Nothing so strong as the dependence effect, especially its active ingredient of advertising, operates to draw attention to these collective wants.

Yet a moment's reflection establishes that private and collective wants are complementary. The increased utilization of automobiles must go hand in hand with increased collective provision of roads and traffic control. Suburbanization in the wake of the automobile age requires a far-flung government apparatus to service and protect dispersed neighborhoods. The resort to an ever greater volume of packaged goods and disposable items necessitates more trash removal and solid waste disposal planning. Galbraith even anticipates the trend toward dual-earner households and notes it too has implications with regard to social balance. Increased participation of both spouses in the paid labor force will generate a need for more collectively regulated and provided environments to occupy the time of children.

The principle of social balance simply states that, for a given level of private consumption, there is an optimal size public sector. The most insistent of the book's lamentations is that this principle is not observed in the contemporary society, so that there exists a debilitating imbalance between our commercial affluence and our collective provision. In forcefully making this contrast between private opulence and public squalor Galbraith issues what is perhaps the book's most famous paragraph:

> The family which takes its mauve and cerise, air-conditioned, power-steered, and power-braked automobile out for a tour passes through cities that are badly paved, made hideous by litter, blighted buildings, billboards, and posts for wires that should long since have been put underground. They pass on into a countryside that has been rendered largely invisible by commercial art. (The goods which the latter advertise have an absolute priority in our value system. Such aesthetic considerations as a view of the countryside accordingly come second. On such

matters we are consistent.) They picnic on exquisitely packaged food from a portable icebox by a polluted stream and go on to spend the night at a park which is a menace to public health and morals. Just before dozing off on an air-mattress, beneath a nylon tent, amid the stench of decaying refuse, they may reflect vaguely on the curious un-evenness of their blessings. Is this, indeed, the American genius? (Galbraith, 1958, p. 253)

Galbraith viewed this paragraph, though not the point it addressed, with extreme diffidence. In his memoirs he enjoyed a chuckle in this regard: 'I lingered over this paragraph. I thought it too patently contrived, too ripe, but in the end I let it stay. It was the most quoted passage in the book' (Galbraith, 1981, p. 340).

There are other serious consequences of the preoccupation with private production and consumption. Personal or human capital is neglected, as is the serious poverty that remains and the continuing but dubiously neces-sary agony of toil. Insecurity, inflation, social imbalance, and the failure to affirm personal development, eradicate poverty, and reduce the burden of toil are the legacy of the obsolete mentality described in *The Affluent Society*. Galbraith insisted that a sane and humane society would make far better use of its affluence.

Galbraith's case is not simply that poor taste in the purchase of goods in the private sector means that public spending would necessarily be bet-ter (Wallich, in Phelps (ed.), 1965, p. 45). He cites many examples of penurious public sector spending and their deleterious effects, such as in-sufficient resources devoted to education, playgrounds, municipal services, and medical care delivery. These incontrovertible limitations on the qual-ity of life are then contrasted with the plethora of gadgets and ostentation in the private sector, not to prove the need to expand collective consumption, but only to argue that the opportunity cost of such an expansion is not as great as is habitually thought because the importance of the private con-sumption that would have to be forgone is not so great as is habitually believed.

In another way, however, the contrast between private affluence and pub-lic squalor does not entirely capture the pivotal forces at work. In twentieth-century capitalism, government has a vastly expanded economic presence, notably in the areas of defense, roads and highways, traffic control, and parking (Baran and Sweezy, 1966, ch. 6). Baran and Sweezy contended that what the government does is constrained and shaped by powerful pri-vate interests so that there are definite limits on public spending in certain areas, such as health, education, and housing, in which higher public spending would conflict with the class structure and business hegemony of capitalist society.

In the later works of his trilogy, Galbraith refines the analysis of social imbalance, recognizing that some public sector spending is favored because it fits the interests of the powerful corporate system. Other collective wants, and indeed some significant private wants, fare badly because there is no strong voice for them amongst the powers that be. The *technostructure*, as Galbraith is to anoint his power elite, promulgates a very distorted set of social priorities as it exercises its undue influence upon both the public and private sectors.

Some mention must be made of the rather curious Chapter 13 in *The Affluent Society* in which Galbraith frets about whether or not the Pentagon would get enough resources to wage an all-out war if called upon to do so. His concern was that so much attention is devoted to private consumption that popular willingness to forego it in order to support a war effort would be undermined.

One supposes that this curious proposition is an extrapolation of Galbraith's experience in the Second World War. It ties into the concern about situations of hyper-full employment aggregate demand and the disequilibrium system that characterized his books in the early 1950s. Then as in the present case this concern obstructed his full attention being applied to the structural edifice of the administered society.

It would appear that in comparison to more radical theorists, Galbraith was slow to come to grips with the phenomena of military Keynesianism and the peace–war double talk that sustains the lunacy of seeking to reduce the prospect that weapons of mass destruction will be used by constructing as many of them as possible. He fares better in comparison to his liberal peers in the Democratic Party, among whom cold war corporate liberalism was all too popular a stance (Markowitz, 1973). By the middle of the 1960s Galbraith had become an ardent critic of the defense establishment. *The New Industrial State* argument in this regard was followed by a pamphlet that concisely set out the indictment of the military and industrial complex that Eisenhower prophesied (Galbraith, 1969).

In retrospect friendly readers should perhaps accord benign neglect to the peculiar Chapter 13 of *The Affluent Society*. But it is interesting to note that for all the 1980s rhetoric about remilitarization, there was little evidence of any popular commitment to reduce consumption to pay for making America number one again in the ability to abort human life as we know it.

The preoccupation with excess aggregate demand is also apparent in the discussion of inflation in *The Affluent Society*. Galbraith (1958, p. 218n) notes that he views the discussion of inflation in the book to be similar but hopefully improved over that of *American Capitalism*. Perhaps, but he still seems to come down on the side of applying some slack to restrain inflation (1958, p. 213), despite going on to formulate the asymmetry of the effects of higher interest rates upon the dualized economic sectors. His discussion seems more to the point that monetary policy will not be applied than that it should not be.

Of course this is not to say that Galbraith is incorrect in the main. The restraint of the economy via aggregate demand is bitter medicine. As we have seen he had already anticipated the asymmetry of fiscal policy in the early 1950s books. In *The Affluent Society*, he again submits the difficulty of combatting inflation by this instrument, observing that

fiscal policy to counter inflation will almost always require an increase in taxes. The importance of cutting or postponing expenditures, however much it may be urged on the more vacuous margins of the conventional wisdom, may on occasion sustain hope. But the accomplishment will invariably be negligible. On this point experience is complete. (Galbraith, 1958, p. 241)

This paragraph is astonishingly apropos to the obdurate discussion over the past two decades with regard to 'the deficit'. As the next section illustrates, this is one of many instances of prescience apparent in Galbraith's 1958 book.

THE TEST OF TIME

Galbraith's vision in writing *The Affluent Society* was uncannily prophetic; he repeatedly raised trends and issues that have since come to the fore. The vociferous criticism levelled at the book attests to its potential significance, much of which remains unrealized and therefore of continuing relevance. The fundamental themes of *The Affluent Society* continue to threaten conservative and classical liberal puffery and neoclassical economic complacency. In part this continuing relevance reflects the uncanny anticipation in *The Affluent Society* on matters of detail that have since emerged as problems or issues.

Galbraith's (1958, pp. 263, 315–20) assertions on taxation and the revenue imbalance in the American governmental structure presaged a revival of discussion of fiscal federalism and important revenue-sharing programs as well as a continuing discourse on shifting to a consumption-based tax. It is not a stretch to connect his observations in this regard to the subsequent fiscal crisis of American government (O'Connor, 1973).

His concern with consumer credit (Galbraith, 1958, pp. 200–9) continued the institutionalist emphasis on the changing character of affluent capitalism, adding the element of consumer finance to the rise of salesmanship activities. This prefigured recognition of discretionary consumption in the analysis of business conditions and economic indicators. Much concern is now focused upon indices of consumer sentiment and investment is no longer the sole source of volatility in aggregate demand models. Indeed, Galbraith (1958, p. 200) hypothesized that consumer debt would be elastic with respect to the growth of consumption and income. Presumably this anticipates a decline in the personal saving rate – a matter that becomes deeply troubling after the capital shortage discussion resurrects classical economics in the 1970s.

The independence of the Federal Reserve Board (1958, p. 227) has been a perennial political economic issue in recent decades. The importance of human capital to economic growth (1958, p. 271), while neglected in the Reagan–Bush era, was a prime concern of the 1960s and is again a leading issue of the 1990s. The rising participation of women in the paid labor force (1958, p. 258) has become perhaps the most powerful element reshaping the nature of American society.

The concern for the degradation of the environment (1958, p. 355) was one of a handful of precursors to Rachel Carson's *Silent Spring* (1962), the book that is deservedly considered to have spawned a social movement. Galbraith's (1958, pp. 97 and 327–8) insistence that the nation not lose sight of the other, poverty-stricken, America was influential toward Michael Harrington's *The Other America* (1962) and the ensuing War on Poverty. Even today, the task of facing the obsolescence of the work and income link remains unrecognized (Galbraith, 1958, pp. 289–91). Nor has much been resolved in the many issues having to do with the quality of work life (1958, p. 334). Likewise, no consensus has emerged on the issue of industrial or structural policy focused on both the demand and supply sides of the economy (1958, pp. 246–7).

In *The Affluent Society*, Galbraith remarked that 'an incipient revolt' may have begun 'against goods or at least a refusal to allow competitive emulation to be the source of wants' (1958, p. 193). Such a revolt seems to have most definitely sprung to life and exerted considerable influence in the 1960s counter-culture, student, and environmental movements and in a heightened concern for quality of life. Galbraith also noted that any such revolt against production would be met by a counter-revolt by those with interests vested in production, who can be expected to 'battle vigorously for a value system which emphasizes the importance of production' (1958, p. 183).

This ideological battle over the relation between quality of life and quantity of output continues. The regulatory programs introduced to secure social and environmental objectives came under severe attack in the Carter, Reagan, and Bush administrations. This attack was conducted largely on the basis of the negative effects on productivity and economic growth of the regulatory programs. This provided a curious spectacle in that benefit-cost analyses were conducted without attention to benefits. Social imbalance is involved here also because many of the programs that moved society toward a better sectoral balance are imperiled by the current attack on the social welfare and regulatory state complex in the name of scarcity, productivity, and growth.

This power of anticipation and the continuing relevance of *The Affluent Society* is not idiosyncratic. It results from the institutionalist method of inquiry in which the economic problem is conceived as the problem of *institutional adjustment*. Galbraith represents the institutionalist logic of reform and its quest to uncover the fundamental social trends and problems of an affluent society. Galbraith (1958, pp. 250–1) poses the three unsolved problems of the affluent society as the process of consumer demand creation and financing, persistent inflation, and social imbalance between the public and private sectors. These problems remain unsolved and continue to serve as major impediments to advancing the development and quality of human life.

The three problems are interrelated. The invidiousness with which the process of demand creation is interwoven cultivates an ideology of consumption in which virtually all human needs are seen as commodity consumption needs. The result is a *treadmill syndrome*, as my co-author and I have termed it (Stanfield, 1995a, ch. 6), in which people pursue income to buy more things to consume, neglecting non-consumption needs in the process, and, feeling dissatisfied due to the neglected needs, set out after still more income and consumption. Galbraith's (1958, pp. 154, 159) suggestion of the squirrel cage metaphor no doubt suggested the treadmill syndrome phrase.

Financing this invidious consumer demand, and the investment to service it, makes it difficult to finance much-needed and highly beneficial collective and private action. The invidious pecuniary calculus is blind to non-commodity, non-income needs. Power wielded by those deluded by this mentality will be used to secure more income to sustain purchases of more commodities. Prices and incomes spiral upward and social and environmental considerations that lie outside the scorer's reach in this game of competitive emulation are neglected. The culture of competitive emulation places so much emphasis on individual pecuniary success that the degree of solidarity and social responsibility necessary for the welfare state to function smoothly is not present. Programs designed to remedy social imbalance and social injustice tend to be exploited by greedy manipulators and their failure written off to some original sin in human nature rather than to a defective culture and institutionalized patterns of behavior which are subject to human discretion (Stanfield, 1979, ch. 6, and 1995a, ch. 9). At the same time, the allocation of time and resources in the private sector is distorted with debilitating results (Schor, 1991).

The relevance of the social imbalance theme to the American present should be quite evident. Much has been said about the need to rebuild the deteriorating infrastructure and to respond to the educational crisis in order to fashion America's response to the new realities of global competition. So also there is growing recognition of a festering *nurturance gap* as Americans sacrifice childhood, intimacy, dignity, and civility in the interest of pecuniary values.

Galbraith foresaw much of this problematic, as when he observed that the unremitting persuasion toward earning income and buying commodities necessarily generates

> strong pressures to have as many wage earners in the family as possible . . . If both parents are engaged in private production [in the paid labor force], the burden on the public services is further increased. Children in effect become the charge of the community for an appreciable part of the time. If the services of the community do not keep pace, this will be another source of disorder. (Galbraith, 1958, p. 258)

Again, the problem of social imbalance is seen to be a version of the problem of cultural or institutional lag. Major changes in gender and family relations, with a powerful boost from advancing knowledge and technique, have not been met with the requisite collective action toward institutional adjustment. This has left a breech in many of the delicate and profoundly important tasks of nurturing labor (Stanfield and Stanfield, 1995).

The continuing problem remains that public amenities, education, and nurturance, if they are valued at all, tend to be so valued primarily as tools for increasing commodity production or increased international competitiveness. Those who have made this link to growth in commodity production have absorbed only half the truth. The full truth awaits complete understanding of the Galbraithian System and the modern liberal thrust. Sadly, in a government that is operated as an adjunct to corporate capitalism, education for the sake of human development as a goal in and of itself remains an external economy (Galbraith, 1958, p. 275), without compensable pecuniary benefits and therefore subject to pathological neglect in a pecuniary culture. Still, one shares Galbraith's hope that 'investment in the things that differentiate man from his animals requires no further justification' (1958, p. 278).

Galbraith's deeper message is the need to subordinate commodity production to the lives of beauty and joy that people should be able and expected to lead in the affluent world they inhabit. In such a scenario, ecological preservation and social continuity would serve as the cornerstone of a culture dedicated to individual development. This is the basic theme of Karl Polanyi's work (Stanfield, 1986), and of Marx before that, and it has enthralled modern worldly philosophers such as Adolph Lowe (1988) and Robert Heilbroner (1974).

There emerges then a hint of Veblenian pall in *The Affluent Society*. The imbecility of habitual patterns of cloying pursuit of pecuniary success is Veblenian. Galbraith's constitutional optimism notwithstanding, his message is most unsettling. The Veblenian mood becomes even clearer in Galbraith's derision of the conventional wisdom in economics and his indictment of the bulk of the economics profession for complicity in the debilitating ideological lacuna. The obsolescence of the conventional wisdom in economics is now woefully apparent as is its rootedness in an ahistorical approach to an essentially historical subject matter (Stanfield, 1979). 'Economics is not durable truth; it requires continuous revision and accommodation. Nearly all its error is from those who cannot change' (Galbraith, 1981, p. 125).

In *The Affluent Society*, Galbraith forcefully raised the specter of the obsolescence of economic thought in the face of social change:

> there are . . . grave drawbacks and even dangers in a system of thought which by its very nature and design avoids accommodation to circumstances until change is dramatically forced upon it. In large areas of economic affairs the march of events . . . has again left the conventional wisdom sadly obsolete. (1958, p. 29)

It should be remembered that this was a time of general complacency in the economics profession. Not long thereafter economists celebrated the great victory of the Kennedy tax cut and seriously debated whether or not the new economics of the neoclassical synthesis had permanently solved the problem of business fluctuations.

The obsolescence to which Galbraith adverted is apparent not only in the general refusal to accommodate the reality of an affluent society but also specifically in the area of macroeconomic stabilization policy. An insistent theme of Galbraith's works, not only in *The Affluent Society* (1958, pp. 224–5, 246–7) but also in *A Theory of Price Control* and *American Capitalism* before it and in *The New Industrial State* and *Economics and the Public Purpose* after it, is the need for a direct intervention mechanism to deal with the wage-price spiral. Such a policy is, however, effectively prohibited by the conventional wisdom because of distaste for the bureaucracy necessary to maintain it and the distortion of relative prices and resource allocation that it would cause. The logic of scarcity and the paramount position of commodity production underlie this hand wringing about resource allocation.

The prohibition of direct controls necessarily links economic security to inflation. Those who would be damaged by the requisite slack in aggregate demand to restrain wages and prices are likely to be the least able to bear such a burden. Their voices and those of observers sympathetic to their plight are raised in support of maximum aggregate demand, along with those voices that simply want maximum output because of the paramount position of production.

The surge in nativistic nostrums in American political economy in the past twenty-five years indicates the danger of the obsolete conventional wisdom. The counter-revolt against the twentieth century that began with lamentation about a capital shortage and government regulation continues with the prospect of abandoning the goals of the welfare state. The clamor about the crowding out of the private sector by government upholds, as a self-evident truth, the superiority of the former.

But the argument of *The Affluent Society* insists upon asking the incommodious question: *What is being crowded out?* How seriously can a reasonable person fret about foregoing the creation of the consumer debt necessary to satisfy wants derived from the corporate-sponsored game of competitive emulation? And, other than its connection to employment security, a connection that could be linked instead to expansion of the public sector, how much concern is warranted about denying borrowed funds to corporate executives to invest in meeting such consumer wants or, perhaps worse, to be devoted to financial manipulation or intensified ostentation in the executive suites? Is it not more distressing that funds are denied public education, parks, income maintenance, and support of the arts in order to service such dubious priorities?

The problem in question is not, of course, limited to the public sector versus the private sector. Within the public sector itself, the counter-revolt is taking its toll. Military expenditures continue to be exempt from the close scrutiny to which a reasonable society would subject such obviously dead-weight drags on human well-being. The call for public investment neglects the truth that *a person rescued from deprivation is a person promoted to participation in society.* Although there is nothing wrong per se with a policy of encouraging technical training and advance narrowly conceived, in this case it is evidence of a deep-seated neglect of the more fundamental crisis facing the affluent society, one which cannot be resolved by technical manipulation. The more fundamental problems relate to the spirit or ideology of the age and have more to do with the folly of continuing the game of competitive emulation than with who succeeds at it.

The major lesson of Galbraith's work on the whole is that realization of the potential of the affluent society would require that the conventional wisdom be discarded. As an evolutionary positivist, he frequently notes that intellectual obsolescence will ultimately yield only to the force of hard fact and circumstance (Galbraith, 1958, pp. 13 and 20). He does not, however, neglect the need for an ideological struggle that strategically makes use of historical circumstance in its quest to overturn the conventional wisdom. Indeed, one of his most important themes is the need for some more or less organized *cultural resistance* to the ideological hegemony exercised by the corporate elite and the complicitous neoclassical mainstream. The myth that expanding production is the central social problem can be debunked only through sustained effort devoted to the 'emancipation of the mind' (Galbraith, 1958, p. 281).

In *The New Industrial State*, Galbraith urged the 'educational and scientific estate' to take the 'political lead' in breaking 'the monopoly of the industrial system on social purpose' (p. 387). Interestingly, this book was published in the same year that Clarence Ayres, in the first article ever published in the *Journal of Economic Issues*, argued that the intellectual's responsibility includes the 'responsibility to understand something of the nature and functioning of the ideology of our own society, and to convey this knowledge to the intellectually less advantaged community' (Ayres, 1967, p. 3).

Galbraith further elaborates this theme in *Economics and the Public Purpose*, devoting a chapter to 'The Emancipation of Belief' that is usefully read in conjunction with his 1969 lecture to the American Economic Association (Galbraith, 1971a, ch. 4). The belief from which emancipation is required is, of course, the ideology that subordinates all other social concerns to the maximization of income and consumption.

The enduring message of *The Affluent Society* is that pernicious effects on the quality of life flow from the fact that democratic industrial society is wedded to an ideology of consumption and economic growth. Human time and other resources are very poorly allocated. Time for reflection and contemplation is usurped by the incessant quest to earn and buy. Education for human development takes a back seat to that which serves to expand commodity production. All of this is reminiscent of John Dewey's argument that the twentieth-century crisis of liberalism is caused by its fixation with one historically specific *means* for human progress to the neglect of the enduring *ends* of that progress. The result is that liberal society utilizes the character and initiative of its people in their least significant realm, expanding economic output, and largely neglects the application of these means to the development of culture and human relations (Dewey, 1963).

Severely pernicious cultural effects and foregone opportunities for human liberation and self-realization are the costs borne in order to expand the production of commodities that bear a highly tenuous and ambiguous relation to human needs and development. The incomes rat race virtually guarantees inflation, social imbalance, and environmental deterioration. The issues of values and public policy raised in *The Affluent Society* remain not only very fresh but also indispensable reading.

Indeed, in the way of all classics, the book offers continuity and invention. It is well within the traditions of modern liberalism and institutionalism but it offers bold new insights that are apropos to pressing anomalies. Its prophetic vision indicates a continuing path of articulating the theme that realization of the great promise of affluent capitalism is retarded by what Karl Polanyi (1968, p. 59) called an 'obsolete market mentality'.

4 The Administered Society

> The difference is a difference of spiritual attitude. . . . it is a difference in the basis of valuation of the facts for the scientific purpose, or in the interest from which the facts are appreciated.
>
> (T.B. Veblen, 1898)

> The study of the capitalist market economy, when restricted to the non-evolutionary aspects of the capitalist process, ceases to be relevant to it.
>
> (A.G. Papandreou, 1972)

The publication in June 1967 of *The New Industrial State* constitutes the maturation of the Galbraithian system. In the 'Foreword,' Galbraith himself compared it to *The Affluent Society* as a window to the house that contains it, the earlier book providing a 'glimpse' into the structure depicted in the latter. Years later he referred to it as his 'principal effort in economic argument' (Galbraith, 1983, p. xiii).

Looking back from the vantage of the fourth edition, Galbraith noted that in the course of writing the book he had come to recognize that he was challenging the established scholarly edifice in economics, which had not been his intention at the outset. In light of the earlier books, this is scarcely credible, but one can accept his further observation that he came by degrees to recognition of 'the deeper culture of economics that causes its errors and myths to be perpetuated and, with considerable energy and indignation, defended' (Galbraith, 1985, p. xxi). The cultural context of habit and belief, and the service provided to the powerful by the obscurantism of the conventional economics wisdom, and thereby the disservice to the public purpose, become resonant themes of the Galbraithian System.

The New Industrial State is the systematic expression of all of Galbraith's precedent works that examine the dissolutely neglected problem of power and political economic structure. The works that followed it, notably the highly readable *Economics and the Public Purpose*, emended and clarified, but scarcely enlarged upon, the 1967 classic which remains the most essential work of the Galbraithian System. Three decades later it rewards the careful and open-minded student with a model of the concrete political economy that no other scholarly work in the post-war period approaches. It is essential reading and will likely remain so for the foreseeable future; as the facts evolve in the directions it anticipated, it will remain vital until a superior interpretation of the trajectory of late capitalism is provided.

Obviously, all due pains must be taken to explain this bulwark of the Galbraithian System; hence two chapters will be devoted to this effort. In the present chapter, stress is laid upon the most imperative lesson that the new industrial state must be viewed as an *administered society*. First, the method that Galbraith employed will be characterized, and cited to be an example of the *critical historical method*. This methodological ingress sets up the discussion that follows of the dominant facts that Galbraith sought to explain and of the technological imperatives that he offered by way of explanation. These imperatives provide the genesis for the dualized political economic structure that is the essential aspect of the Galbraithian System.

The *social predicament* of our endeavors to improve upon the performance of the administered society is the subject of the next chapter. The characteristic operational performance of this structure, while far from being abjectly disagreeable, is not wholly unproblematic. Galbraith's critical examination of this social predicament and his optimistic eye for the genetic forces toward its amelioration revolved around the intelligentsia and their potential for vanguard political action.

THE CRITICAL HISTORICAL METHOD

In *The New Industrial State*, Galbraith employed a method of analysis and communication that deserves a label. The method is found in works as diverse as Max Weber's *The Protestant Ethic and the Spirit of Capitalism* (1958), Paul Baran and Paul Sweezy's *Monopoly Capital* (1966), and Sam Bowles's, David Gordon's, and Tom Weisskopf's *Beyond the Wasteland* (1983). In a sense even Keynes can be seen as an example to the extent that one takes the maturation of the capitalist economy into a complex industrial system subject to stagnation as his basic vision.

This methodical procedure will be referred to as the *critical historical method*. Its characteristic features are, first, to commence analysis with an adumbration of the significant facts-to-be-explained; second, to move on to examine alternative explanations for these facts; in turn, and third, to select or offer an alternative that corresponds most closely to the facts; and, fourth and finally, in light of well-articulated value premises, to draw implications for thought and action from this explanation.

This method is fully compatible with the approach that has been labelled *evolutionary positivism* or *radical positivism* and said to be a central strand of liberal and pragmatic thought (Markowitz, 1973, p. 14; Veblen, 1948, p. 24). In this view the potential for progressive social change occurs almost spontaneously as knowledge and information increase (Stanfield, 1981). Realization of this potential requires the social will to put institutions to the test of social usefulness. Clearly the view that experience and knowledge undermine resistant attachment to habitual outlooks is a primary theme of institutionalist economics. This is especially true of Galbraith, who refers often to his sense that the ideology and the academic scribblings to which Keynes accorded considerable force, tend to yield eventually to the 'march of events' or pressure of changing circumstance.

The critical historical method outline permits the construction of a succinct reader's guide to *The New Industrial State*. The book's first chapter provides an overview of the trends of modern capitalism which, though cast specifically in the American context, are eventually said to be representative of generic modern industrial societies. These trends are the facts for an accounting must be made. And, this account must yield insight that is relevant to the conduct of collective or private life.

Chapters 2 through 20 of the book contain Galbraith's explanation of these trends, the facts to be explained. This recounting is frequently juxtaposed to the conventional wisdom in economic thought. Chapters 21 through 32 then detail the major problems society faces in light of these political economic trends and their underlying causes. Chapters 33 through 35 provide the reader with Galbraith's prospect and strategy for change or action to ameliorate these problems.

THE FACTS TO BE EXPLAINED

Galbraith began *The New Industrial State* with a list of six commonplace facts or trends in the political economic organization of the twentieth century. The growth and development of the corporate form of organization is one obvious change. The bulk of manufacturing output, in particular, is generated by enterprises organized as large corporations. Their ownership tends to be widely dispersed and largely invisible and their operational managers tend to be qualified almost entirely by virtue of professional credentials rather than ownership. Nor do the managers perform the visible social functions of ersatz royalty the way their industrial predecessors once did – the managerial equivalents of the public recognition associated with 'Carnegie, Rockefeller, Harriman, Mellon, Guggenheim, Ford' and the like are few and far between. Although there are a few corporate executives who have a high profile, the vast majority are unrecognized by face and name to the general public. The organization has displaced the individual decision-maker in so far as repute is concerned. The reputation of the corporation is important, that of its management less so.

But even the names of corporations are less visible than the brand names of the products they purvey. Publicity is far more importantly attached to the products. Another, the second, of the basic trends to be explained in a realistic model of modern economic life is the major increase in the promotion of products by advertising and sophisticated forms of marketing design. The cost of this growing effort to persuade the consumer is now readily accepted in the conventional wisdom as a necessary expense of doing business. It was not always so nor has economic theory made peace with the new reality on capitalist business conduct. The widely influential Cambridge School (England) once emphasized the concept of prime cost in discussing supply functions. It seems that Sraffa would have placed selling costs on the demand side rather than on the side of cost and supply (Sraffa, 1926).

It is far from evident that economics has established the consistency of such costs with the doctrine of necessary supply price which remains the basic rationale of market economies. The ambiguity implicated by the fact of selling costs and other administered components of prices and incomes for the doctrine of necessary supply price has been given scant attention in conventional economics, wherein the impression remains that the discussion concerns prime or production costs despite the presence of distinctly non-prime costs in the activities of large corporations.

Institutionalists have criticized this neglect. The older institutionalist tradition has used this in its cultural criticism and its case concerning the apologism of conventional economics (Stanfield and Phillips, 1991). The more recent institutionalist tradition, as well as neo-Austrian economics, have developed *transactions cost analysis* to include advertising (North 1990; Ekelund and Saurman, 1988). These new departures, plus the field work into the symbolic impact of advertising (Schudson, 1984), are exciting and should be monitored closely by the older institutionalists.

A third fundamental and very visible trend is the increasing technological sophistication applied to the production process. Machinery has replaced human energy to an increasing extent and the machinery has become ever more intricate. The machinery is often possessed of automation capacity so that the immediate intelligence in control of the productive activity is often embodied within it.

Importantly, intelligence is the key to the matter because technology is the 'systematic application of scientific or other organized knowledge to practical tasks' (Galbraith, 1967, p. 24). This definition of technology is not the same as the habitual parlance which tends to identify technology with things or mechanical instruments. When precisely stated, and neither Galbraith nor other institutionalists are as consistent in the matter as one would like, the Galbraithian definition, like that of other institutionalists, emphasizes *mentality* or habitual attitude, habitual procedural recourse to 'scientific or other organized knowledge.'

The reference is back to Veblen's emphasis on the displacement of animistic prejudice by cause and effect knowledge (Veblen, n.d.). As we shall see, Galbraith also echoes Veblen's pursuit of the 'cultural incidence' of the 'machine process,' though Galbraith is at least more explicit than Veblen about the technocratic prospect in which engineers and scientists govern society by default of the democratic process.

A fourth fact to be explained is the dramatic increase in the extent of state activities in social and economic life. As a share of national income, as a proportion of the labor force, as an issuer of regulations and a dispatcher of the inspectors to audit compliance, and by numerous other measures the state's accepted role has grown in the course of the present century. And this is not mere quantitative growth, the state is now involved in many matters that it previously was not. The quality or nature of the state has changed along with the increase in its size and the extent of its role.

Education has grown along with the increased technical sophistication of production, though perhaps it has not done so to a proportional extent. The adequacy of the state's accommodation of education to the dynamics of the economic process is an issue of great and currently growing importance. But certainly education has expanded. More students go on to the next level of the formal educational process and the per capita years of education has increased.

In Galbraith's view, it could not be otherwise since the expansion of systematic intelligence devoted to practical tasks obviously requires that such intelligence be present if it is to be so applied. And of course a good part of the increase in the role of the state has to do with expanding this systematic intelligence through the financing of education, research and development, and the dissemination of information.

The final fact to be explained is the 'beginning of the decline of the trade union' (Galbraith, 1967, p. 15). Though perhaps not widely recognized at the time of the first edition of *The New Industrial State* (1967), the peak in the growth of union membership had been reached a few years earlier, in 1956. Institutionalists had early on identified deeply-rooted structural tendencies that would necessarily tax the ability of union leaders to adapt their strategies (Barkin, 1964).

Galbraith considered the decline of unions to be a secular trend that flowed from the reduction of hostility between unions and management (Galbraith, 1967, p. 271). In effect these changes reduced the antagonism between the workers and unions in their negotiations with the capitalists and corporate fiduciary management – an argument he advanced as early as 1955 in *Economics and the Art of Controversy*. The displacement of the entrepreneurial firm by the corporation in the dominant administered sector, and the concomitant development of the regulation of specific and aggregate demand, have reduced the antagonism over workers' compensation versus profits. This has reduced apace the importance of the union's functions in economic life (Galbraith, 1967, ch. 23).

As discussed below, in its quest to reduce uncertainty, the technostructure may well situate the placation of unions above additional profit, so long as the minimum profit consistent with its autonomy is secure. This, plus the maintenance of high employment as a goal of economic policy, increases the income and employment security of the worker and thus significantly diminishes the task of the union in advancing the worker's interests in these regards.

So also identification of worker loyalty to the organization reduces both industrial relations conflict and the union mission. Galbraith (1967, p. 274) asserted that mechanization erodes barriers to this identification by reducing the drudgery of work and displacing many of the craft skills upon which strong union identification arose. The later development of efficiency wage theory adds an explanation for employee loyalty that is not based upon decline of entrepreneurial sentiment.

Most important in the decline of the unions, Galbraith noted, is the technological change that shifts the occupational structure away from the heavily organized occupations. But this is not to introduce technical change as a determinant. Galbraith went on to cite the bias of the technostructure toward this substitution and their possession of the power to effect it.

In terms of recent institutionalist litany, Galbraith here applied the concept of *encapsulated technology*. It is the same key as Marx's insistence that not industrial technology but the social relations of production induce the alienation of industrial work. Much to the same effect does Karl Polanyi insist that not industrialism but its institutionalization within a commercial society induces the need for a socially protective response.

Galbraith did not expect that the union will disappear; its traditional functions do retain some significance, notably in the market sector of the economy. New functions also arise but, as is elaborated below, Galbraith contended that unions will come to function more as an adjunct to the corporate elite than as its resolute adversary.

Galbraith claimed no originality in citing these trends; to the contrary, 'these changes, or most of them, have been much discussed' (1967, p. 16). This is an important aspect of the critical historical method that is of much significance toward understanding the characteristic methodological controversies in economics. There is not generally disputation about how one arrives at a fact nor even a bevy of facts. But much controversy surrounds the manner in which significance is imparted to facts, and this includes selection of facts that are germane to the scientific enterprise.

For example, no economist can fail to see the increasing significance of the corporate form of economic organization, but the significance of this fact and how or whether it enters one's analysis in any important way is another question altogether. Conventional economic theory largely ignores the change in market structure and models the economy upon the assumptions of perfect competition. As Galbraith observed in a retrospective commentary on *The New Industrial State*, conventional economics assumes a competitive market at the onset of the analysis and the 'validity of the result then depends not on congruity with what exists, with reality, but with whether it derives in a valid way from the assumption' (Galbraith, 1981, p. 514). There is a striking similarity of this sentiment to Veblen's insistence that not the facts but the 'spiritual coherence' assigned to them differentiates conventional and evolutionary economics (Veblen, 1948, p. 219).

Obviously conventional economists are not unaware of the facts of market structure; they act not from ignorance but under the aegis of methodological precept, the conviction that the structure of the economy as a whole remains sufficiently competitive for its behavior to be significantly revealed by the competitive market model. This continuing controversy should in any event be understood as a difference in the interpretation or 'spiritual coherence' applied to the facts.

Social scientists should be mindful of the tendency for any theorist to become committed to a theory and to promulgate it even when some wishful thinking is involved by way of the convenience of the facts chosen and the meaning assigned to them. Social theory is the extrication of a coherent story from the chaotic particulars of the unfolding historical process. Paradigm battles or the competition of research programs are exercises in persuasion as to the coherence and correspondence of one's narrative (Stanfield, 1979, ch. 2). Commitment is necessary but it must not extend so far as to remove doubt in the correspondence of one's interpretation. For all reflective individuals, existential *angst* must remain. The recent surge of literature on 'rhetoric' appears to be aimed in this direction; if so the wheel has yet again been reinvented.

Galbraith's purpose in citing these trends was to draw attention to their interrelatedness and to the need for a holistic model to elucidate their intertwined evolution and its significance for the way human beings make their living and carry forward the dramas which comprise their living. He sought these explanations in 'the imperatives of technology and organization, not the images of ideology' (Galbraith, 1967, p. 19). In effect, he sought to emphasize the necessity of pattern modelling or story-telling to the enterprise of social theory (Ward, 1972; Wilber and Harrison, 1978; Heilbroner, 1981).

Indeed, the images of ideology have generally been contrary to the enlargement of the business enterprise, the expansion of its selling activities, and the extenuation of the role of the state. The habitual predilection of liberalism, including its erstwhile populist variant, is toward small scale competitive economic structure. A century of antitrust activity has putatively been dedicated to this predilection. Nor is advertising accorded a favorable place in doctrine. It is at best a waste of resources and at worst a potentially dangerous interference with the formation of preferences in the organic social process of kinship, friendship, and community life. Even more definitely, the role of the state, by all habitual liberal precept, is to be circumscribed and minimized.

This paradox, the course of apparently ineluctable development in the face of contrary ideology, is frequently noted (Hamilton, 1957; Harrington, 1966). It played a major role in Karl Polanyi's (1944) splendid model of the nature and development of market capitalism (Stanfield, 1986). It stands as the major counterpoint to the popular notion that the democratic capitalist societies are faced with a 'creeping socialism' animated by the ulterior forces of leftwing ideological predisposition. The best of the arguments to this effect remains that of the great classical liberal, Friedrich von Hayek, whose *The Road to Serfdom* is usefully read in contrary conjunction to the equally great statement of modern liberalism provided by Polanyi, *The Great Transformation*.

To summarize, the constitutive facts to be explained, adumbrated above, have arisen despite the absence of systematic ideological support. Therefore they may be supposed to have lacked intentional design in any overall sense, though of course they were the results of myriad individual acts of decision which had purpose in the particular context of time and place. As noted, Galbraith accounted for this apparent paradox by citing the force of deeply-rooted technological and organizational imperatives, the factual exigencies of the times.

Present attention will turn shortly to a review in detail of Galbraith's model in this regard. First, however, it is necessary to settle a terminological matter as to how best to refer to the fundamental aspect of the Galbraithian System.

THE ADMINISTERED SECTOR

Galbraith's model of the modern economy turns upon a basic structural duality between the dominant large-scale oligopolistic sector and the remaining small-scale market sector. In early editions of *The New Industrial State*, he used the term *industrial system* to refer to the dominant sector, but in *Economics and the Public Purpose* and later editions of *The New Industrial State*, he converted to the term *planning system*. The only explanation one encounters from him is that the prior usage was 'an unduly bland designation' (Galbraith, 1981, p. 515).

Either usage fails to satisfy. The first seems to say too little and the latter too much. The industrial system is too amorphous and leaves many a conundrum as to the naming of earlier eras of capitalist development and of the activities of the market system which seem highly industrious. It says nothing very specific about the *differentia specifica* of the large-scale sector. Plus, in general usage the term has a well established reference to the overall economic system of the democratic industrial society.

The planning system is specific enough in demarcating the oligopolistic sector from the market sector, but here too common usage has established the term to mean overall direction of the economy by the state. Certainly this is part of the point, that corporate activity resembles the collective activity habitually associated with economic planning, even that the public and private are not so separable in principle as habitually imagined. But the term in the end may say too much since the corporate activities in question definitely do not add up to the collective governance to which the term habitually refers. The lacunae are fundamental and should not have to be readmitted by resort to *ad hoc* adjectival admonishment such as the insertion of the word partial before the word planning.

Galbraith himself frequently employed a third term, the *corporate sector*, in later discussion (Galbraith, 1979c, ch. 1; and 1981). Perhaps this indicates some doubt on his part about the planning system term, perhaps though it was only to relieve his prose of drone. The corporate sector is an adequate synonym to use for this purpose but it is not sufficient to carry the principal burden. There are hundreds of thousands of incorporated enterprises that are not part of the advanced, concentrated sector of the economy. Rather they reside in the market sector. The structure of incorporation is necessary but not sufficient to the phenomena under concern.

Accordingly, some literary license must be taken. Herein reference to the advanced portion of the economy will be termed the *administered sector*. This is more habitually neutral with respect to the planning and collective action issue. It has the added advantage of parallel usage to the important term administered pricing. This usage makes reference to bureaucratic command-and-control, hierarchic, or redistributive systems of integrating behavior without welcoming confusion with collective action through the public sector to improve the correlation of behavior to the tools and knowledge of the day.

Incidentally, the alternative may occur to some of using the term the oligopolistic system. But there is first the clumsy roll of the word from the tongue and its curious literary appearance. This is sufficient per se for its disqualification, especially in relation to Galbraith, the wordsmith *non pareil*. Its employment would also overtly invite confusion with models that emphasize a theoretical pattern of corporate behavior quite distinctly at odds with that of the Galbraithian System (Galbraith, 1973a). Hence, though occasional reference to oligopolistic structure should not confuse, it would invite confusion to designate the examination of the systematic function and performance of this sector as oligopolistic.

The administered sector then refers to the dominant political economic sector of *The New Industrial State*, or to have resort to parallel synonymous usage, to the dominant sector of the *administered society*. The administered sector is the complex of corporations of considerable size and diversity that produce the bulk of a nation's output under market structural conditions generally conforming to the textbook structure known as oligopoly, though as noted, the textbook model does not satisfy Galbraith in its interpretation of the facts of this structure with respect to performance.

Far from it, as already noted, Galbraith insisted that the conventional wisdom dramatically misses the point in this regard (Galbraith, 1973a). In many ways his work is a critical examination of the conventional industrial organization analysis of market structure, conduct, and performance. This is true of his work at all phases, from the early defense of bigness against the vagaries it faced at the hands of classical competitive enmity, to the profoundly critical attack on illegitimate corporate political economic power.

But as noted, it has seldom been the facts of political economic structure but rather what these facts meant that separated him from his more conventional peers. Once again it is less the facts than the 'spiritual attitude' by which the facts are appraised that separates institutionalists from their conventional neoclassical colleagues. So also it shall be this difference that ultimately divides the present century from the next. The *road to the future* must be paved with the reconstruction of our habitual political economic responses to the evident exigencies of living and making a living in a complex commercial and industrial society. This reconstruction must necessarily turn upon a reinterpretation of the place of economy in society (Stanfield, 1986, ch. 6).

The demarcation between the administered sector and the market sector is not exact. More often than not, Galbraith referred to the 200 largest manufacturing corporations and cited the shares they comprise of sales, assets, and employment. The specific number of firms matters little to his analysis so long as the general pattern of concentration is as he described, and there seems to be no reason to doubt that the largest 100, 200, or even 1000 corporations do in fact dominate measured productive activity.

Further it seems clear that there is sufficient bimodality in such measures to speak of a dual economy. There are millions of firms in the economy that cluster at the opposite end of the spectrum of measured size. This does not establish the dominance of the administered sector over social choice in the manner Galbraith ascribed, but it does establish a useful demarcation for theoretical effort.

Galbraith argued that the administered sector has been evolved in response to specific requirements of correlating behavior to the requisites of modern industrial technology. Such evolution in the face of the consequences of technology has generated a change in the structure of social relations, notably within the corporation. This change is sufficient to warrant a new term, for which Galbraith offered the *technostructure*. This mutation in the means of correlating behavior has given a distinctly administered character to much economic and social behavior. Such a profound change deserves terminological recognition in systems of symbolic logic which structure thinking about the sequential relations between the business firm and the household. In this regard, Galbraith offered the *revised sequence* and asserted that it must be recognized if the social predicament is to be met head on analytically and institutionally.

The Consequences of Technology

Galbraith discussed six interwoven imperatives or consequences of modern technological and organizational forms. First, there is an increase in the passage of time from initiation to completion of an industrial task. This has much to do with more rigorous specification of the material basis of the product. The work of design reaches backward in the vertical structure of the industry to carefully specified if not made-to-order inputs. The life-cycle of a product is lengthened by the more exacting engineering standards applied to it as well as, one assumes, the more elaborate preparation for its marketing.

Second, the size of the corporate operation grows along with the time element. This of course means that ever larger amounts of capital are committed to the operation of an enterprise. Inputs need to be kept on hand so that production is not stalled by a bottleneck in some more or less important input. The intensified division of labor embodied in this interrelated machine process requires a considerable structure of integration in terms of equipment and devices for monitoring and control. All of this contributes to capital-deepening of the enterprise, though not, one supposes, necessarily of per unit product since the volume of production from the fixed plant rises many times over as the scale expands.

Capital and labor grow more and more specialized in this process. Equipment and the knowledge which is inevitably wedded to it become more committed to particular tasks and the specifications of particular product cycles. Labor too becomes more inflexibly committed as it shapes itself to the niche it occupies in the overall industrial scheme of things. Galbraith's discussion here is remarkably reminiscent of Marx's powerful model of the systemic capitalist tendency toward the socialization of capital and labor as the rationalization and centralization and concentration of production unfolds. It also echoes Veblen's frequent discussion of the intensifying standardization and interdependence of the production process.

Increased specialization of knowledge and skill, and its embodiment in ever more dedicated equipment, requires ever more sophisticated organizational forms to bring them to bear and integrate them into a coherent interdependent mechanism. Specialized activity requires specialized organization that runs on specialized information about the operation of the particular production process. Organizational expertise is an admixture of general and particular knowledge. This is somewhat reminiscent of Walton Hamilton's insistence that there is no substitute for detail about particular institutional arrangements if one is to formulate useful insight into the making of policy to maintain the going concern (Hamilton, 1919). The details of a given concern are different because the details of technical exigency are different; so also do corporate cultures differ, in part as a result and in part as a cause of the exigencies of the knowledge and skill that are applied within the production process they contain.

Large, inflexibly committed amalgamations of specialized knowledge and equipment call for reliable combination and reasonably accurate expectation of circumstance. The application of foresight and the exercise of contingency adjustment are critical to avoidance of costly shutdowns and delays involving many expensive components with little else do other than what they are designed to do within the processes they are designed to work within. In a phrase, such expense and bother mandate planning to see that things go right lest they go expensively awry. Research and development is an apropos procedure, and an apt expression, of problem-solving to bring specialized knowledge to bear on these processes before the uncertainty presented by unsolved problems creates expensive errors. Guesswork, no matter how educated, and rules of thumb, no matter how experienced, give way to organized intelligence dedicated to the anticipation of potential problems and the investigation of their resolution in advance.

Corporate enterprises exercise planning by replacing spontaneous market forces by administration. By vertical integration they reach backward toward the sources of necessary inputs and forward to secure necessary outlets for their products. Inconvenience of price or the details of supply or distribution represent possible surprises that are expensive in the waste of inflexibly committed, expensive inputs. An even more disturbing surprise would be the extreme inconvenience of finding that these inputs cannot be financially reproduced.

Administered pricing allows large firms to control the exigencies of much that they buy and sell. The amount sold remains a threat but size allows some actuarial anticipation as well as a ready war chest of funds to deploy in market research, advertising, and similar missions to seek and captivate buyers. Size affords power over what one buys as well. Sales that are large in volume in relation to the size of a firm are lucrative; therefore smaller enterprises will think more than twice about quantity or price actions that might jeopardize future patronage from large customers. Such satellite status may not be wholly intolerable but it is no great honor either. As Galbraith was to argue later in *Economics and the Public Purpose*, this not so great honor is often maintained by dedicated, indeed puritanical exploitation of one's self as well as one's employees (Galbraith, 1973b).

Where size faces size, long term contracts resemble military alliances and potential adversaries negotiate, amicably or not, to establish the security of each from the actions of the other. Power begets countervailing power because those who lack power are reduced to dependency upon, if not servility toward, those who have it. Lack of size and power is an inconvenience that begs for correction whenever possible. As noted in the discussion in Chapter 2, the government may well be called upon to render this correction possible where it would not be so otherwise.

In the aggregate, matters are more complicated. The administered sector requires state intervention to manage the overall volume of demand within which the individual enterprise seeks its fortune in the form of well-heeled and willing customers. The corporation sees to its funds to invest and plans for the customers it needs to refinance its existence as a going concern housing in its overhead costs inflexibly committed, and not altogether inexpensive, knowledge and equipment.

The Keynesian specter of an excessive rate of saving that leaves too little left over to buy the output and therefore secure the comfortable refinancing of the going concern is a threat that exceeds the reach of even the largest corporation. Hence accommodation is made to the vicissitudes of modern circumstance so as to permit the state to manipulate aggregate demand. That this accommodation is made grudgingly and with considerable expenditure of Veblenian (1953) surplus energy to achieve the creative social act of cultural change should not blind the observant to the fact that it is nonetheless made.

The data on public budget deficits in relation to corporate profits leave little room for doubt as to the powerful vested interests of the administered sector in Keynesian economic management (Minsky, 1986). This is not to say that the deficits serve only or even primarily the corporate financial interests of the administered sector, only that these interests are not so ineluctably disserved and disinclined in this regard as habitual thought portrays them to be.

The support of such programs by unions is evidence both of labor's interest in the programs and of the useful political function the unions thus provide their corporate employers. In the process, the state undoubtedly has expanded in ways that would probably have surprised Veblen for whom a democratic government is a business government (Veblen, n.d.); no doubt it would also occasion surprise for the angry Prussian for whom the capitalist state must remain nothing but the executive arm of the ruling class.

It should also be noted that the increased scale and sophistication of production brings with a rise in the scale and refinement of correlating human behavior. This is most clear in the operation of the paid labor force in the manufacturing sector. Scientific management and more recent techniques of personnel administration come to mind. But the household is also engaged in productive activity that must be brought into concert with the pattern of commodity production. The generation of action patterns appropriate to living through commodities cannot be left to chance, nor can social control in anonymous urban-industrial areas be left to the less formal forms of accommodating behavior that prevailed in rural and village life. Mass society and mass media are as much a part of industrial society as the machines that run upon inanimate energy (Harrington, 1966). Much of this is anticipated in Marx's discussion of the 'socialization' of labor and capital and Veblen's 'cultural incidence of the machine process' (Marx, 1967, Vols I and III; Veblen, n.d.).

The Technostructure

Such fundamental structural changes as those stemming from the exigencies of modern technology cannot leave matters of social class and social outlook unaffected. As effective control of the modern corporation shifts to those who possess the expertise to exercise it, the social landscape is transformed apace. Status, prestige, income and the other social perquisites of importance attach to the fragmented functionaries of the corporate edifice as surely as they once adhered to the land barons or the captains of industry and later the captains of finance.

The separation of ownership and control received forceful expression in the seminal 1932 classic of Berle and Means, which along with Means's later work on administered pricing, is credited by Galbraith as having exerted major influence on his own work (Galbraith, 1985, pp. xx–xxi). Marx's anticipation of the separation of ownership and control more than a half century before Berle and Means was not, alas, seminal. His disciples perhaps abandoned this insight in a mistaken belief that because it implies a diminution of class conflict, it also implies a decline in the tendency toward socialism. Marx saw matters differently and mentions the separation of ownership and control in the context of the joint-stock company as the principal institutional form taken by the transition to socialism (Marx, 1967, vol. III).

The separation of ownership and control refers to the tendency of the modern corporate form to disperse ownership very widely so that owners of necessity settle their economic interest in the hands of a fiduciary agent, the management, who then operate the day-to-day affairs of the enterprise. This impact of ownership dispersion is powerfully reinforced by the rising technical sophistication of the enterprise's means, organization, and output. Increased sophistication in process and result requires increased sophistication in direction. Together the scale and technological consequences of modern industry necessitate a coordinating force that can apply specialized and differentiated expertise over a vast organizational range. This expertise and scope cannot be ordinarily brought to bear on the conduct of business by one entrepreneur nor even a small cluster of entrepreneurs.

Galbraith's technostructure refers to the committees or teams of specialists who staff the corporations and in whom reside the effective power to exercise discretion over the substantive decisions of corporate operations. Teams of specialists, empowered both technically and institutionally, are needed to assemble and correlate the knowledge applied in the corporation. These teams must be relatively unimpeded by interference from their formal superiors in the corporate organization. Discretion and autonomy pass not only from the owner to the management of the enterprise, but also from the more visible managerial chieftains atop the enterprise to the anonymous and functionally fragmented professionals within it. These professionals through teamwork and committee counsel bring their variegated expertises to bear upon the many lines of activity that are critical to the enterprise, its financial and personnel management, marketing, accounting, product development, and so on.

The technostructure is then an 'apparatus for group decision-making – for pooling and testing the information provided by numerous individuals to reach decisions that are beyond the knowledge of any one' (Galbraith, 1967, p. 88). The technostructure is composed of 'technicians, engineers, sales executives, scientists, designers and other specialists' (Galbraith, 1967, p. 163).

The technostructure proper apparently does not include the upper echelon of the firm's executives or management. Of course, these top managers are recruited from, or climb the ranks through, the technostructure (Galbraith, 1967, p. 165). The basis for separating the upper management lies not in background, say, technical versus business, but in their relationship within current decision-making. The technostructure requires autonomy to function as teams of experts who provide tested solutions to the problems of corporate conduct. The top executives cannot comprise all this expertise and must therefore devolve much decision-making.

Galbraith should probably have left no doubt on this score; at the very least, it is curious that his list of the technostructure included no mention of business backgrounds except the sales executives. One would think that the technostructure would be staffed aplenty with experts in law, accounting, and finance. And indeed the similar adumbration in *Economics and the Public Purpose* is replete in this regard with its inclusion of corporation executives, lawyers, economists, controllers, advertising and marketing men. In the later work, Galbraith also mentioned the technostructure's allies and satellites in organizations offering services in law, advertising, accounting, business consulting, and business education along with their like in scientific and engineering fields (Galbraith, 1973b, p. 162).

Galbraith's discussion of the motivation of the technostructure is surely prominent among the most controversial areas of *The New Industrial State*. He questioned the logic of profit maximization as a goal because managerial control is separate from ownership. Profit maximization, even conceived not in the short run but as an optimal long run concept, is logically in the self-interest of the equity owners, subject to some risk constraint; but even thus qualified, it is not logically associated with the managerial interest without further specification of the agency relationship.

Absent compelling empirical evidence that the ownership interest has developed strong success indicators to persuade management to pursue return on equity as a paramount goal, one should revert to assessing the interest of the managerial agent. This was Galbraith's approach, though, of course, he insisted that the technostructure is the relevant agent whose interest must be assayed.

Personal profiteering by the upper echelons of management might be logical were they to be the seat of effective day-to-day power. But with the passage of this discretion to the wider technostructure, this interest is diluted in the nature of the case. The whole of the decision-making structure cannot self-aggrandize at the expense of itself. No doubt there is much oligarchic flavor here, these are well-paid and well-expensed people, but there are inherent limits to the potential avarice. Law and regulation regard matters of executive compensation and insider trading of equity and goods and services with a look askance, that here and there more or less zealous, but ever present.

Moreover, the technostructure develops professional standards and is enjoined by more or less automatic peer review, given the nature of collective decision-making, which militate against an ethos that is unduly oriented to one's pecuniary income. Finally, even were their own income their principal objective, the technostructure would more likely be able to divert income their way by sales and revenue maximization than profit maximization – they are after all part of the cost of production to be subtracted from revenue to derive profit, not participants in the residual itself.

Galbraith argued instead that the technostructure's motivation must be understood as a complex admixture of identification with the organization's goals with a desire to adapt these goals to one's perceptions. Individuals who identify with the organization's goals internalize them and make them their own. Other individuals rightly or wrongly believe they have or can yet adapt the organization's goals to their own. Either way, there is a merging of interest as the individual members of the technostructure identify with the organization and seek to adapt its goals to their view of priorities. It should be noted that in this discussion of the psychology of motivation, Galbraith anticipated the later interest in corporate culture.

He extended the discussion with a direct discussion of the goals of the corporation in relation to the interests of the technostructure. This hired salariat is served by corporate security because this underwrites the financing of itself as an overhead cost. Thus financed, the technostructure can continue, a desirable objective for normal organisms and organizations. To function, the technostructure requires autonomy – interference in its decision-making by those presuming to have the knowledge to do so is a threat of vital proportions. If indeed the technostructure *in toto* solely possesses the requisite information to make the key decisions, interference from outside the technostructure could be disastrous for the corporation.

Beyond its primary goal of securing organizational existence as a going concern, thereby securing self-preservation, the technostructure pursues enhancement of its status by maximizing the growth of sales, subject of course to the security constraint which is primary. Its status and the inherent integrity and quality of its work are further served by technological virtuosity – the tendency toward dynamism in the techniques and outputs of the corporation. A steadily rising rate of dividend payouts is also desirable in that it reinforces the primary goal of securing technostructural autonomy – 'why fix it if it ain't broke?' Finally, a reputation for social responsibility and public service is both satisfying directly and a purchase of public image which again reinforces the aura of being a well-managed company, interference into which invites errant deflection of a going concern that is doing well.

Corporate Autonomy

The primary need of the technostructure is to protect its autonomy, to preserve its discretion to pursue its goals without external interference. Of course, it is powerfully assisted in this objective by the notion that its apparent discretion is chimerical because it is ultimately subject to the discipline of market competition. The corporation's boundary conditions are mostly the concrete conduits by which the market forces would contravene its apparent discretion – the notable exception in this regard being the state with its implicit threat of regulation. The means by which the technostructure pursues its goal of autonomy provide the most telling arguments of Galbraith's performance.

One possible source of interference with the technostructure, the corporation's top management layer, as already discussed, stems from the technostructure and is presumably therefore generally cognizant of the necessity of this autonomy. The various financial interests that threaten technostructural autonomy include the stockholders directly or as represented by the board of directors or the corporate raider or takeover artist. The banking community, including such specialized elements as pension and trust fund managers, are also distinct threats.

Galbraith asserted that the board of directors is generally in a cozy relationship with the upper echelons of corporate management and will not interfere unless more or less forced to do so by a failure of steady earnings. The ordinary stockholder is seldom large enough nor actively engaged enough to intervene in any major way beyond parting company with the equity of portfolio non-performers. Large stockholders who take an active managerial interest directly or via directorial membership are a declining breed in Galbraith's view. Then too, if they function as part of the administrative strata, they become social typically managerial. By virtue of close approximation with the technostructure they would presumably learn the lessons of team decision-making and technostructural autonomy. If not, if Galbraith's model well serves, they would become vanishing breeds along with the companies they sought to manage, since such interference would manifest itself as a weak corporate culture.

Investment banking interests routinely limit themselves to portfolio decisions about equities. Direct interference would take them into the details of industrial conduct to a distracting extent in terms of managing their own highly specialized entities, with presumably, similarly specialized teams of decision-makers. Corporate raiders are notorious bottom feeders, seeking their prey among underperforming equities that do not satisfy the steady earnings proviso.

In all cases, the technostructure's security is rooted in its ability to sustain a minimum earnings pattern. This minimum is set at a level sufficient to ensure substantial internal financing of corporate investment. Beyond retained earnings, access to credit is rendered more facile by a good earnings record. Moreover, to fail to secure this minimum is to invite interference from large shareholders, trust funds, mutual funds, or takeover specialists.

The state is a possible interloper into the technostructure's affairs, but it is enjoined by severely stringent ideological antipathy. The market mentality by which businesses are routinely guided in the public interest by forces all the more powerful by being unseen is deeply rooted and not infrequently celebrated by corporate officials and 'advocacy advertising'. Citizens may affect the corporation directly through its public image or by influencing the state in matters of importance to the corporation. The technostructure does not lack vanity with respect to its public image and expends considerable resources to exercise positive spin control and undermine the credibility of those who seek to influence the public mood in another direction, especially one suspects if state action is a possible response to the citizen concern. Again, ultimate resort may be made to the mythology of ineluctable market forces in the face of which no real power resides within the body corporate.

It is interesting to note that the presence of various citizen social movements – environment, peace, civil rights affirmative action, even consumer product safety – that aim to influence corporate behavior, is evidence of public belief in the existence of managerial discretion. So also is implied the public perception that controlling corporation behavior is essentially a political problem, a problem of governance (Hamilton, 1957). The corporate response is to cite its record of social responsibility in the areas being pressed upon it and to point to the ineluctable pressure of market forces which prevent its doing more in the good and noble cause.

This is a deeply paradoxical response. To claim to be exercising social responsibility is to recognize the power to administer. To simultaneously cite market forces as one's reason for not doing more in the desired direction is to deny the power to administer. That the corporate response is ambiguous should occasion no surprise; the Galbraithian System makes clear the corporate need to escape the market in practice but to advert to it in principle. The result is enigmatic to be sure, but may serve all the better for it. On some matters it is best not to cast the light of day.

The demand for its products is a vital concern for the corporation and its activities in this regard do not well support the view that it is the more or less willing servant of genetic market forces. The corporation does not allow its deep commitment to the ideals of the market to dissuade it from extensive efforts to safeguard its sales volume. Advertising, design obsolescence, survey research, and other marketing techniques seek to identify and persuade potential buyers. The flow of such strategies, their main themes and symbols, is a popular history unto itself.

Government spending also serves to maintain demand. Baran and Sweezy (1966) were critical of Galbraith's concept of social imbalance because it overlooked the presence of much government spending. They argued that social spending to alleviate the condition of the working class tends to be given short shrift but not public spending which serves to promote the interests of capital. In *The New Industrial State*, Galbraith acknowledged that much public spending serves the technostructure and is well funded, while other spending, though potentially of great service to the quality of life, tends to be neglected. The theme of social imbalance is thereby made into a distortion of priorities within both the public and private sectors, rather than simply a problem of public versus private sector. The distorting influence is the power of corporate America which generally manages to get its interests advanced.

Galbraith also contended that the technostructure is far less inimical than is often supposed to Keynesian fiscal policy. The task of this policy is to maintain aggregate demand at a volume high enough to ensure that there is sufficient revenue available for the corporations to carve up by their micro-demand management activities. The areas of public spending that are most important to the technostructure, notably defense and space activities and research and development generally, do not come in for a great deal of criticism from the technostructure. Nor does highway construction and projects to build such infrastructure as airports.

Evidence to the contrary concerning the technostructure's views is, in Galbraith's view, an overestimation of the reach of entrepreneurial lament about the growth of government. It is true that the entrepreneurial sector of business, compared to the corporate element, has less interest in increased government. Government programs serve it less and it pays more of the taxes to finance them. In the administered sector, government contracts and maintenance of the overall level of demand are far more important. Moreover, the taxes are far less onerous because, with tax shifting of the burden of corporate taxes, someone else pays them. Galbraith concluded that there is a nostalgic tone to much corporate dissent from active government.

The union and its workers represent possible boundary constraints upon the technostructure's autonomy. Here the decline of union importance, already noted, is an outgrowth of the same forces that have tended to create the technostructure. Nor is the latter beyond weakening the union by automation and similar process innovations which tend to reduce the numbers employed of the type of employees who are likely to engage in union activity. A technostructure may well pursue such capital-deepening innovations even to the extent that costs rise on average as a result – it will be remembered by now that not profit maximization but organizational security is the primary goal.

For the period of the post-war era covered most directly by *The New Industrial State*, there was considerable peace in American industrial relations. The social compact that obtained was supported by realistic union leadership who stressed the lunch pail issues and eschewed divisive issues such as opening the corporate books or intruding into the prerogatives of management. At the same time, the technostructure, bent first and foremost upon minimum earnings to secure its own existence, and administering prices to cover costs, was a poor choice to impose society's interest in wage-restraint.

The union actually functions in a somewhat *ministerial* fashion, administering the corporation's interest by explaining its operation and culture to the production workers. No doubt identification generally works with less force among the production workers than their pecuniary interest applied by supervisors who seek to maintain the intensity of labor effort. Still some identification among this strata is to be expected and a good working relation between the union leadership and the technostructure's representatives in the human relations process is a factor likely to be of some import in some corporate cultures.

The union also serves a ministerial function in explaining to its members the bargaining process and justifying the complex gradations of pay for a differentiated structure of employees. The workers are less likely in general to see such status-driven differentials as arbitrary, which they largely are, if they perceive that their representatives have participated in their derivation (Galbraith, 1967, ch. 24). Unions serve further by a tendency toward standardizing wage costs at the industrial level, which facilitates corporate cost planning, as does, of course, long term wage contracting per se.

Union support of state maintenance of aggregate demand and of the specific demand for corporations that sell importantly to the state is also a considerable service to the technostructure. Similarly welcome is the union voice in favor of the protection of domestic markets against import penetration.

Technostructures in other enterprises who supply inputs or purchase output represent potential threats to a given technostructure. Forward contracting and vertical integration, already discussed, allay much of the problem in this regard. There would also likely be a certain chumminess owing to the similar social and educational backgrounds but this does not appear to have figured prominently in Galbraith's argument in *The New Industrial State*. Indeed, the nature of these relationships has generally been neglected by scholars of the American corporate scene, and it is possible that attention to such networks or systems of informal reciprocities would prove to be useful research areas. Where price stability fails in these relations, the technostructure has some latitude in administering its own prices to offset surprises imposed by others.

The technostructure has the need to control its boundary conditions less they change unexpectedly in untoward directions, thereby damaging the autonomy required for it to do its job. And insofar as possible it develops the means to exercise this control. This dynamic is apparent in its relations to finance capital, to its workers and their unions, and to its suppliers and distributors.

So also is this pattern to be seen in its relation to the state. Antitrust enforcement is muted. Weapons procurement is a ready source of reliable demand to an important fraction of the administered sector. So also does the research and development effort of the state, much of it related to the military purpose, abet the technostructure. So also education, at least part thereof. So too are relatively adequate funds available to socialize much of the overhead costs of commodity production, notably in the area of highway construction and maintenance without which the present social landscape is simply unimaginable.

So too must the administered sector rely on the state to regulate the volume of aggregate demand. The administered sector must complement that effort by expending prodigious sums of money toward assorting the aggregate demand among the various purveyors of commodities. The management of specific demand via advertising and marketing is a major aspect of the Galbraithian System and the source of its most troubling implications. It is given more detailed in the section to follow.

The Revised Sequence

The compelling turn that Galbraith's work began to take with the *dependence effect* in *The Affluent Society* emerges in more somber form in *The New Industrial State* with the concept of the *revised sequence*, which serves as a core concept of the mature Galbraithian System. The conventional wisdom in economic thought has at its core the competitive market which empowers the sovereign consumer or household. In this original sequence the flow of causative influence in the production process is from households, as ultimate consumers of commodities and ultimate suppliers of resources, to the productive organizations. The existence of a secondary, weaker flow from producer to consumer in the form of sales effort activities was either not acknowledged or dismissed as unimportant in the mainstream development of economic theory, notwithstanding discussion of related issues by Romantic critics of classical economists, such as John Ruskin.

With the revised sequence concept, Galbraith sought to shift the analytical focus to the flow of influence from producers to consumers – though he took pains to emphasize that the reverse flow of influence from the household cannot be ignored. The organic society of relations in friendship and kinship, and within educational and religious organizations, persists and no doubt remains important in the formation of consumer preferences. But this is no reason to ignore the issue of the influence exercized upon these preferences by the corporate elite. Indeed, such as with the news industry, bad news is news because it is unsettling of what we expect or hope to be the norm.

If Galbraith's notion of the revised sequence has a degree of validity, there is an important asymmetry to be noted. The accepted sequence conception is reassuring to the degree it is true but its degree of truth does not moderate the consternation evoked by whatever degree of validity that must be accorded the revised sequence conception. The latter negates the former but the converse does not hold. Evidence to support the notion of the revised sequence indicates a social problem exists. Evidence that the original conception exists alongside the revised sequence does not support the conclusion that there is no problem. Such is the asymmetry of apologetic and critical doctrine, born of the logical impossibility of proving the negative by example.

The revised sequence concept applies only to the administered sector and not to the market sector in the dual economy of the Galbraithian System. The market sector, comprised of the vast majority of business organizations in terms of number, is still organized more or less upon the original sequence in that the firms within it are not the source of consumer attitudes nor do they find themselves to possess the ability to make prices. There are many firms in a given industry in the market sector; for example, the various retail trade and agricultural production industries. This structure does continue, as in the classical faith, to protect consumers from exploitation at the hands of sellers.

But here also Galbraith subsequently departed in important respects in the 'spiritual attitude' by which he appraised the facts. As discussed in Chapter 6, the market sector protects consumers from exploitation but serves up ripe for the taking its labor force and even its entrepreneurs. The demanding character of small business survival is a notable addition to the Galbraithian System as depicted in *Economics and the Public Purpose.*

In the administered sector, again roughly comprised of the two hundred or so largest manufacturing corporations, traditional price theory leads only a red herring expedition. Its emphasis on price-taking firms constrained by market conditions obscures the relation to the price system of the large, industrial corporation. Exchange processes still visibly operate to clear markets but much of the underlying preferences are influenced by the corporate elite. The principal function of the market in the administered sector is not to constrain the power of the corporate behemoths but to serve as an instrument for the implementation of their power (Papandreou, 1972).

The decisive significance of the concept of revised sequence is its relation to the legitimacy of corporate production and distribution of output, its effects on income distribution, and the broader consequences of its various charitable, political, and media activities (Stanfield, 1979; Dugger, 1989). The original sequence conception 'supports the conclusion that the individual is the ultimate source of power in the economic system' (Galbraith, 1967, p. 226). This conception has the further implication that state regulation is in most respects an unnecessary violation of the sovereign rights of the individual, that is, an abridgement of the *liberal sphere.*

Thus a wide range of collective action that would be inconvenient to the corporate elite is ruled out by virtue of the doctrine that upholds the natural rights of individuals. Transportation planning, product design, environmental protection, the vagaries of the marketing effort, media programming, city planning, and so on are left to the market's monitoring of individual preferences.

To the extent that the market is inaccurate in this monitoring or that the preferences are suspect by taint of corporate influence, collective action could very well improve the sum of individual welfare. Yet the ideological scheme of individualism is said to enjoin collective action. The power exercized by the corporate elite is effectively obscured, as well put by the forceful phrase from a later book, the *imagery of choice* (Galbraith, 1973b). Galbraith issued the scathing charge that conventional economics is a system of belief which tends to systematically exclude 'speculation on the way the large economic organizations shape social attitudes to their ends' (Galbraith, 1967, p. 77).

The revised sequence could not be more radical in that the original sequence is the root of traditional economic thought and the fount of legitimacy for the organizations that produce the daily bread. With it, 'Galbraith raises the question of whether the American people actually want the particular kind of material progress their system delivers' (Kristol, 1967, p. 90). With it, Galbraith raises 'the fearful prospect . . . of a nation in deep servitude to corporate power with respect to both the ends and means of life' (Hession, 1972, p. 179).

Thus Galbraith sharpens the attack on the tendency of economists to explain so much by *scarcity* without examining the concrete cultural context in which economic decisions are made. Relative prices certainly exist but what do they mean? In a given historical context, institutional analysis of concrete cultural patterns is necessary to assay their significance (Stanfield, 1995a, ch. 1 and 1995b). This analysis must necessarily be holistic and evolutionary in scope. And as such, as the next chapter illustrates, it can be linked to socio-cultural criticism that delves deeply into the fabric of social life.

5 The Social Predicament

The American people can afford everything but beauty.
(E.D. Stone, 1959)

What counts is not the quantity of our goods but the quality of life.
(J.K. Galbraith, 1967)

The critical historical method, to remind, begins with a set of facts to be explained, for which explanation is then provided. The third dimension of this method is to demonstrate the significance of the foregoing by examination of social problems or issues that stem from the explanation given. The *useful economist* will see that commercial, industrial society embodies core tendencies that chronically undermine the quality of human life and threaten to acutely diminish it in a flash of military or ecological bedlam. These untoward tendencies comprise the social predicament of the New Industrial State and the road to the future lies in the responses chosen in the effort to subordinate them to the quality of human life.

As discussed above, the reorganization of social relations into an administered mold has done much to meet the correlative behavioral changes associated with the ongoing development of tools and knowledge. But this social evolution has met these challenges incompletely, so that critical unresolved problems remain which taken together form a definite social predicament that demands vigorous attention and earnest commitment to further reform. The dual economic structure retains serious problems of aggregate instability that staunchly resist resolution by habitual recourse to aggregate demand policy, thus posing a *macroeconomic dilemma*.

There are further, profoundly debilitating aspects of the social predicament in that the administered society relentlessly misallocates a large fraction of its collective wherewithal. This obdurate error is best captured in the relation between *social imbalance and the quality of life*. Institutionally, the correlative requirements of the New Industrial State offer occasion for hope as to the possibility of further reform that would effectively attend to this social predicament. The administered society is a part of an ongoing process, the modern phase of which began with the rise of industrialism within commercial capitalism. This reform logic expresses the social necessity of securing a stable pattern of economic provisioning that is consistent with ongoing social existence. Commercial industrialism offered such peril to social stability that the experiment with the disembedded, self-regulating market economy had to be abandoned in practice, the persistent and deep-seated emotional and ideological commitment to the contrary notwithstanding.

As already noted, this has been powerfully expressed by Karl Polanyi's notion of the *protective response*: collective action within and without government auspices to protect social interests against disruption at the hands of market forces (Polanyi, 1944; Stanfield, 1986). This theme has also been prominent in the American institutionalist literature (Gruchy, 1967). Indeed the *logic of reform* has served to connect many generations of institutional and historical economists to the central reality of institutional adjustment (Stanfield, 1986, ch. 5). Institutions are adjusting to the sweep of technical change and the social and ecological quandaries thereby propagated; the task is to manage the process so as to control its pace and deflect its trajectory toward desirable futures. This requires an imagery that is realistic and evolutionary, necessarily emancipated from the preternatural sense of propriety and normality that characterizes the market mentality.

The corporate and union organizations that are so very visible on the modern political economic landscape are part of this logic of reform or protective response (Hamilton, 1957; Stanfield, 1986, ch. 5). Galbraith's model of this ongoing change, of which the corporation is itself a key ingredient, offers as well considerable insight into the manner by which further reform may come into being and how it may be subjected to responsible social direction. Reliance cannot be made upon the forces of *institutionalized drift* (Stanfield, 1995b, ch. 7) to accommodate our humanity with more than desultory interest nor to resist with reasonable energy the expansive banality that represses the quality of life.

Galbraith called upon the essential estate of research and educational professionals to take the *political lead* in resisting this tendency toward comprehensive insipidness. The shape of this resistance is given by the nature of its task. Organization is required to guide the reform of our correlative behavior toward the public purpose of achieving economic progress that is equitably distributed, ecologically feasible, and aesthetically meaningful.

THE MACROECONOMIC DILEMMA

The matter of macroeconomic stability was for a very long time neglected in mainstream economic thought, under the aegis of Say's Law. This classical proposition maintained that supply creates its own demand because productive activity is rewarded with income identical to the value of output and that this income will in one way or another be spent to buy the output. Macroeconomic instability was brought to center stage by Keynes and the economic exigencies of 1930s and 1940s. The Great Depression induced the lasting impression that Say's Law left much to be desired by way of accuracy. The Second World War implanted a further powerful impression that Keynes was correct and that fiscal policy could indeed affect the level of macroeconomic activity.

A sea change ensued in economic theory and political economic philosophy. Theoretical examination of the determinants of aggregate employment, income, and output became the growth industry in the profession. The conduct of macroeconomic policy became a largely unquestioned responsibility of government, and so it remains despite much atavistic sentiment within academic economics in recent decades.

For a quarter of a century after 1945, the focus of mainstream economic thought was upon the aggregate relations of income and product flows with very little theoretical attention to the question of the microeconomic foundations of these aggregate relationships. Structural or frictional considerations were appended in an ad hoc fashion to the policies advocated. Around 1970, the matter of microeconomic foundations began to be reintroduced into the theoretical consideration of macroeconomic stabilization policy, but alas it was the obsolete microeconomic foundations of ancestral precept that were utilized. Recently, the discipline seems to be intent upon escape from this antediluvian illusion. A New Keynesian revival is afoot that is considering real world, real time macroeconomic stabilization problems in the context of real world, real time microeconomic conditions (Ferguson, 1993).

The microeconomic basis of macroeconomic issues has always been a prime concern for institutionalists, and as seen above, Galbraith is no exception. Indeed, he has been among the most forceful of advocates for the manifestly rudimentary but extremely consequential notion that the actually prevalent economic structure matters in any discussion of what to do in order to improve its performance. His 1957 article was extremely explicit in this regard and especially sought to indicate the untoward effects of recourse to monetary policy in a dualized microeconomic structure. His series of articles from the OPA experience that reached a second fruition in *The Theory of Price Control* provide further testament to his prescience on the matter of the need for structural policy. Further, it is worth recalling his declaration that inflation should be regarded as the most pernicious threat to the tranquility of democratic industrial society.

In *The New Industrial State*, Galbraith advanced the argument in this regard and in others. The planning provided by the administered sector and the symbiotic state is, in principle, incomplete, partial planning. In principle there is no means available to the technostructure to coordinate interindustrial relations. Moreover, as Galbraith (1985, p. xxxi) was to notice in retrospect, in practice it is not possible to assume uniform competence in the staffing of the technostructure. Hence, even where the means exist for the exercise of administration, their actions may not be applied in practice with the acumen requisite to the task.

Most of the matter of macroeconomic stability has to do with the employment of labor and price stability. Wages being a large fraction of the costs covered by prices, the latter too is importantly bound up with labor market conditions. Structural economics emphasizes the matching of the supply and demand structure for output and for labor and other inputs. Obviously, bottlenecks that induce price increases and surpluses that result in unemployment can exist alongside each other in an economy that is structurally maladjusted.

The oil price shocks of the 1970s made this difficult to ignore for the profession at large, though again Galbraith and other institutionalists were insisting upon a realistic supply-side economics even before the signal turning point of the 1958 recession in which disinflation but not deflation accompanied a definite reduction in the aggregate level of economic activity. The very oil bottlenecks that caused inflation to rise in the 1970s also rendered idle much plant and labor. In Veblenian economics, the attempt to find or create such imbalances that work to one's advantage is the key entrepreneurial strategy for pecuniary success. The opportunity to practice such legitimate extortion is the centerpiece of the power theory of income distribution.

The administered sector requires considerable government support to secure its purposes. The technostructure is not in a position to accommodate the labor force to its needs and the task of financing education by classical economic precept falls to the state. Education is to some extent a public good in that its beneficent effect does not fall entirely upon its recipient but to the advantage of society generally. Such external benefit means that private market decisions as to the desired level of education would fall below the level that is best for society. In practice the state has produced much of this educational service in public institutions, though this is not necessary by economic principle, as all manner of voucher proposals elucidate. The dependence of the administered sector on the state in this connection figures strongly in Galbraith's appraisal of the prospect for reform. It also figures importantly in his somber assessment of the prospect for democratic process if the requisite reconstruction of habitual precept is not accomplished. On these matters, there is much more below.

For now, it is sufficient to note that the need for educational accommodation adds a dimension to the operation of the administered society that the technostructure cannot plan directly. The control of the supply of properly socialized, properly educated, properly assorted labor power rests in large part with the financial activity of the state in concert with the decisions of households. As in many areas, the wheels of social change respond but only belatedly or with a lag. The state has greatly increased educational and social services in the present century. No doubt in so doing it has attended to much of the need of the administered sector for technically qualified personnel. The habitual bias against the state does induce a lag in this accommodation. This is forcefully evident in the persistence of structural unemployment which results from a poor matching of the worker's skills or location with the needs of potential employers. Labor and the output it produces become more differentiated in the New Industrial State and excess capacity for some types may coexist with excess demand for others (Galbraith, 1967, pp. 253–4).

The incidence of unemployment, in good times or bad, remains inversely correlated to the individual laborer's years of formal education. In itself, this fact tells us only that educational credentials are a screening device for employment, not that the education is technically necessary for the job to be performed. But coupled with the presence of a changing industrial structure and an increasing sophistication of the means of production, the impression is that more than an inflation of credentials is at work.

So also much structural unemployment reflects the social discrimination against minorities which can be found even if educational levels are controlled statistically (Shulman, 1987). Still, in terms of the overall magnitude of the racial problem, a great deal can be attributed to differences in educational opportunity and attainment. The problem of racial discrimination is part of the lag in cultural development. With respect to the accommodation lag in the face of economic change, formal educational remains a key aspect, especially if one includes therein the need for a program of lifetime education and training.

The accommodation lag means that much unemployment persists when the economy is in macroeconomic balance, or even in inflationary imbalance. If openings for qualified employees exist alongside people who want but are unable to secure jobs, then the problem is not the amount of capital per se but its structure in relation to that of the available labor. Nor should it be supposed that the capital is obsolete; it may be, but what of the labor? The argument here is that labor being more specialized than

before, the matching of educational background to the tasks to be performed is far more complicated than suggested by the simple aggregation
of openings and unemployed. With the increased technological sophistication of the system and the increasing pace of its technological development, one should surely be more surprised were this matching problem
not to become more important than the fact that it has become so.

The effect of a mismatch, a failure of the accommodation of supply
to demand will be the presence of frustrated job seekers in the face of
employers who are unable to hire the labor they require. Any concerted
effort to employ those not employed by a quantitative increase in the
number of jobs will intensify the shortages of those desired by the industrial system without solving the frustrations of those left out.

Of course the proportion of various kinds of labor is not fixed in concrete. Technical or organization changes alter the mix on the demand side
and workers augment their skills on the supply side. But the technical
trend seems to be toward an inflexible commitment to production capacity that requires a particular assortment of labor for its operation. Indeed,
any bias that the technostructure is likely to have would move away from
structural accommodation of surplus labor. Unemployment tends to be
higher among those with lower education and skill. Structural accommodation would require that corporations move to employ shift to more
intensive use of less skilled labor.

In the Galbraithian System, several factors militate against this result.
These include the prestige of technological virtuosity, the desire of the
relatively skilled to have more individuals like themselves to work with,
and tax incentives to investment which tend to raise rather than lower the
technical level required of the labor force. In recognition of this, Hyman
Minsky (1986) has proposed an alternative policy of providing employment rather than investment incentives but such a policy redirection, however wise, would require a sea change in political economic orthodoxy and
public commitment to override the sentiment of the technostructure.

It is plausible that redesigning aggregate demand policy could moderate the structural tendency. Fiscal policy could be designed to favor the
market sector of the economy. The market sector employs a greater proportion of less skilled labor and is populated with small entrepreneurs
who seek from a competitive environment the profit for their livelihood.
These entrepreneurs cannot afford the bias to investment and technical
credentials that permeates the administered sector.

Relative ease in monetary policy might moderate the structural bias
somewhat if the market sector were helped more by the lower interest
rates than the advanced sector. However, it may be that credit at high

or low interest rates is rationed more by bankers' judgment about credit worthiness than by the effect of interest rates on the demand for credit (Wray, 1990). If so the market sector may be expected to be at a disadvantage at all interest rate levels. To this must be added the conventional Keynesian asymmetry of monetary policy as expressed in the metaphorical phrase 'you cannot push on a string'.

The political economic currents flow strongly against any such revision of aggregate demand policy. Again, dominant economic thinking would have to incorporate the dual economic structure into its models and the power of the technostructure would have to be counteracted. As discussed below in Chapter 7, Galbraith proposes a reconstruction of aggregate demand policy to favor the market sector. But he recognizes that fundamental changes in political economy would have to occur before this reform could be enacted.

Government policies to improve labor supply structure are also necessary to counter the structural tendency. Government could facilitate the retraining and enhanced education of workers. It could subsidize workers who relocate to find new jobs. It could expand its activities in providing information about openings to workers and about available workers to business. So-called active labor market policies are one of the best kept success stories of the times. They operate in the main to improve the efficacy of markets and should likely enjoy the ringing endorsement of those who are pro-market as opposed to simply anti-government.

Active labor market policies could go hand in hand with an expansionary fiscal policy as transfers were given to structurally unemployed workers and payments made to the personnel providing the educational services. However, active labor market policy should not be linked to expansionary fiscal policy. If economic conditions militate against fiscal ease, labor market policy should be pursued with tax increases to cover the transfers and expenditures or cuts in transfers or expenditures elsewhere.

However financed, this approach would also favor the market system in the short run and reduce the structural tendency. In the longer term, given the expansion of technically advanced labor, the advanced sector would also benefit by a reduction in the bottleneck it faces in labor supply. This enhanced accommodation and the decrease in payroll taxes necessary to support those unemployed would also improve competitiveness internationally. Further impetus in this regard might occur if enhanced re-employment prospects reduced worker resistance to innovation that threatens disemployment.

Structural considerations then suggest that combatting unemployment with aggregate demand policy beyond the area of macroeconomic balance is likely to kindle inflation without doing much to eliminate unemployment. The use of aggregate demand policy beyond macroeconomic balance to combat inflation is equally dubious. The unemployment brought about by high interest rates and budget austerity will tend to fall hardest on the market sector and lower skilled workers. The cold bath policy will moderate inflation at the cost of high distress in the short run and a worsening inflation and unemployment tradeoff in the long run.

On the significance of structural unemployment there would seem to be growing agreement within the economics profession. The so-called natural rate of unemployment is surely no more nor less than a level of unemployment that is not usefully attacked by aggregate demand policy. The argument that the natural rate of unemployment cannot be reduced by aggregate demand expansion or that it can be reduced only by a ruinously inflationary process, is surely no argument that this number of supernumerary workers is socially acceptable much less somehow optimal or desirable. The only conclusion to be reached is that the problem be attacked by means of more precise instruments, if it be attacked at all.

The wage and price spiral that results from primary reliance upon a buoyant aggregate demand policy is all too familiar. Corporations which can pass cost increases along in their administered prices are not a very effective front line against wage push pressures, much less are they an obdurate front versus the salaries and perquisites of their own kith and kin in the corporate structure. Intent upon sufficient earnings gains to appease stockholders, pension fund managers, and the like, corporate leaders will likely exercise prudent foresight in factoring into their price markup a band of inflationary expectation so to avoid the public embarrassment of taking too little from the buyer's purse. Furthermore, union leaders may be expected to seek a risk premium in case inflation over the contract period occasions surprise.

Control of the wage-price spiral in the administered sector requires that wage increases be held within productivity increases. This an unresolved problem of the New Industrial State. The issue of wage restraint from within the industrial relations complex or its *constraint* by some form of incomes policy will remain on the agenda for the foreseeable future. The more successful national economies in this regard, such as Japan in recent decades, will prosper in the global economy. That Japan has achieved wage restraint with low unemployment because of the culture of its industrial relations is a fact that should occasion much interest from the other democratic capitalist nations (Stanfield, 1994).

SOCIAL IMBALANCE AND THE QUALITY OF LIFE

Beyond stabilizing the aggregate system of output, employment, and income by which society materially and financially reproduces itself, Galbraith has been persistently concerned with the quality of life that is lived on the basis of that livelihood. The concern for the question of *lives and livelihood*, that is, the effects of the pattern of earning a living upon the quality of that living, is a fundamental issue for social or institutional economics.

The place of economy in society is a focus not only upon the necessary institutionalization of the economy by socialization but also upon the effects on society of particular forms of instituting economic regularity. This was the central concern of prominent economic theorists such as Karl Marx, Thorstein Veblen, and Karl Polanyi (Stanfield, 1986, ch. 1).

Galbraith has long been concerned with the predominance of economic considerations over aesthetics. The modern economic model is dedicated to spurring economic growth by financial vulnerability. Beyond the obvious psychological misery of economic insecurity, this entails cultural deprivation or distortion. In effect, this model is a blueprint for making the 'pecuniary motivation as nearly pre-emptive as possible' to the detriment of aesthetic considerations (Galbraith, 1960, p. 49). With regard to its interest in aesthetic development, society cannot confidently rely upon the attention or the competence of the organized interests of the administered sector (Galbraith, 1986, pp. 139–51).

His concern about the fate of the arts in the absence of an effective state response is part of Galbraith's extension and emendation of the concept of *social (im)balance*. As noted, the imbalance is not solely one of the public versus the private sector. In many areas of public provision the interests of the administered sector militate toward adequacy, perhaps even sufficiency or profusion. But in other important areas that require public provision the result will be penury because the administered sector has no viable interest or understanding. Indeed the administered sector may be expected not only to neglect important areas which do not abet its purposes but to actively spurn other concerns which are seen to defy its purposes.

Galbraith (1967, ch. 31) cites transportation and urban development design as a major instance of the *planning lacunae*. Planning is here required but it falls outside the organized intelligence of the administered sector. Much of the benefits involved would lie in social or public goods so that there would be no effective means for their capture in the revenue

functions of the administered sector. Resistance is likely to be active because the autonomy of the technostructure is threatened whenever the state
presumes to enforce the public purpose in ecologically conscious modes
of mobility or in aesthetically cognizant built environments.

The aesthetic dimension generally is most notable in regard to the planning lacunae. Aesthetic concern threatens the autonomy of the technostructure by insinuating the criterion of good taste into its physical installations
and threatening regulation of its activities. Even more galling to the technocratic prospect, any semblance that individuals be concerned with beauty
and meaning in adorning their lives with commodities undermines their
submission to the systematic inveigling ministered to them by the corporate edifice to assure their compliant pursuit of copious quantities of money
and things (Galbraith, 1967, ch. 30).

The matter of toil is likewise a concern when one is examining the
achieved versus the potential quality of living. Echoing *The Affluent Society*, Galbraith (1967, ch. 32) again questions the wisdom of continuing
the link between income and labor that is productive in the pecuniary
sense. The concern is not addressed with characteristic clarity, but one
supposes it lies in recognition of the freedom from want and agony of
toil that is possible. More and better leisure as well as improved quality
of work life are possible. To continue to spur labor effort by employment
insecurity and income deprivation in the face of this potential is a social
concern for which the technostructure can have no sensitivity, no tolerance even.

Galbraith also evinces concern for the threat this 'organized public bam-
boozlement' must surely have upon the frequently affirmed values of individual liberty and political pluralism. The vitality of the individual's exercise
of discretion in matters of taste and judgment in affairs of state rests upon
educational cultivation. The hegemony of the administered sector impends
the subordination of this cultivation to its inordinant interest in commodity production. 'One is led to inquire whether education remains education when it is chained too tightly to the wheel of the industrial system'
(Galbraith, 1967, p. 329).

The concern for enlightenment and pluralism is vastly increased by
consideration of the cozy relation between the technostructure and the
military establishment (Galbraith, 1967, ch. 29). The easy access to R&D
funds and secure profit centers that the military procurement system
affords to influential portions of the technostructure is understandably
irresistible. The possibility that our policy and even our images of the
seeming implacability of geopolitical discord are shaped more by this
irresistible cozy relationship than the facts of the matter reasonably

assessed is very disconcerting. The problem here of course goes far beyond waste of resources to the possibility of ultimate catastrophe.

The humanistic concern is thus evident. In matters of aesthetics from artistic endeavor to the simple pleasure of a pleasant urban environment or workplace, in matters of community and civic participation, in matters of meaningful existence and sense of purpose, in matters of peace and the specter of ultimate human peril, Galbraith offers somber admonitions with regard to the bearing of the administered society upon the quality of human life in the late twentieth century. Lives and livelihood indeed. Incredible heights have been scaled in the latter, but at what cost, and what is there to show for it in comprehension and application of the art of living?

TOWARD REFORM

In Chapters 33 and 34 of his classic, Galbraith turns to the final step in the critical historical method. This final step is to indicate the significance of the explanation offered for the facts from which the inquiry began. This significance is to be drawn more or less explicitly with respect to relevant social values, and to comprise suggestions as to the further relevance of the work to the attainment of social purpose and to the conduct of social inquiry.

As is clear from what has been said about Walton Hamilton's classic article and about the nature of institutional economics generally, this approach insists that lucid relevance is among the most important tests of social science. For *instrumental* social science, beyond the tests of logical coherence and empirical correspondence, there is the additional test of relevance or praxis (Eichner, 1983; see also Lowe, 1966; Stanfield, 1979, ch. 9).

The relevance criterion means that social behavior must be examined in relation to a workable conception of social values. Only thus can the instituted organization of that behavior be cast in a relevant relation to social action. Social problems arise from dissonance between social values and the dominant patterns of social interaction that regulate behavior. Operationally, this implies that social scientific paradigms must incorporate instrumental or control variables into their explanatory models. These variables are such that they are functionally related to perceived social problems and are amenable to policy manipulation. These instrumental variables are the tools of social policy that can be used in the service of collective action to modify and control individual action.

Social science in this view merges into the task of social reform (Tilman, 1987). Social reform is the incessant goal of a vital and liberatory democratic process. For modern liberalism, anything qualitatively short of such an essential democracy is more sham and pretense than substance. The task of directing social reform requires a clear frame of reference as to the attendant social problems, that is, to disparities between social values and prevalent patterns of instituted behavior. Social science in the service of social reform must identify these problems, the priorities among them, the explanatory and instrumental variables, and any relevant constraints imposed by social values upon the tools to be utilized.

This need not be scientistic or constructivist in the manner alluded to by Hayek (1944, ch. 1). *Scientism* in his view is the transfer of natural science methodology and its technical derivatives to the social process, so to suggest a social engineering that mirrors the engineering concomitant to the physical sciences. Such technocratic images of social policy do indeed tend to neglect the element of human will at work in the social process. *Constructivism* is a related tendency that manifestly envisions, more or less, a radical refashioning of the social process. This imagery of reconstruction necessarily relies upon faith, or at least hope, that human character can be reconstituted to match the potentialities immanent in some new system for instituting social behavior. This is potentially a dangerous ideological tendency, not least because it may invite notions of infallibility of the vanguard intellectual and political leadership (Heilbroner, 1981).

It must be quickly said that if the ethnographic record does not support the notion of fully malleable human character, it offers even less comfort to the habitual contrary ideological tendency which sees human character as essentially invariant. The fixation of human character and the consonant institutional pattern is the bedrock of conservative or classical liberal capitalist apologism. The doctrine of invariant human character maintains its own version of infallibilism in the form of what is, or ought to be.

Galbraith and the institutionalists seek to avoid both of these extremes. Present institutional patterns are not regarded as inviolate incarnations of ancestral wisdom. That which has come to be accepted as proper and just may have the most sinister or haphazard of origins (North, 1990). Institutional adjustment to redistribute power may be freely undertaken insofar as the reasonable expectation exists that such change will ameliorate well-understood social problems. But utopian constructions of radical institutional change are to be resisted insofar as they lack this reasonable expectation. The concrete problem to be dealt with, not overarching teleological vision, sets the frame of reference for the institutionalist.

In the Galbraithian System, the logic of institutional growth and change does more than beget the constitutive facts that are explained by the dualized, power economy model, with its characteristic social predicament. This logic also begets the potential for reform to resolve the dilemmas of this predicament. One of the constitutive facts is the growth of higher education. This has been seen to be bound up with the technological and organizational imperatives that bring the corporate form of economic organization to its characteristic role in the modern political economy. The growth of the economic presence of the state has been similarly related to the imperatives. The personnel of higher education and research are therefore expanded and potentially empowered.

The *scientific-intellectual* estate has a fundamentally indispensable function in the Galbraithian System. Expertise is necessary to the technostructure of the New Industrial State and those who possess it can only come into being through the scientific-intellectual estate. Thus the estate is positioned to exert influence directly through political and organizational activity and indirectly through its research and educational activities. In the latter the instillation of the critical attitude in students and the refusal to purge research of humanist concern and idle curiosity are immensely important.

As modern higher education is in large part an accommodation to the requirements of the administered sector, so also it is necessarily in large part organized to accomplish this accommodative function. Characteristically, that which is not an immediate or visible aspect of this accommodation tends to be relegated to secondary status in deliberations as to the structure and coordination of the higher learning. The arts and humanities, notwithstanding their ancient pride of place in the higher learning, nonetheless tend to be accorded secondary status in the modern edifice. So also, it must be said, this relative neglect extends to many of the applied and interdisciplinary studies programs concerned with the delivery of social welfare, the understanding of the ecological predicament, and so on.

The Galbraithian System maintains that the criterion for neglect or sufficient support does not in the main turn upon the *public purpose* but upon the importance of the field to the technostructure. That which offers no apparent advantage in this regard tends toward neglect; that which portends a threat to the autonomy of the technostructure is subject to vigorous adverse selection. This is evidence of the administered sector's perception of its interests and of its power to induce society to attend to its felt needs.

But this tendency has not passed into fact without resistance and the matter is far from settled. The academy is by immemorial tradition the repository of human values, erudition, and wisdom. The insistence upon the value of a good or liberal education as an end in itself is habitually asserted by the academic establishment. More than occasionally such adverts extend beyond mere academic ritual into the substance of the academic curriculum. The need for a general, liberal educational foundation seems to be widely accepted, notwithstanding the fact that the core features thereof continue to be hotly contested.

Of late this has taken the form of the furor over the pursuit of multiculturalism and political correctness versus the preservation of traditional pillars of excellence in the academic program. This is most likely a propitious discourse. In any case, the adversaries are in substantial agreement on the fundamental point presently at hand: there exists a core educational curriculum that configures the process of becoming an educated human being. Debate of the nature of this liberal educational core is rightly the subject of heated controversy because it comprises the essence of the academic entity as such.

Significantly, this debate over the core curriculum represents the distillation of several centuries of academic experience. Hence, its character has definition that preceded the present era with its tendency toward hegemonic dominance of social life by the administered sector. The nuances of this debate have stature independently of the vagaries of the administered sector, are often expressed in a litany which is virtually incomprehensible to its crackpot reality, and frequently contradict its most notable tendencies. It cannot be otherwise. The aspiration to empower the human intellect and imagination as the unique right and responsibility of every person, is necessarily incompatible with subordination to the purposes of the administered sector. The cultivation of the self, of the 'entire human personality,' is expressly in conflict with definitive preoccupation with the earning and spending of incomes. Yet precisely in such preoccupation with commodity flows lies servitude to the purposes of the administered sector.

No case can be made in the Galbraithian System that the resistance to the corporate purpose is automatically sustained nor inevitably victorious. Only the potential for such resistance is ineluctable. Its exercise is latent and remains so unless it is vigorously prosecuted by an appropriately constituted and focused scientific-intellectual estate. This estate must be securely funded to perform its most vital social functions, those apart from the technostructural purpose. Penurious support for its service to the public purpose will leave the estate beholdened to the considerable resources that the administered sector has to offer. But a share of this largesse will be forthcoming at a dreadful price. Heavy reliance upon support from the administered sector would necessarily deflect the functioning of the estate's supposedly independent organizational edifices to corporate purposes and away from those of the public (Dugger, 1989).

Adequately funded on its own terms, thus empowered to autonomously conduct its affairs, the estate must in so doing insist not only upon the inviolate nature of its essential mission but also upon the preeminence of this mission relative to the interests of the administered sector. Contrary to habitual sentiment, which emanates from media shaped by the administered sector rather than the *public cognizance*, the organizations of higher learning, at least those securely funded on their own terms, fulfill the most critical functions for the continued health and vitality of a free and pluralistic society.

The litany of natural rights and free private enterprise that operates so powerfully to obscure this fact is among the more resolutely insidious threats of the age. Resistance to this threat cannot be overdone and is most certainly less than well done presently. Nor are recent trends in political behavior encouraging (Galbraith, 1992). The matter of belief and the empowerment of pluralistic sources of influence is further considered in the next chapter when attention turns to the *emancipation of belief*.

The matter extends beyond the estate's protection of its turf from encroachment by the administered sector's power elite. Galbraith argued that emancipation from the hegemony of the administered sector will require a *political lead* from an emancipated scientific-educational estate. He made it clear that nothing short of direct political effort will save the day. Intellectual debate and conversation, the natural mien of the estate, are mere 'political surrogates'; they are not the functional equivalents of the political lead. The latter will require the application of cohesive and disciplined effort, patiently sustained toward effective compromise.

The estate is not naturally suited to this role. The intellectual and artistic temperament so celebrates the dignity and worth of the individual and so cherishes precision that its constituents do not take readily to the coordination and compromise of the political campaign.

Moreover, the estate's habitual sense of itself places great stock in its nonpartisan, even aloof, juxtaposition to the contemporaneous issues of society. By virtue of its political neutrality it is said to defend its political autonomy. This *scientific separatism*, to employ Clarence Ayres's (1962) aptly descriptive term, has a hallowed if largely unexamined place in the academic retinue. John Dewey (1948) critically examined it in his call for a reconstruction in philosophy, to which much kinship is evident in the contemplated revision in thought of the Galbraithian System. Galbraith pilloried without mercy those who uphold the doctrine of scientific separatism:

In the last millisecond before the ultimate nuclear fusion, a scientist will be heard to observe that the issue of nuclear control and military security is really one for the politicians. . . . And as the last horizon is lost behind the smoke, gas, neon lights and detritus of the industrial civilization, men of self-confessed artistic sensitivity will be heard to observe that, unfortunately, none of this is the business of the true artist. (Galbraith, 1967, p. 391)

No doubt the notion of an ivory tower of sages who dispense wisdom impartially and with no need to examine its remote social consequences holds fewer in its thrall than in the era from which Galbraith's classic emerged. But its essential effect upon the scientific-intellectual estate remains powerfully in force and leaves the way open for the corporate elite to determine social priorities and hence to shape them to the corporate rather than the public purpose.

The neglect of power by economists may be the most telling dimension of scientific separatism. It is very convenient to the political economic powers that be. As the next two chapters indicate, Galbraith was to renew and sharpen his criticism of the *convenient social* virtue of his peers with regard to the exercise of power by the administered sector. The *imagery of choice* conveyed by conventional economics opinion obscures the reality of power and defuses popular dissatisfaction with the quality of life provided by the administered society. Habitual economic sentiment thus blocks the development and application of the *public cognizance* to the formation of public policy.

6 Economic Doctrine and the Public Purpose

The persistence of a way of thinking which somehow fails to take account of what are proving to be the basic realities of modern economic life is itself one of the great economic mysteries of our civilization.
(C.E. Ayres, 1944)

In *Economics and the Public Purpose*, Galbraith slightly emends the overall model of *The New Industrial State* and sharpens and elaborates upon its implications. The development of his thinking that he integrates into his model of the new industrial state in this book was foreshadowed by two important essays initially delivered to the American Economic Association, 'Economics as a System of Belief' in 1969 (republished in Galbraith, 1971a) and 'Power and the Useful Economist' in 1972 (also republished, 1979c). Galbraith regards the latter essay as 'the best short account of my general economic position' (1979c, p. 3).

In these essays he began to assign a larger role to what he was later to refer to as 'conditioned power' that operates by persuasion or by habitual belief (Galbraith, 1983). He was also becoming more confrontational with the neoclassical synthesis because it was a powerful underlying expression of the habitual mentality that allowed such unfettered and unexamined reign to the conditioned power of the administered sector of the economy.

In *Economics and the Public Purpose*, he was much more systematic in his criticism of the neoclassical synthesis (Stanfield, 1995a, ch. 3), and seemed to attach a far more sinister significance to its role in the social process. The dualistic structure of the economic order was given more systematic conceptualization and the international sector was incorporated into it. This permitted more systematic formulation of the grave distortion exercized upon the quality of life by the refusal to cope with the bifurcated structure of the economy. The theory of the state was more carefully presented and more attention was given directly to the matter of consciousness, i.e., personality and culture. Galbraith offered the ingenious *test of anxiety* to draw attention to the implications of the Galbraithian System and outlined a specific agenda for reform (on the latter, see the following chapter).

THE IMAGERY OF CHOICE

The theme by which Galbraith organized *Economics and the Public Purpose* is to contrast the purposes of various interests with the general purpose of the political economic system, to wit, the public purpose. The common view that the economic system exists to serve the wants of the population is sufficient so far as it goes but in its simple form it begs a question of profound import. This is the question of power and hence the issue of whose wants are being served.

The purpose of economics as a discipline is a major and explicit theme in the discussion. The conventional view is that economics as a science has 'no purpose except to understand that behavior' that follows from axiomatic scarcity and the imperative of choice thusly mandated. Presented with ineluctable scarcity, households and business firms make choices and engage in exchanges that advance real income by the gains of specialization. Economists have no agenda other than the comprehension of this choice behavior.

But Galbraith detected a hidden agenda, not one intended by economists but vitally important nonetheless. People do not make choices solely as individuals, they organize and make some choices collectively. In so doing, they acquire power. Galbraith expended little energy defining power, in his view its essential and commonplace meaning is that one can impose one's will on others (Galbraith, 1983, p. 2). He earlier gave similarly brief definitions such as 'the privilege of controlling the actions or affecting the income or property of other persons' (Galbraith, 1952b, p. 25) or 'to command the efforts of individuals and the state' (Galbraith, 1973b, p. 3). Far less evident are the sources and uses, and therefore the implications, of power (Galbraith, 1983).

Power structures the economic process toward outcomes that are amenable to powerful, organized interests. At the very least the exercise of power changes the alternatives available to others as they make their own exchange decisions. The exercise of power to effect the prices at which one buys or sells and therefore one's own relative income ramifies throughout the system of relative prices and impinges upon the decisions made in light of these relative prices (Stanfield, 1995b). The relative distribution of income is effected and so also the structure of life chances.

Political power is highly significant in this regard. Much of the national income in a modern industrial economy is devoted to public goods and services and to redistributive programs of one kind or another. It is a mistake to view such transfers as solely inclined toward to those with lesser earned incomes. Moreover, very often collective decisions structure the tendency of private decisions. Recall the theory of social balance. If private consumption in many instances stands in a joint goods relationship to public goods, then the relative success of possible private goods will be influenced to some extent by the collective decision whether or not to supply the juxtaposed public good.

The heavy reliance upon automobile transportation is the most important case in point. It is surely not in doubt that had the government allocated the funds to alternative transportation modes that it has to supplementing the automobile mode, America would move about in a much different fashion. And the matter is dynamic. Once a given technology is given a lead by such collective action, it may enjoy economies of scale that effectively bar the entry of alternatives in the future. Note that given the relative inequality of power, the original path chosen may not have been the preference of the majority, nor the most efficient in any social sense (North, 1990).

Nor does majority rule in collective action dispose of the matter of power. Power may extend to the exercise of a degree of influence over the attitudes from which those who are less organized make their own decisions. This is a profoundly sinister possibility in a liberal society and it is precisely the thrust of the Galbraithian System. The foundation of a liberal society is the *liberal sphere*, that space within the private domain in which the individual's preferences are presumed to be supreme. The preferences developed in the liberal sphere are the source of the commitment to democratic governance of collective action: pluralism is significant because of the assumption that there is a multiplicity of life experiences that then come to bear as the multifaceted individuals engage in political discourse. If the preferences are seen to be shaped by centralized mass media then the liberal sphere loses much of its verve and the idea of pluralism is lost. The essential concern is for the *self-authenticity* of the preferences or the extent to which they arise from the experience and reflections of psychologically mature individuals.

If organized interests effect the relative prices and perhaps even the preferences of those less organized, then the emphasis on individual choice within the conventional economic model exposes that model to a sinister possibility. If organized power so operates, then the choices which are habitually presented by the conventional model as the culmination of myriad interacting individuals become, to some degree, the administered outcomes imposed on the process by the powerful organized interests. Such is not acceptable within the liberal culture, as already noted. By obfuscating inconvenient facts, the conventional model may be doing yeoman service to the powerful interests that exercise essentially illegitimate power (Stanfield, 1995a, ch. 4).

To nominate this implicit and socially pernicious service, Galbraith coined the phrase *imagery of choice* – inexplicably he did so without resort to his habitual capitalization. The two basic ways by which the imagery of conventional economics serves the powerful are well-known to Galbraith's readers of earlier works. The imagery of scarcity renders important all who march on the front lines of resistance to its limitations. Great status and prestige most surely is legitimately accorded to the soldiers who daily renew the battles against nature's obstinate niggardliness.

This applies with most especial force to those who are the generals in this holiest of wars – corporate CEOs and their technostructural staff. No doubt it applies at some remove to the economists who form a part of the liaison staff. The related imagery of the self-regulating market reinforces the power of the economic commandants by limiting it to the technical issues of the battlefield. It is the population's ultimate wants that are served in the fray, not those of our generals. As surely as the military-industrial-complex has no interest and no sway over how much defense is applied with regard to political enemies, those who command the great economic organizations have no interest in the amount of defense chosen in the war against scarcity. They have no power in this regard because they are subordinate to individual decisions to supply productive resources and purchase consumer commodities.

The imagery of choice effectively renders nugatory any suggestion that a 'dominant economic interest' exercises influence over wants and the habitual ways and means by which they are satisfied. All who would press the case in this regard are but crackpots of one kind or another, conspiracy fantasists and would-be taste czars who would be dangerous were they not so divorced from reality as to be self-evident lunatics.

The state is not without a place in this imagery. Much is done through the public sector, especially in areas that are useful and lucrative to the technostructure. Here again the individual rules through choices, herein made politically but no less independent of any organized effort at persuasion. In particular, the corporate organizations have no bearing upon the amount and character of public goods. They have their lobbyists in the pluralistic fray, to be sure, but the effort to understand even such obvious collective efforts at taste deflection has been belated and originates outside the highest citadels of neoclassic orthodoxy in economics.

The Public Choice School, so powerfully influenced by James Buchanan, is a very important development in contemporary economic thought, but it too is severely limited in its sense of the issues that Galbraith raises with regard to the formation of wants. True to its classical liberal roots, the Public Choice School takes preferences as given and examines the political behavior of the abstract individual seeking to maximize utility. Still the attempt to endogenize the state is a welcome effort, deserving of the attention it has received. The Platonic problem of dealing with the own agendas of those who staff the offices of the state remains a serious issue in political economy.

THE DUAL ECONOMY REDUX

In *Economics and the Public Purpose*, Galbraith carefully elaborated the dual economy. He included a discussion of the causes by which some activities remain in the less organized, market sector of the economy and he provided a more systematic examination of the interaction of the two sectors.

The Market Sector

No sharp quantitative line separates the market and administered sectors in terms of sales, employees, assets, or profits. On average the administered sector firm is certainly larger, vastly so, but no threshold of size alone sets it apart from its smaller companion. A few hundred corporations dominate the commercial landscape. A thousand account for around one-half of all economic activity. In manufacturing, two hundred account for that percentage and then some. More than twelve million firms overall scramble for the other half of economic activity; in manufacturing the total firms number in the hundreds of thousands and the share left over by the largest 200 is a fraction far less than one-half.

The dividing line is essentially qualitative, made on the basis of conceptual nuance rather than size alone. The market sector enterprises are amenable to control by an individual or a small number of individuals in partnership. As seen above, in the Galbraithian System, no such individual control is possible in the administered sector. Therein the scale and technical sophistication of operations militate strongly in the direction of organizational control, and hence, of course, the technostructure.

Firms in the market sector tend to be those which face inherent structural obstacles to development of the size and technical and organizational character that comprise the administered sector. Productive activities that tend to be geographically dispersed and resistant to standardization, and that involve artistic creativity or personal service, make up the bulk of the market sector. There is an additional limiting factor where law or custom inhibits the development of organization.

Activities which must be performed on site in various parts of the world are poor candidates for the advantages that modern technology and organization confer. Construction activities are an example, though one cannot sort out altogether the influence of the productive activity itself from the effect of trade unions and local government regulations. Personal service carries with it the expectation of a personal nature although here again law and custom operate to limit organization in legal and medical fields. And there has been some development of organization as professional corporations replace the old-style family practitioner with a number of clinicians who are variously on-call. But the numbers are small relative to the massive scale of cooperation in the administered sector and the advantages lie largely with scheduling of the professional's leisure time. This is more an antidote to the tendency of the market sector to self-exploitation (see below) than a nuance of forthcoming organizational revolution.

Even where scale is increased, such as in university lecture halls with hundreds of students, the matter is less one of the benefits of organization than the necessities of compromise given budget constraints. Few maintain that the educational service provided in a class of four hundred students is comparable to that in a class of twenty five. That it is cheaper, even that it may be good enough, does make it the same in terms of quality. So it is with haircuts, interior design, and the like. Some accommodation to competitive cost pressures may induce restructuring and packaged programs, but the economies gained tend to be limited by the deterioration of quality.

The artistic element is another influence. The creative impulse of an individual is unique in principle and legendary in its resistance to organized control. So also is much made of the eyes that behold the beauty of the result.

Where organization confers no particular advantage, most especially where it is selected against by the vagaries of detail, the market form of integration remains forceful, and with it the market model of neoclassical faith. However, even in this regard one must issue the caveat that the presence of the administered sector distorts the eventual outcome, as recognized long ago by J.M. Clark (1940). State activity, much of which occurs at the behest of the administered sector, also alters the outcome of the operation of the market in the unorganized sector.

Profit maximization is a reliable motivation within the market sector.

The force of the individual remains where organization has not intruded. The individual as the energizing force, is also the motivating force, and profits accrue to the entrepreneur. Little opportunity exists for abnormal profit on the basis of the ability to administer relations with customers, suppliers, or the state. Absent secure rents to finance it and the difficulty of differentiating products, advertizing tends to be informational and frequently oriented to price. Suppliers tend to be larger than oneself, which presents problems for a would-be oligopsonist. Where the state can be influenced in one's specific behalf, laws and regulations tend to be broken and one faces the distinct possibility of ultimate ruin when the graft is exposed by some journalist or whistle blower affected with an undue sensibility as to the public interest.

The opportunity for abnormal profits of the classic Schumpeterian type are present in principle. Such rents as are captured are gained by entrepreneurial innovation, and tend to be fleeting because barriers to entry are insignificant. A small firm that innovates in its product, market area, or production process can enjoy a time-band of profitability that exceeds that normally available. This time-band will likely be less for small firms that face constraints to organization or otherwise lack the ability to grow in step with the market for their innovation. Barriers to entry are notably minimal in the service, retail, construction, farming, and light industrial manufacturing businesses that comprise the market system. New market areas are the innovations most available to such business and also the most difficult to protect from new entrants in search of a share of excess profits.

In the major product and process innovations for which the time-band is more pronounced, Galbraith has of course long been a staunch participant in the debate over the source of innovative activity. He tends to the Schumpeterian view that the large corporation with its scale and monopoly profits has a distinct advantage when it comes to financing and bearing the inherent risks of innovation (Schumpeter, 1962). Such advantages were part of the Schumpeterian theory of the bureaucratized entrepreneurial function. The secure rents of the large firm provide a fund to support research and development on a scale large enough to afford the misses on the basis of the rents that derive from the successful projects. In addition to R&D risk, there is the necessity of teams of specialists utilizing specialized equipment that adds to the expense of conducting modern R&D.

The inability to sustain an important volume of excess profits subjects the market sector firm to the discipline of the market in a further significant way. Retained earnings for reinvestment are unlikely to be large and are direct subtractions from the household's living standard. The market sector firm is therefore likely to be dependent upon the financial intermediary system for financing. Accordingly, as has been observed above, the market sector firm is potentially very vulnerable to the repercussions of monetary policy.

The many firms in the market sector face great uncertainty. The more obdurate and successful endure and succeed by intensive exploitation of themselves, their kin, and their employees. The rules that govern organized behavior in the administered sector do not operate in the market sector. Labor effort within the large organization is standardized within limits set by more or less precise formulae and expectations. Arrant sloth is likely to draw attention, so also unmitigated diligence.

Matters are different in the market sector. The non-absentee entrepreneur continues to resemble the jungle fighter of popular legend (Maccoby, 1976). Here one's hard work and dedication to business has direct bearing upon one's survival and personal prosperity. So also does reward follow success in personal oversight to intensify the efforts of employees. Long hours with intensive concentration on the business at hand is profitable for the owner of the firm in the market sector.

Of course, there remains the possibility of windfall gains and losses that may intrude upon the relation between effort and reward. Circumstances beyond individual control can, on occasion, defeat the most worthy and escalate the most undeserving. Arthur Okun's (1975) 'shifting sands of technology and taste' still operate with great force upon the market sector. Indeed, to them must be added the repercussions of decisions made in the administered sector which add to the vulnerability of the market sector firm and therefore to the necessity of intensive exploitation.

Such then is the market sector. Organization, and with it the ability to control the enterprise's boundaries, while no doubt desirable, are not feasible. Organization therefore does not supplant personal control of the enterprise, which continues so that there is maintained a direct if somewhat uncertain bearing of personal effort to personal reward. Products are only slightly differentiable, requirements for capital and expertise minimal, the gains of innovation fleeting, and barriers to entry low enough that any sense of enterprise security is likely to be false. The exigencies of competition render life Hobbesian, especially in a world of countervailing leviathans, between which one may be constricted. The struggle of the state and the administered sector to control and co-opt one another to the other's purposes leaves strong currents among which the ships of the market sector must chart a course.

The Administered Sector

In *Economics and the Public Purpose*, Galbraith made few changes from *The New Industrial State* in the analysis of the administered sector. This permits brevity in the present discussion.

That the corporate organizations in the administered sector are large and growing occasions no dissent. But the conventional wisdom in economics seems to be disinterested in explaining the basic tendency toward expansion of corporate size. The received pedagogy rather firmly instructs its novitiates to the counter-empirical proposition that there are external constraints upon the growth of the corporate enterprise. Like all enterprises, the corporation is depicted as bent upon profit maximization. Thus engaged, its decision-makers seek to equate revenue and costs at the margin.

These decision-makers select from a menu of technologic possibilities given by spontaneous invention or publicly supported R&D, both of which are exogenous to the corporate enterprise. They face cost relationships such that inevitably their per unit costs rise as they decide to produce greater output. Again these are matters beyond their control save to hold costs to a minimum by searching out the lowest available input prices and using the inputs as sparingly as possible for a given level of output. Likewise are their per unit revenues external; consumers decide their preferences for what might be produced by the corporations for consumption markets, other firms decide what they seek to buy in producer goods markets, and government, or, better, individuals wearing their citizen hats, decide what shall be produced in the way of public goods and services.

Ultimately, so the conventional story goes, the size of any firm is constrained by the objective of maximizing profits. A more or less unique optimal output will occur, graphically speaking, at the intersection of the rising cost function and the horizontal or falling revenue function. A firm which exceeds such optimality is operated by distinctly irrational decision-makers, megalomaniacs presumably soon to be dumped by astute directors who uphold the sacred interest of the owners in equity of the corporation.

This textbook model that a firm will reach its optimal size is based upon external constraints of costs, demand and price, and technology. Its conclusions vanish with the introduction of the notion of administration. If corporations can to some extent administer their boundary conditions, that is, influence the demand for their output, the price at which it sells, or the costs at which it is produced, the notion of external constraint in practice becomes an empirical rather than an a priori matter. This follows even if profit maximization remains the goal.

If the objective of the enterprise is also open to empirical examination, which it must be if there is reason to suppose that interests contrary to those of the owners in equity may be dominant, then the necessary presence of external constraints upon optimal firm size is further compromised.

To emphasize, to the extent the corporation can administer these boundary constraints, the textbook model of external constraints on firm size is rendered nugatory. In the Galbraithian System this administrative extent is said to be very wide so that there is no apparent limit to the size of the corporation.

Further, in the Galbraithian System, within the corporation, power tends to reside with the technostructure. This team of 'corporation executives, lawyers, scientists, engineers, economists, controllers, advertising and marketing men' (Galbraith, 1973b, p. 162) effectively runs the organization on a day-to-day basis. The technostructure also wields political power broadly speaking and influences national consciousness on matters of political economy and public policy. This influence it shares with satellite constellations of similarly trained and similarly minded specialists who are housed in universities, think-tanks, management and marketing consulting enterprises, law firms, and government.

The strategy of the corporation and the state policy that emerges largely under this influence has as its most determinant goal the protection of the technostructure. To secure its existence and autonomy the technostructure requires steady, minimal earnings to satisfy stockholders and cover the salariat. Beyond security, growth of sales and earnings affirms the prestige and finances the expansion of the income of the technostructure. Moreover, it helps finance the further affirmative purpose of technical virtuosity or innovativness to which prestige is attached and from which growth is secured.

Some constraint on the size of the firm exists because of the primary objective of protecting the technostructure. Some growth strategies are risky in this regard, notably growth by agglomeration (Galbraith, 1973b, pp. 104–5). Yet agglomeration is a path to rapid growth and therefore an ever-present temptation and tendency for the administered sector. The 1960s agglomeration growth was high-risk growth. Subsequently many of these agglomerations were taken apart in the restructuring and downsizing of the 1980s.

Accordingly, the rise of the raiders and takeover artists associated with the merger and acquisition activity of the 1980s is not so alien to the Galbraithian System as is sometimes supposed. Indeed, the hiring of external consultants to appraise the competence of the technostructure, and further hostile action if indicated, is one of the alternatives that Galbraith (1973b, pp. 88–9) cited as still available to the owners in their quest to subordinate fiduciary agency to the equity purpose.

There is an added aspect of which Galbraith seemed not to avail himself. The scale economies available to agglomeration mergers and acquisitions cannot be represented as so-called real economies of scale. They are necessarily the gains of political clout and market power and hence serve the profit interest by redistributing income, not by any saving in resource use to society. This opens the way for a possible ideological vulnerability. Galbraith's assertion that conventional economics dismisses the pursuit of size beyond some point as irrational giantism is not an altogether accurate depiction. Indeed, especially with respect to his comments regarding a quote from Walter Adams, Galbraith (1973b, p. 106) seemed to ignore the distinction between real and pecuniary economies of scale and hence between social efficiency and profit maximization for firms with power.

It is in any case the corporation's ability to administer that is critical, not the goal of its administration. The effects of the technostructure's pursuit of its own agenda would be ultimately constrained as would its profit quest were its costs and revenues independent of its control. Serious questions of the legitimacy of power arise if the administered sector and its constituent organizations have the ability to administer these putatively external constraints to *any degree* (Galbraith, 1973b, p. 91 and 145). For, to that degree, to the extent of this power to administrate, corporate behavior becomes *self-legitimating* (Stanfield, 1995a, ch. 4). As discussed above and to be discussed again below, this prospect has unsavory implications that extend far beyond economic efficiency in any narrow sense.

The Transnational Context

In *Economics and the Public Purpose*, Galbraith was far more systematic in regard to the international economy than in his earlier work. Not that he altered the basic Galbraithian System; instead, he extended but did not modify the model to encompass the external sector. He treated the transnational system primarily as a relationship between the industrial democracies or, more precisely, between their technostructures. In so doing, however, he accorded attention to the issue of uneven development and the plight of the less developed countries.

The technostructure necessarily attempts to extend its reach into the international sector. In part this is but the fickleness of providence lacking the foresight to distribute raw material resources equably among the locales into which human beings imposed their economic development. Technostructures are large-scale users of materials and they reach out to secure their supplies globally via contracting, vertical integration, and political influence.

But apart from raw materials there is further need to reach out and establish operations transnationally. Other costs of production, notably labor costs, and of late, costs associated with compliance with environmental and other social regulations may also vary internationally. Political and social systems for various reasons may ebb and flow in accommodating themselves to the needs of the technostructure. The movements in exchange values of currencies present further but similar problems. A corporation operating primarily in one or a few countries is subjected to cost disparities that could be ruinous and is at the least inconvenient with regards to keeping abreast of one's corporate Joneses.

But diversification in the locales in which one produces and markets one's products averages out the exposure and allows rapid adjustment of production and marketing should differentials occur. This does not of course protect the nation's labor force or its market sector; to the contrary it exposes them to international pressure to a greater extent than if production were primarily national, because in that event the technostructure would have a much greater stake in the cause of protectionism. The great influence of the technostructure would then come fully to bear behind the same interests as the market sector and the representatives of labor.

Galbraith detected the cost disadvantage of American industry and related it to the distortion of American industrial structure by an implicit industrial policy toward the weapons industry. Faced with these cost disadvantages in civilian industries, especially in relation to Germany and Japan, the American technostructure shifted operations to lower cost foreign locales. What was visible to the farsighted in 1973 has since become a national scandal (Thurow, 1992).

It is instructive that in the matter of industrial policy, as in the matter of planning, the debate has been miscast as whether or not there should be government intervention. Any government of the size that obtains in the modern industrial societies necessarily has an industrial policy. It is inconceivable that the public sector could account for one-fifth to one-third of national income without differentially affecting the structure of industry within its borders. The issue is which industries are favored and which not, just as planning is reality and the issue is by whom and for whom.

The American government continues to favor weapons development, automobile transportation, agriculture, health care technology (but not its effective delivery), and residential and commercial construction with its implicit industrial policy (Kash, 1989). The pernicious symbiosis between the military technostructures of the superpowers is now widely seen to have very seriously strained the American economy and contributed in no small manner to the bankruptcy of the economy of the former Soviet Union.

The nature of imperialism, or obstruction of the development of another country in one's economic interest, is centered in the need for raw materials. Galbraith argued that what is thus described is not chauvinistic national conceit but the extension of the dualistic economic structure to the global system. The less developed countries (LDCs) are disadvantaged in the same manner and by the same processes as the market sector in the advanced countries. The inequality that persists internationally is mirrored by that nationally. The exploitation by which the market sector survives and the instability by which it perishes in the advanced countries is likewise the fate of the LDCs.

Galbraith (1973b, p. 175) apparently did not deny that uneven development in its modern form derives from the legacy of colonialism. Nonetheless he accounted for the persistence of the development gap by the tendency of the LDCs to specialize in the economic goods and services not amenable to organization. Notwithstanding that this geographic specialization is a legacy of colonialism, the dissolution of that legacy requires comprehension of current context. In particular, Galbraith's model indicated that the development gap is not to be overcome merely by removing any sort of vestigial neocolonialism. The inequity is rooted in the nature of the administered economy and does not require state repression of development, nor will it evaporate spontaneously. It is the result of covert administration by the global technostructure and its transcendence will require concrete political action on a scale appropriate to that power elite.

This is not to deny that the multinational corporations obstruct the sovereignty of the nation-states in which they operate. They most certainly do. The technostructure everywhere wields enormous economic clout which cannot for a moment be supposed not to confer political influence. Nor is there lack of evidence that the technostructure uses this influence in pursuit of its interests. But this is not limited to the LDCs; the technostructure exercises such influence wherever it does business. To this, the *co-opted state*, the discussion now turns.

THE CO-OPTED STATE

The consanguinity of the state and the technostructure became much more forcefully articulated as Galbraith's work developed. In the foreword essay to the fourth edition of *The Affluent Society* (1984), he alluded to this increasing sense of the role of power and to the unwitting service provided by conventional economic thought in obscuring it. Although *The New Industrial State* was quite clear on the technostructure's political needs and the influence it wields to secure the state's service of these needs, even in this regard Galbraith later became much less sanguine on the capacity of the state for independent action to contain the technostructure. In the introduction to the fourth edition of that work (1985), he referred to a decline in his optimism regarding the potential influence of the educational-scientific estate. An especially disturbing consequence of this influence is the 'dark shadow' that is cast by the military lobby and the arms race. Galbraith came to believe that had been rather too optimistic in this regard, notwithstanding his short essay on controlling the military (Galbraith, 1969).

Bureaucratic symbiosis is one of the basic sources of technostructural influence upon the state, and it is especially marked in the military and intelligence areas where the claim of necessary secrecy provides it yet another blanket to shroud it from the public eye. There is already a useful discretion in the technostructure's tendency to relate to the government through its executive branch, in contrast to the market sector's resort to the much more highly visible processes of the legislature.

The staff agencies of the executive branch are generally the focal point of this symbiosis of the technostructure with the public's nominal agents. The technically trained in the one move freely in the world of the other. Their backgrounds are similar, they work well together, they understand each other. Bright people in each who are realistic in assessing the symbiotic relationship can move through the infamous revolving door to important, and not altogether unremunerative, careers in the other side.

The tendency of the regulated to reverse roles with their regulators is now commonplace, but its deeper meaning is not. The manner in which big business and big government do business remains obscure to a public schooled in pluralistic apologia, and reports of transgressions tend to be regarded as extraordinary. Of course, they are extraordinary only in the sense that there is no excuse for the symbiotically related to be caught in anything remotely resembling a scandal. The ways and means of getting results within the bounds of strictest propriety are far too ordinary for anyone of normal intelligence and guile to be detected in the employment of improper influence. Where proper influence suffices, only the chronically ignorant or congenitally conspiratorial risk impropriety.

The members of the legislature, their influence as governmental bodies declining no matter their protests, frequently make similar resort to their own minor-league version of symbiosis within the technostructure. They add technical staff to be able to more adeptly appraise the jargon testified before them, but such staff is technostructural in its background and view of the world. Nor is there untoward penalty in terms of money and prestige for the legislator who speaks realistically about the wisdom of accommodating the needs of the technostructure.

The union, declining steadily in any event, is no longer the implacable class enemy of the directing force of the corporation. Nor is there more than residual political conflict. Economic growth is vital to the jobs of the union's members and a directly affirmative and indirectly protective purpose of the technostructure. At every level of political consideration, there is what might be called a *growth lobby* that militates toward decisions that ratify and promote the growth of commodity production. That sustaining the growth trend is supremely in the interest of the technostructure is not in doubt. That the growth lobby includes many other, perhaps unwitting, elements is likewise clear.

The news media are no doubt staffed with experienced, objective reporters who are unaware or at least unconcerned that their paychecks are met with revenues from the technostructure's dedicated effort toward mass persuasion. But objectivity requires one to be conventionally realistic, for to swim against the current of respected opinion is to be noticed as having a point of view. The hegemony of the technostructure rests upon control of that which is realistic. The ordinary business of society revolves around strategies for winning in politics and economics that are familiar and unexceptional. The curiosa of dissent need not be routinely suppressed, especially if coverage of deviant opinion may boost ratings. Dissent can be safely reported so long as it is ignored, as it must be by the conventionally realistic in the workaday worlds of business, politics, and journalism.

Which leads to the fundamental source of the technostructure's political influence – *belief.* So long as the public mind is securely attuned to the needs of the technostructure, no important opposition to the latter's sway can be mounted. On this point Galbraith's work has been consistent from *The Affluent Society* forward, notwithstanding the increasing urgency of the message. The basic power of the technostructure stems from the public's acceptance of its mission. So long as more goods and services are perceived to be the cure for all that ails, and for so long as the market is perceived to be the impersonally functional device that induces the augmentation of output, the technostructure can rest easy at the prospect of having its cake and eating it too. It can administer its market relations to its liking and deny all suggestions of having any administrative power because it is subject to the discipline of the market. All who are conventionally realistic will agree, especially if they struggle in the market sector under substantial subordination to the market's discipline, or if they prosper in the administered sector in splendid transcendence of that discipline.

Thus does the *imagery of choice* continue to serve, notwithstanding its inability to explain to the critically conscious observer so much that is so important. The emancipation of belief is the prerequisite to reintroducing the technostructure to the public purpose. The debunking of the imagery of choice is the prolegomenon to the drama of emancipation. Galbraith offered the *test of anxiety* to motivate this critical reassessment of economic doctrine.

THE TEST OF ANXIETY

An important component of *Economics and the Public Purpose* was an explicit, detailed contrast of the conventional economics model to the administered economy model of the Galbraithian System, the so-called *test of anxiety*. This strategic artifice had been prefigured in the 1969 lecture to the American Economic Association in which Galbraith asked the profession to confront the prevalent social unease by abandoning the presumptions of consumer and citizen sovereignty (Galbraith, 1971a, ch. 4).

The test of anxiety is based upon the pragmatic principle that economics as a useful social science should treat the issues about which citizens are anxious.

> The ultimate test of a set of economics ideas . . . is whether it illuminates the anxieties of the time. Does it explain problems that people find urgent? Does it bear on the current criticisms of economic performance? Does it bear on the issues of political debate? (Galbraith, 1973b, p. 198)

Obviously, the case can be made that popular anxiety is an imperfect guide, that it is focused on the wrong issues. This is perhaps some validity to this objection, but in a liberal society popular sentiment is of necessity the point of departure. False consciousness is an issue but the available evidence strongly suggests that it must be handled by a cultural criticism not by a dictatorship of a revolutionary vanguard. Moreover, the demonstration of misplaced concern would per se pass the test of anxiety. At any rate, the present discussion will go on to review the Galbraith's application of the test of anxiety.

Economic Instability

The matter of economic instability is the most visible failure of the neoclassical synthesis, if only because economic stabilization is its major promise. Common knowledge of the record of the aggregate economy since 1970 is sufficient to indicate that conventional opinion of the post-war synthesis has been impaled on the dilemma of inflation and unemployment. Opinion polls routinely indicate that one or the other, or both, of these macroeconomic ills, are among the most urgently perceived problems or our time. The experience of stagflation in the 1970s severely impacted the neoclassical synthesis and there has been no clear consensus or orthodoxy in economics since that time.

In the face of this popular anxiety, the neoclassical synthesis offers a theory of aggregate income determination grounded upon the presumption of smoothly functioning microeconomic behavior. To be sure, problems of frictional adjustment and structural imperfections are offered to explain the simultaneous occurrence of inflation and unemployment. It is equally certain that this explanation is valid, insofar as it goes. But it does not go far enough. It cannot meaningfully account for periods of stagflation in which observation can be readily made of the presence of high, and at times simultaneously increasing, rates of both macroeconomic ailments.

Most significantly, the neoclassical synthesis does not offer a theory upon which to base an effective structural policy. Such structural policy proposals as it offers – wage-price controls and human-power development – are haphazard or piecemeal in character and temporary or emergency in mood. Moreover, many such interventions are proposed with reluctance, indeed apology, as they must be from a perspective that emphasize the self-regulating character of markets.

For surely direct state intervention is more likely to worsen than improve the structure by which necessary economic adjustment is signalled and mandated more or less smoothly by relative price movements. Hence from the neoclassical synthesis perspective, much, but certainly not all, direct intervention is likely to worsen the frictions that give rise in the first place to simultaneous inflation and unemployment.

At the very least, this presents a vast opening for the more classically liberal of the profession to mount their highly reactionary monetarist and expectationist counter-revolution against the Keynesian element of the neoclassical synthesis. Then too there is the curious episode of of the rise of so-called supply-side economics in American political discourse. To their partial credit, because they must be held in part responsible for this nativistic recrudescence of Social Darwinism, most economists of conventional sensibilities refused to accredit this intellectual distemper of the Reagan years, trusting no doubt that the fever would burn itself out if isolation curbed the spread of the virus at fault.

In contrast, Galbraith's institutional economics offered an historical viewpoint and a demand for a new (structural) departure in theory and policy. The orthodox theory of the market economy was evolved to fit the nature of a very special institutional configuration which prevailed for a century down to the latter part of the nineteenth century. The profound technological and institutional changes since that time have invalidated that special theory. The microeconomic motives and expectations now extant no longer add up to aggregate stability in the absence of systematic social control.

The Keynesian Revolution, as comprised in the neoclassical synthesis, is incomplete because it does not provide the groundwork for that systematic control. A new theory expressing the socioeconomic configuration of administered capitalism is required. The technostructure's decisions have displaced market discipline in the economy's commanding heights. But its administration is only partial planning; it cannot coordinate the interstices between industries. Nor do its ministrations stabilize the market sector for which it bears no purview of responsibility nor means for administration.

Nor is the accommodation of the structure of labor supply closely attuned to the technostructure's choices of technology. The wage-price spiral is attacked only at great long and short run cost by the crude methods of aggregate demand management. In the short run output is lost and income denied, especially to the denizens of the market sector who already have less than the administered sector by way of income-access to life's chances. In the long run, denial of life chances worsens the very structural problems that the technostructure is unable to administratively avoid. The population becomes more segmented and the accommodation of the structure of labor supply is slowed down as school and family budgets suffer recession and reduced ability to provide human capital.

Increasing segmentation and secular slowdown or decline in real income growth is also in part responsible for the rise in dual earner and single-parent households which face severe obstacles in providing preschool and after-school superintendence, quite apart from the further ministrations necessary to socialize a new generation in the practical arts and sciences of social and economic life. School systems faced with such poorly socialized brigades necessarily become exercises in crowd control, which necessarily displaces much of their presumed academic instruction (Stanfield, 1994).

More will be said of Galbraith's macroeconomic model in the chapters to follow. For now the reader is apprised of the main dimensions of the test of anxiety in this regard. Instability that flows from the operation of a system of administration requires countervailing intervention that, mindful of power, turns that power to account in terms of the destabilizing effects of its decisions. A direct adjustment and intervention mechanism is required to control the wage-price spiral and facilitate the structural adjustments of the economic process. Public planning of the broad dimensions of investment policy and price/income relations is required.

Corporate Hegemony

In the address to the American Economic Association, Galbraith (1971a, p. 76) referred to the social unease and 'tension and discontent' of democratic industrial society and the 'commonplace explanation' in this regard 'that the individual feels himself in the grip of large, impersonal forces whose purposes he senses to be hostile and in relation to which he feels helpless.' Moreover, and here Galbraith made a telling point, this sense of disarray is often marshalled by various protest movements aimed at major constellations of power, such as General Motors, the National Aeronautics and Space Administration, or the Department of Transportation. This indicates that the citizens thereby organized recognize the reality of power and administration! Otherwise their protests would be aimed at changing the sovereign popular consciousness that controls these apparent loci of power.

A major component of administered capitalism is the modern corporation. Corporate power is a source of anxiety not only for its pivotal importance to the stabilization dilemma, but also due to its enormous influence over matters of ecology, work routine, political decision-making, and culture. Beyond particular problem areas, the reach of corporate influence is, in a word, illegitimate, because there are no well-defined, dependable mechanisms which hold corporate power accountable (Stanfield, 1995a, ch. 4).

In the face of this multifaceted anxiety, the neoclassical synthesis offers the view that the corporation is a firm with market power. Corporate profits and prices are too high, i.e., greater than they would be under competitive conditions. Production and resource utilization are too low, again relative to the would-be of competitive conditions. The policy alternatives which are offered relate simply to resurrecting the competitive conditions.

But there is little evidence of popular preoccupation with the issue of static supply restriction. The wider influence of the corporate behemoths, and indeed the massive production they generate, is more the focus of popular anxiety. Corporations are perceived as too large rather than too small and their cumulative influence on political decision-making and popular tastes is the source of popular anxiety.

In the Galbraithian System the modern corporation and its surrounding milieu are portrayed as a fundamental historical mutation. The corporation is a new historical phenomenon which requires a new departure in theory and social control. Its power reaches beyond the concerns of the market to the basic realm of opinion formation. The modern corporation is a governing institution and must be dealt with as such (Hamilton, 1957). The imagery of choice is again revealed to obscure essential questions. If the comforting illusion of citizen and consumer sovereignty is set aside, profoundly unsettling questions with regard to the structure of output and the quality of life emerge. One can then entertain the very basic question about the level of cultural achievement attained with the disposition of the unparalleled affluence available (Galbraith, 1971a, p. 78).

The clear conclusion is that consumer decisions buttressed by antitrust activity are inadequate; new institutional departures are required, and they must be political because the corporation is an agency of (private) government. The state is the only forum for the scale of the collective action needed to countervail the influence of the administered sector. The myopia of the self-regulating market mentality and the continuing suspicion that any public intervention in the affairs of the corporation is a dangerous transgression of the liberal sphere is revealed to be a powerful barrier to the reform that is necessary.

Inequality

The unequal pattern of not only income and wealth distribution, but of life chances in general, is also a major source of popular concern. The conventional explanation for the pattern of income and wealth distribution is, of course, that market forces are determinant. These forces are held to operate outside the influence of the participants. So, high techno-structural incomes are but the necessary supply prices of scarce technical and managerial talent. Competition for this scarce talent is necessary to secure its apportionment to its best uses. That this results in an unequal pattern of distribution may be ethically lamentable, but as such it is of no concern to the economic scientist. Of course, given a popular taste for greater equality, it is within the parvenu of economic science to trace the disincentive effects of a redistributive program.

In contrast, the Galbraithian System asserts the institutionalist insistence that the pattern of income and wealth distribution is a basic element of socio-economic organization, inseparable from the issue of economic effectiveness. A perception of reasonable justice is required for the social bonding essential to a functional social economy. Efficiency in the narrow sense, as the degree to which the preferences of the those empowered by income are met in the allocation of resources, is socially efficient only so far as the distributive pattern is efficient. Efficiency is a vacuous concept if it is not grounded in the basic substantive economic function of provisioning the continuity of social life and the participation of the populace therein. To focus upon a pattern of distribution as the result of the market mechanism in isolation from the structure of social and political power is to emphasize epiphenomena and neglect the phenomena that determine them (Stanfield, 1995a, ch. 1).

Galbraith insists that tradition, notably the customary hierarchical precept that those higher on the totem pole should be paid more, is a major factor in determining the structure of income distribution. Power also increases as one proceeds up the pecking order, including the power to augment one's own compensation (Galbraith, 1973b, pp. 264–5; see also Peach, 1987; Dugger, 1992a, ch. 32).

Here again the imagery of choice conveniently serves the powerful. The matter of executive compensation and expense accounts, so also the higher pay of the technostructure and others in the administered sector relative to the market sector, are conveniently hidden from view. Popular resentment would surely swell were the economics profession more ingenuous in dealing with the basis of the necessity of much corporate expenditure. The doctrine of necessary supply price, basic to the imagery of choice, renders the issue largely nugatory. If, however, inequality were to be seen as the outcome of administration, it would likely to be challenged; indeed such compensation issues would become 'a question of much interest and the proper subject of public policy' (Galbraith, 1973b, p. 264).

Ecology

A persistent source of popular anxiety, if here ebbing, there flowing in the last forty years, has been that associated with issues of ecology and environmental protection. The anxiety over resource depletion and environmental degradation runs a gamut of concerns from an individual's health to the moral responsibility to subsequent generations. The anxiety transcends the concern for any particular resource or waste-sink problem and embodies the specter of a civilization gone pathologically parasitical and functionally illiterate in its production of inane output to the detriment of the habitat that bears along human, as all other natural, life.

In the face of this humiliating and agonizing disgust, orthodox opinion offers the concept of externalities and market failures. The strategy of internalizing external costs and benefits so to achieve competitive market outcomes is dubious on its own terms since the measurement with any precision of the relevant marginal social costs and benefits is well nigh impossible. Moreover, still on its own terms of seeking accuracy of preference monitoring, there is a bias imparted to individual choice by the exercise of power in the process of collective decision-making. As North (1990) has emphasized, institutions matter precisely because decisions are incessantly made which alter the rules of the game and select technologies for development and deployment. North's notion of 'path dependence', that instituted procedures may be adopted and technologies selected by accident or because they serve powerful vested interests, is reminiscent of the older school of institutional economics' emphasis on the process of circular and cumulative causation. Both would agree that no presumption of efficacy can be made for any aspect of the observed institutional pattern or technological configuration.

Yet such decisions structure future decisions. As already noted, a compelling example of the exercise of power in the collective limitation of individual alternatives is the heavy reliance of America on the automobile, which is by any reckoning a major aspect of the environmental problem (Sweezy, 1972, p. 661; Galbraith, 1973b, p. 106n). This heavy reliance has come about via the exercise of power in political decisions to invest in the social overhead costs of automobile transportation rather than collective transportation systems.

Incremental private and collective decisions form a vicious circle in that

> as public transportation deteriorates, we are given an extra incentive to use our own private mode of transport which in turn results in further deterioration and a worsened position of public *vis-à-vis* private transportation. The choice is posed at each stage in a dynamic process; there is no chance of selection between the states at either end of that process. (Hirsch, 1976, p. 18)

Similar concern exists for the neglect of some sources of energy, such as solar power, and of conservation in the face of heavy reliance on petroleum and nuclear sources. Calculations of the social rates of return on investment in R&D and production capacity in these regards are biased by power and path dependence.

As noted above, beyond the accuracy of monitoring preferences there is the issue of the formation of the preferences themselves. Powerful media largely under the aegis of the technostructure incessantly drone with the cant of the consumeristic culture, at least reinforcing the ideology of consumption (Stanfield, 1995a, ch. 6).

In the face of such powerful socialization, the task of insinuating ecological concern into the unfolding political economic process is exceedingly difficult. Nothing short of a comprehensive confrontation with the 'high intensity market setting' is required (Leiss, 1976). This confrontation is necessarily a psycho-cultural exercise. The issue involved is no less than the habitual perceptions and inclinations of people as to what is valuable, and as to what modes are available by they can pursue solutions to their problems and development of their faculties. The ecological crisis is ultimately a crisis of social character (Stanfield, 1995a, chs 2, 9).

THE EMANCIPATION OF BELIEF

The problem of ecology then merges into the universal and deepest problem: the general concern for the quality of human life and the institutional configuration which best suits its pursuit. Galbraith's analysis of the process of wants articulation pointed toward a fundamental ambiguity of human needs in relation to the production of commodities (Leiss, 1976; and Stanfield, 1995a, ch. 6).

The power arrayed on the side of the growth lobby seems virtually unsurmountable, yet Galbraith was not without hope. He drew again on the notion of an operant antagonism that may yet bring the public purpose to bear on the technostructure. He repeated the original idea from *The New Industrial State* that the lamentations of disaffected youth require leadership and focus for effect, and that such can only be provided by the 'political lead' of the 'educational and scientific estate' (Galbraith, 1967, p. 387).

It may be more than a sign of the times, a sign of Galbraith's foundering optimism, that the paragraph on the anti-establishment youth movement was excised from the fourth edition (Galbraith, 1985). Nonetheless, the operant antagonism remains in that 'the state not only educates those who accept and defend the values' of the administered sector. 'It also nurtures its critics – for there is no practical way of doing one without the other' (Galbraith, 1973b, p. 156). The 'educated proletariat reflects the values of the educational system' in which it is lettered with the credentials necessary to enlist in the technostructure (Galbraith, 1973b, p. 211).

If liberal, humane precepts prevail in academia, these values are constitutionally alien to the needs of the administered sector in that they are grounded upon the idea of self-worth and independent thought. Students are thus imbued with a 'sense of personality' and instructed in the social doctrine that ultimate power resides in the individual calculus of good and bad, right and wrong. But outside the universities students encounter a world in which organization and entrenched interests seem to exercise plenary power over individual action (Galbraith, 1971a, p. 77).

Galbraith placed much hope on the resulting cognitive dissonance. 'Thus, in effect, the technostructure cultivates the criticism of its own need to override personality – to harness people to its purposes. This is a fact of first importance, a fulcrum on which much reform must rest' (Galbraith, 1973b, p. 211).

It would seem no exaggeration to ascribe to Galbraith the conviction that this 'fact of first importance' is the moral and analytical equivalent of Marx's inveterate contradiction or antagonism between the classes of owners and non-owners. That this was clearly Galbraith's intent was indicated by his denial of any notable stridency or conflict in the relation of the industrial proletariat to its technostructural masters as well as his selection of phraseology, the 'unlettered proletariat.'

For this operant antagonism to become effective in the redirection of social effort to social purpose, the way must be cleared for public regulation of the administered sector. This requires that the public mind focus on the normal condition that the purposes of the technostructure diverge from the public purpose. This being normality, regulation to affirm the superiority of the latter shall also be normalized. Only then can the strategy for emancipating the state from the administered sector emerge so as to permit, when accomplished, the regulation of the administered sector by the state.

Again, the first step, the emancipation of belief, is likely to be exceedingly difficult. The belief which must be contested is clear enough but so also is the inordinately powerful sway of the imagery of choice upon the public mind. The acceptance of the purposes of the technostructure as identical to those of society must be contested; the preoccupation with growth in the production and consumption of commodities must be challenged. People who have capacities to develop and relationships to nurture and cherish need not subordinate themselves to the treadmill of an incomes race of emulative, competitive consumption.

To emancipate belief from this self-justifying commodity expansion, the mythology that identifies the public interest with the purposes of the administered sector must be contested at four basic nodes. The present economics pedagogy must be subjected to the excruciating embarrassment of the test of anxiety. The doctrine of inexorable scarcity must be countered by the inordinant attention devoted to manufacturing wants.

The educational system must devote itself to critical thought and throw off its most basic assumptions about the social value of educational achievement. The pecuniary interpretation of achievement and the identification of money income with social purpose must be broken. At the university level, students bent on efficient self-commodification must be challenged in their selection of majors and curriculum. That which separates them from the other beasts in nature as sentient and aesthetic beings must be celebrated for its own sake. Making money is surely a fact of life in a society that commercially governs and accounts its material provisioning. But making money need not therefore be confused with life itself. Making a living is the means of living; it is surely a malicious misconstruction to pursue it as the end of living. A good society must subordinate livelihood to living (Polanyi, 1944; Stanfield, 1986).

The way people respond to overt persuasion and to the manufacture of public policy in the interest of the technostructure must also be a focus of the cultural resistance. Alternative financing of media will free popular entertainment from the enervating commitment to the mundane and allow niches of excellence to replace the marketing niches so popular in the cable industry. Differentiation of programming, it is now clear, should not be confused with discriminant programming. Resigned acceptance of the commercial pollution of entertainment must be converted to resolute resistance.

Here again the service of economic doctrine is not without import. The doctrine of necessary supply price informs us that competition allows only necessary costs to be covered in the prices of commodities we purchase. But it is difficult to see how financing the provision of commercial television and radio is technologically essential to the hygienic purpose of a tube of toothpaste or the mobilizing function of an automobile. Consumers surely pay for commercial media but how their doing so is an exercise of their celebrated sovereignty is a sweet mystery upon which the conventional economics pedagogy is becalmingly silent.

The *public cognizance* is Galbraith's term for the development on the part of American citizens of a healthy suspicion toward their elected representatives and other government officials. He asserted that the public cognizance must presume that the interests of the administered sector diverge from the public purpose. This means that in the absence of contrary evidence, citizens should assume that the positions advocated by the technostructure are not in the public interest. Likewise, government officials should be assumed to be active in the technostructure's interest without proof to the contrary. Galbraith held this to be of especial import for the legislative branch which he considered to be the focus of emancipation. Recapture of legislative initiative for the public interest would create an opportunity to enlist the executive branch.

After the emancipation of belief has progressed, the state can be emancipated and turned back to its task of overseeing the public purpose. Galbraith adumbrated the general outlines of substantive policies to be pursued. These will be taken up in the next chapter in the context of a general overview of the policy implications of the Galbraithian System.

7 Social Reform and Economic Policy

The next step toward perpetual prosperity is the provision of a basis for the coordination of firm plans, particularly in key industries, to assure a rough equality between *industry capacity* and *industry demand*.

(R.T. Averitt, 1968)

We now affirm that that direction is forward which provides for the continuity of human life and the noninvidious re-creation of community through the instrumental use of knowledge.

(M.R. Tool, 1979)

The Galbraithian System seeks to clarify the complex matter of social and economic reform in late capitalism. Much of the focus rests upon the social predicament of turning the vast influence of the mature corporation and its administered sector of the economy to the human, public purpose. This effort runs aground upon the twin shoals of the crisis of the state and the sway of the conventional wisdom. The extent of mandated collective action is increasing amidst a widespread discontent not only with the prevalent forms of collective action but also with collective action in principle. This discontent is rooted in an intellectual confusion that obscures both the nature of the social predicament and the character of its resolution.

The state is in a crisis which is at once fiscal, organizational, and ideological (Stanfield, 1995a, ch. 9). The conventional economics wisdom, the neoclassical synthesis and its policy mix of haphazard manipulation of incentives, offers little to assuage the anxiety that results. The standard dicta aver that the state bureaucracy is inefficient due to the absence of the discipline of competitive market forces and the inveterate human tendency to free ride and collect the rents available in the interstices of collective action.

Problems of preference-monitoring and perverse incentives of state interventions are certainly prevalent, but there is more to the story. The intellectual failure to advance an effective notion of the modern political economy with its symbiotic relationship between the public and private sectors casts a stultifying obscurity both upon that which is observed and that which is imagined to be desirable.

129

Macroeconomic stabilization policy is the search for 'a reliable flow of income and product at reasonably stable prices' (Galbraith, 1973b, p. 303). For institutionalists such as Galbraith, stabilization policy is necessarily examined within the context of power and microeconomic structure. Moreover, it is to be conducted with an eye to the social reform that embodies the progressive spirit of modern liberalism.

The macroeconomic limitation of the self-adjusting capacity of the market economy arises because its microeconomic structure becomes more concentrated and less competitive. Economic crises which once would have been eliminated in relatively short order become protracted declines which are self-correcting, if at all, only at very great cost, a cost that by all indications exceeds the tolerance of modern democracy. Of course, the earlier crises which were eliminated more quickly had social repercussions that were unacceptable to economic and political interest groups. Indeed, many of the structural changes that reduced the automaticity of the market were aimed precisely at ameliorating or avoiding the social disruption attendant to the operation of relatively unfettered markets.

Neither the concerted efforts of an insidious left-wing conspiracy nor the malingering profit-mongering of greedy capitalists created the drift away from the rigors of the competitive market (Hamilton, 1957). The marked tendency toward *institutionalized drift* (Stanfield, 1979, ch. 5) arose from the actions of various interests who sought to protect their social existence from the exigencies of the disembedded market economy (Polanyi, 1944). Polanyi's notion of *protective response* and the *logic of reform* evinced by Galbraith and the other institutionalists indicate the rise of the administered economy (Stanfield, 1986).

In an ironic historical twist, the state intervention that seeks to reduce the crises manifested by capitalist organization has come to be stigmatized as the cause of the crisis (Heilbroner, 1985). There may be some truth to the notion that inadequate or inappropriate intervention exacerbates the critical situations of capitalism. But whatever truth could be gotten thereby is habitually buried in an of atavistic market sentiment.

As discussed above, Galbraith examined this failure to understand the historical forces at work in the context of the *imagery of choice*, by which the conventional wisdom obscures the powerful machinations of the corporate oligarchy. Absent the emancipation *of belief* and the exercise of the *public cognizance*, policy formation serves the interests of the technostructure. The claims of the wider body political economy are pressed forward but the initiatives instigated to meet them are turned to the narrower interest of administered sector. The crisis of interventionist drift is then viewed as a crisis of intervention (Stanfield, 1979, ch. 5 and 1995a, ch. 9), with the apparent presumption that matters could have been better without the intervention. The possibilities that matters could have been a great deal worse or that better intervention could be devised tend to take short shrift.

The logic of reform encompasses far more than stabilization alone. The concern for macroeconomic stability is part of a larger concern to improve the lot of humanity generally. Relief from the enervating vulnerability of economic insecurity is one cornerstone of a renascent surge of inhuman ingenuity and dexterity. The reform thrust seeks to release human initiative from its dogged subordination to economic survival, a subordination long since rendered artificial in the extreme by the advance of the technologic arts and sciences (Dewey, 1948, p. 211; Baran and Sweezy, 1966).

This liberation of human vitality can only be accomplished by an alteration of the relations upon which human beings deal with one another (Dewey, 1963, p. 27). This in turn must be stolidly the goal of unremitting social reform based upon the application of unfolding human intelligence in the democratic process. This was John Dewey's quest and it is that of all institutionalists, prototypically Galbraith. So too was it the thrust of Polanyi's ruminations.

In this chapter, before summarizing and commenting upon the policy agenda of the Galbraithian System, it is appropriate to reset the institutionalist reform agenda by discussing the doctrine of *evolutionary positivism*. This doctrine maintains that fact and circumstance guide the social reformer engaged in the democratic process to accomplish the *institutional adjustment* requisite to advancing the fuller unfolding of the generic human life process. Thereafter attention is given to a summary of Galbraith's views on policies to achieve economic stability and affirm the quality of human life.

EVOLUTIONARY POSITIVISM AND INSTITUTIONAL ADJUSTMENT

Institutionalists offer not simply an alternative method nor even this plus an alternative policy regimen. They offer a different definition of the economy itself (Ayres, 1967; Polanyi, 1944; Stanfield, 1986, ch. 2). The economy is viewed as a technological process and a social or institutional process with which the technological is interwoven.

The definition of technology is critical. Technology is not the machines, it is the relevant knowledge in correlation to the machines. Discussion of technology as the machines per se is a mind-numbing abstraction from the reality that any tool is such only by virtue of its correlation to human knowledge.

The application of the technologic arts and sciences involves division of labor which must be integrated; the divided behaviors must be rendered compatible one to another and all to all. This is accomplished by a more or less habitual or institutionalized pattern of interaction. An economic *institution* is a cluster of mores that configures power or authority over things and people that are relevant to the material and social continuity of human life.

The family unit engaged in the practice of house-holding is a universal but variously significant element of the integrative institutional cluster. Beyond the family, the institutional system that integrates the division of labor seems almost universally in the modern world to have become a stratified, invidious ordering of people by their worth on some metaphysical scale. This institutional configuration motivates and provides incentives in circular fashion because it socializes the emotional response patterns of people so that they do indeed respond to the eliciting signals of invidious distinction. So too is the characteristic employment contract a pivotal institution, as well as the artifices of finance, high and otherwise. Incidentally, retirement is an institution and one that will likely be critically examined in a number of ways in the near future.

This formulation of the integrative process is consistent with the institutional analysis of the famous Veblenian dichotomy between the technological or non-invidious and the ceremonial or invidious aspects of culture, the Marxian notion of the economic base consisting of the forces and relations of production, and Polanyi's tool-kit of reciprocity, redistribution, and exchange. Despite differences in mood and detail, each of these seminal traditions of institutional analysis insists upon comprehension of the concrete historical phenomena of power and habit in the conduct of economic theory and policy.

In so doing each rejects procedure based upon a universal human nature that implicates current institutional forms. No doubt there is a human nature but it is a far cry from the specific attributes often deposited under the label. The variable element in social life is the institutional interaction that shapes and selects the manifestations of human nature. Hence power and habit are crucial to the comprehension of a particular socio-historical system. In short each of these traditions is political economic in the sense of *examining the effects of power and culture on the economic process.*

The institutionalist is not a revolutionary socialist, there is no call to overthrow *in toto* the operant invidious system. This is not a matter of lacking the aberrant temperament that allows one to be a radical, for institutionalist dissenters are at least as cantankerous as their Marxist colleagues. But they lack the teleological vision and constructivist tendency of the committed revolutionary socialist. The institutionalist social criticism seems radical enough to its detractors who often counter with the charge that the institutionalist offers nothing to put in place of the existing order of relative prices. Certainly institutionalists do not offer an answer to this question as posed; one only wishes the detractors would recognize that institutionalists *do not ask it!*

Institutionalists do not seek to administer the entire edifice of prices. They do not counter the metaphysics of utilitarian general equilibrium with another metaphysical equilibrium, such as that involving labor embodied; they have no metaphysical scheme for what the general relation of prices ought to be, no scheme of perfect normality in the economic system.

But, and this is important, nor are they bound by any such scheme. Prices are cultural artifacts. Human societies are constantly in flux as people strive to solve the problems daily life presents them. For institutionalists, where the relation of relative prices poses a specific problem, there is no metaphysically based reluctance to tinker with the prices in an effort to improve matters. If a strata or sector receives too little income, change the prices and income flows to remedy the shortfall. If socially functional behavior is inadequately recompensed and society has too few that are competent and willing to undertake it, then up the ante by intervention into the pricing framework. The institutionalist embraces no view of a natural order of prices, violation of which is sure to result in unspeakably vile if altogether unspecified consequences.

Accordingly, the institutionalists share neither the institutional fixation of the static conventional view nor the teleological view of those intent upon displacement of capitalism with socialism. Rather, they insist on the more truly dynamic focus of *institutional adjustment*. If the prevalent power distribution is leading to specified problems, the task of policy is to redistribute power to resolve the problem. The task of economic theory is then to sort out the power process and identify wherein it is causing the problems in need of redress. The problems are revealed by a procedure such as Galbraith's *test of anxiety*. The test suggests that which people feel anxious about should influence the variables in the social scientist's models.

The test of anxiety exemplifies the pragmatic commitment of institutionalism. Dewey's instrumentalism calls for social science to play an influential role in the democratic process, which itself should be viewed as no more no less than applied intelligence in action. The institutionalist's faith in democracy is not founded upon its consonance with the natural rights of people nor in the absolute sanctity of the majority rule as ends per se. It is rather a confidence in the self-correcting process of inquiry (Dewey, 1960 and 1963; Ayres, 1961). Thus focused social science merges into social reform (Tilman, 1987).

Speaking broadly of the Western liberal tradition, this has been referred to as 'evolutionary positivism' (Markowitz, 1973, p. 14) because it is based on the principle that fundamental errors of outlook will be corrected as their discordance with reality becomes more pronounced with the passage of time. Galbraith's work is replete with expressions of evolutionary positivism, though his insistent optimism became more tempered in the years following the publication of *Economics and the Public Purpose*. The Galbraithian System is based on the promise that circumstance will eventually get the upper hand upon antediluvian precept and clear the way for the thought and action necessary to achieve a stable economy that affirms human ontology.

MACROECONOMIC STABILIZATION POLICY

Whatever self-regulating capacity the nineteenth-century competitive market economy possessed has certainly been rendered nugatory by changing circumstances. As noted above, this reduced self-adjustment capacity results from changing political economic structure. Of particular importance is the growth of oligopolistic market structures in the core manufacturing sector. The ability to restrict downward price and wage movements in this core limits the discipline of the adjustment classically imposed by the market. This discipline persists elsewhere in the economy, in the market sector, which therefore bears the brunt of macroeconomic instability.

Indeed, for institutionalists, the dual economic model may be a cause of crises not merely an explanation for the retarded and inequitable adjustment to a crisis set in motion by other factors. As discussed in Chapter 2, the consolidation of the financial control of manufacturing industry around the turn of the century was a major focus of Thorstein Veblen and Rexford Tugwell. This consolidation had the effect of raising the profit margins in the advanced sector. Falling costs of production coupled with downward price rigidity affected this result.

The traditional or market sector, and this includes the supply of labor prior to the institutionalization of unions and income support measures, suffered a relative decline of its income. This restricted mass purchasing power precisely when the relative increase in the incomes of ownership in the advanced sector generated booms in investment and in speculative increases in the value of financial assets. The rise in the incomes of the wealthy by the speculative boom in asset values further reinforced the income distribution trend, and added to the financial overhead of production that had to be covered in prices, either directly in the form of debt service or indirectly in the form of validating the nominal values of corporate equities (Minsky, 1986).

Eventually, this tendency in income distribution became untenable. The ability to realize profit by selling the output is the ultimate rationale for productive capacity in a monetary economy (Dillard, 1987). The declining purchasing power of the masses became a barrier to the investment boom. For institutionalists, this led to the lesson that the flows of income in the economy must remain balanced if macroeconomic stability is to be maintained. Much of the New Deal policy worked toward correcting such an imbalance, including the support of unions and collective bargaining, agricultural price and income supports, unemployment compensation, social security programs, and perhaps even programs to support small business.

As we have seen, Galbraith initially posited this rebalancing as the generation of countervailing power. In that effort and in later work, the measures designed to increase equality of income distribution are part and parcel of macroeconomic stabilization: 'equitable performance and effective operation of an economy go together' (Galbraith, 1973b, p. 303). The necessity of viewing macroeconomic stabilization policy in the context of the dual economic structure was emphasized in an important article in the late 1950s (Galbraith, 1957).

In his major trilogy, Galbraith (1958, 1967, 1973b) emphasized that stabilization measures that favor the administered sector are ultimately destabilizing because they exacerbate obdurate tendencies for income and prices in this sector to outpace those in the market sector.

Such imbalances, which per se represent distributive inequities and allocative distortions that limit the quality of human life, also pose macroeconomic instability problems because the market sector is the customer for much administered sector output. Attempts to maintain aggregate purchasing power in the face of this maldistribution between the two sectors is fraught with difficulty in that the wage and price spiral is increasingly validated by the additional purchasing power created.

Nor can stabilization policy based solely upon aggregate demand manipulation remain the unpalatable choice between unemployment and inflation. The wage and price spiral and the structural difficulties of matching labor supply and demand are dynamic processes. Validation of wage and price inflation imbeds additional inflationary expectations and layers of overhead costs into the structure of the economy. Retrenchment to stop the inflationary momentum penalizes the more vulnerable market sector and households on the margin of economic sustainability. The inability of smaller firms and marginal households to revalorize their economic positions increases the structural impediments to normal participation in the economy of the future.

The Role of Aggregate Demand Policy

To ascertain the role of aggregate demand policy in the Galbraithian System, it is necessary to establish the concept of *macroeconomic balance* in an operational manner. From his earliest books in the post-war era, Galbraith warned about the dangers of inflation and rejected the crude inflationism of a populist Keynesianism. It is no accident that revolutionaries such as Lenin sought hyperinflation as a means to undermine the context of capitalism. Inflation is a corrosive force in its arbitrary effects on economic decisions which destroys the communication and sanctions system upon which much of the division of labor integrated.

Although institutionalists likely agree with the neo-Keynesians, such as Paul Samuelson and James Tobin, that nominal inflation is preferable to unemployment, they dissent from the view that we should accept the bounds of aggregate demand policy and the unpalatable tradeoff of the Phillips Curve. Moreover, as noted already, given the dynamics of cumulative causation, institutionalists do not think that it is possible to make choices within acceptable bounds because the choices made worsen the tradeoff.

Hence, as a matter of stabilization and barring some national crisis, it seems unlikely that Galbraith would favor significant expansion of overall demand beyond macroeconomic balance. In the books of the 1950s, indeed, he favored aggregate demand slack when possible to avoid the negation of the salutary effects of countervailing power on inflation (Galbraith, 1952b, pp. 196 and 199). If 'limited mobilization', something less than all-out war, or its moral equivalent one supposes, rendered the slack option nugatory, he then favored controls exercized alongside macroeconomic balance (Galbraith, 1952a, p. 69). By 1967 Galbraith had changed his mind in this regard and had come to the view that it is not 'socially and politically tolerable' to apply slack as an antidote to inflation (Galbraith, 1967, p. 268). Hence he advocated wage and price controls and considered them inevitable for a long time, though this position too he subsequently altered in light of further political experience.

It should be noted that macroeconomic balance should be taken to

Table 7.1   Stabilization Policy Indications

Economic Condition	Market Sector Prices Rising		Market Sector Prices Falling	
Qualified-labor surplus in administered sector	(1)	Structural Policy	(2)	Increase Aggregate Demand
Qualified-labor shortage in administered sector	(3)	Decrease Aggregate Demand	(4)	Structural Policy

mean merely a dividing line for aggregate demand policy; there is no sug-gestion that balance represents an equilibrium tendency in the economy. Macroeconomic balance means that aggregate supply and demand are in approximate balance, so that there is no significant tendency for excess demand to generate inflation nor for insufficient demand to lead to unem-ployment. This does not preclude imbalances in particular markets in which either excess or insufficient demand in relation to current capacity may occur. The intent is to isolate these structural imbalances from the problem of aggregate imbalance, and to suggest that structural policies be deployed to deal with them in so far as the forces of the market are seen to be dilatory or ineffective in doing so.

The Galbraithian System implies that the indicators of macroeconomic balance be dualized along the lines of the dual economy (Galbraith, 1952a, p. 74) so that diagnostic indices would focus upon prices in the market sector and the balance of employment of qualified labor in the adminis-tered sector. Falling prices in the market sector coupled with an excess supply of qualified workers in the administered sector indicate an insuf-ficiency of aggregate demand and imply the need for an expansionary aggregate demand policy. Excess aggregate demand would be indicated by rising market sector prices and shortages of qualified workers in the administered sector. Other cases are possible which indicate structural pol-icy rather than any change in aggregate demand. These considerations are summarized in Table 7.1.

Cases 2 and 3 indicate that the condition of the economy would man-date application of the familiar tools of aggregate demand policy. In case 2, both sectors display slack and there is a need to increase aggregate demand. The opposite is apparent in case 3.

Matters are different in the other two cases. Consider case 1. An excess supply of qualified labor in the advanced sector could occur with rising prices in the market sector. Shortages in some product lines in the market sector should be very quickly eliminated by spontaneous market forces and hence should not be a problem of economic policy. Rising prices in the advanced sector could occur despite the labor surplus – administered prices are not directly governed by market conditions. Nor is there guarantee that the structure of qualified labor matches its demand; hence particular shortages of qualified labor could exist alongside particular surpluses.

Again there is no reason to expect falling pay scales in response to the surplus and every reason to expect rising pay scales in the areas of shortage as corporations seek to recruit the best available staff. Administered pricing softens the budget constraint and creates a situation of resource hunger not different in principle, though certainly far different in magnitude, from the experience in the centrally planned economies (Kornai, 1992, pp. 140–5).

These increasing prices would represent an increase in costs to the firms in the market sector. Assuming no increase in the degree of self-exploitation and exploitation of employees, the outcome should reflect the standard supply and demand analysis. Initially, the expectation would be an increase in price and a decrease in quantity. If the higher incomes in the administered sector and the market sector increase demand for market sector goods, then part or all of this decline in quantity would be offset.

For present purposes, the key is that this price increase, stemming from the administered sector, could occur regardless of the macroeconomic balance. Rising market sector prices alone do not signify that a macroeconomic imbalance of excess demand exists since they can occur along with a surplus of qualified labor in the administered sector. Here structural policy, some form of wage-price constraint and improved matching of labor supply and demand, would likely be the most effective policy response.

So also with the occurrence of falling market prices and a shortage of qualified labor in the administered sector (case 4). This could occur if the supply of educated labor was insufficient to meet the demand in the advanced sector but labor was in surplus in the market sector. The likelihood of rising prices in the advanced sector and hence rising input prices to the market sector would then be offset to some extent by excess labor and downward competitive price pressure in the market sector. The labor imbalance would have to be extreme to offset entirely the rising cost pressures, but in principle this is possible.

Galbraith's implicit dualization of the operant indicators of the economy's condition faces severe operational problems. Labor market segmentation is likely visible only with respect to those employed. It could be difficult to assign an unemployed worker to either sector, especially in an economy so dynamic that life-long preparation becomes the norm.

Also, the above discussion indicates that rising prices in the market sector would not be definitive, as Galbraith (1952a, p. 74) seemed to have believed in the early 1950s. This conclusion holds even in the unlikely event that effective price indices dividing the two sectors were to be devised. Administered increases in the wage-price spiral would raise input prices in the market sector which, in a competitive context, would be reflected in the prices of market sector output, so one could not conclude that excess demand is present. Nonetheless, it would certainly be a worthy effort to attempt to develop operational indicators reflecting supply and demand conditions in the two sectors.

If dualized indices cannot be developed, it may be that an aggregate indicator of macroeconomic balance may suffice. The need is for an indicator that reveals whether the economy is in need of a change in the state's aggregate demand policy posture or in need of direct structural policy action. For this purpose, the overall balance between total job openings and total unemployed may serve. The number of unemployed would need to be adjusted to include 'discouraged workers' and to exclude the 'phantom unemployed'. The former are those who desire work but have given up on finding it. The latter are those who are taken advantage of unemployment compensation or other reserves to enjoy a spell of leisure but who qualify under official definitions as involuntarily unemployed. Entitlement crises and moral calculus aside, and practicing for one's retirement may be morally defensible, those thusly enumerated as unemployed should not bias our macroeconomic policy toward excess aggregate demand.

At macroeconomic balance, cyclical unemployment is by definition equal to zero; in principle, any observed unemployment is structural or frictional and does not result from inadequate overall demand in relation to potential output. Likewise, any shortages of labor will be structural, resulting from a mismatch or misinformation between the supply and demand for labor, not from an overall excess in that demand.

The positive frictional and structural unemployed is essentially the so-called natural rate of unemployment that is commonplace in the literature. But there is a major difference. In the Galbraithian System, there is no reason to assume zero inflation at the natural rate of unemployment; there is no private sector force limiting wage settlements to the level of productivity increases and administered pricing allows higher wage costs to be passed on to consumers.

Hence there is what might be called the *natural rate of inflation* that occurs when the economy is in macroeconomic balance. Its level is determined by institutional forces, including the culture of industrial relations, corporate culture and the psychology of the technostructure, the nature of the social regulatory and welfare complex, the effectiveness of capital markets and public policy in targeting investment to productivity enhancement, and the context of global openness and competitiveness.

Use of the designation of natural is not intended to suggest normality, fixity, or inevitability in the manner of the astute purveyors of nineteenth-century wisdom. Parallel usage is proper, but the term natural would be unfortunate in both cases. Notwithstanding the High Priests of the Long Gone By, the Galbraithian System indicates the need to develop structural interventions that promise to reduce the natural rates of *both* unemployment and inflation.

The rates of inflation and unemployment that occur at macroeconomic balance would be better referred to as *structural*, which suggests the obvious acronyms SRI and SRU. In principle, the SRI is no more volatile than the SRU that will occur at macroeconomic balance. The latter is also subject to institutional factors which may or may not be stable.

The critical point is that aggregate demand policy in the face of these twin structural rates can do no better than impale society on the horn of the inflation versus unemployment dilemma. And such a policy regime is likely to do much worse because the choice made in either direction sets in motion perverse dynamics. Austerity to reduce inflation penalizes the market system in particular and the areas of social reproduction for which reliance is placed on government. The provision of education, job training, infrastructure, and income support for those currently not valued on labor-commodity markets are absolutely necessary to nurturing the continuity and productivity of society. There is an essential complementarity of human and physical capital formation (Ranson, 1987; North, 1990).

Inflationism in an effort to eliminate unemployment will exacerbate shortages of qualified labor and validate an acceleration of the wage and price spiral. Inflationary expectations will come into play. Meanwhile those unemployed because they lack the skills to qualify for or the resources to locate the advanced sector openings will be employed only as the income effect increases the demand for market system output.

To the extent that retraining qualifies some of these unemployed to move up, or to the extent that qualified immigrant labor enters the technostructure, the overhead salariat of the advanced system is increased during the heady days of the boom. The salariat would then be reluctant to sacrifice any of its membership as times became leaner in the future, and administered pricing would allow some degree of freedom in this regard. The result over time would be a growing salariat that is maintained as a quasi-overhead cost, except in times of severe recession or restructuring in the face of import penetration.

Even if macroeconomic balance persists, the effect is to steadily increase the division of economy, and hence society, into privileged and disadvantaged sectors. This will have effects on both the ability of those in the market system to provide human capital for their children and the political cohesiveness and social solidarity which is necessary to maintain social order. The vicious circle effects of dualized economic opportunity are well known. The disadvantaged pose social problems even for those who would ignore their plight unless forced to pay attention because of the spread of urban malaise. Then too worsening structural unemployment implies higher unemployment at macroeconomic balance.

Recent concerns about the declining middle class and the declining representation of the non-affluent in political processes indicate the sense that perception of some minimal degree of social justice is necessary to maintain social bonding. Galbraith contributed to the examination of this political economic trend with *The Culture of Contentment*, which had begun to take hold in his mind no later than 1979 (Galbraith, 1979a and 1979b; see also Edsall, 1984; and Kuttner, 1987). It is important to realize that maintenance of social bonds is necessary for the market economy to function even on its own terms (Stanfield, 1994 and 1995b).

Structural Policy

The first structural policy measure is a continuation of the aggregate demand policy discussion. The manner by which adjustments in overall demand are accomplished is significant in the dualized economy, at least so long as the emancipation of the state is not completed. Galbraith argued that aggregate demand policy should be designed not to exacerbate the inequality or imbalance between the two sectors. To reduce aggregate demand, tax increases are the favored remedy, more so to the extent taxation is progressive and comprehensive. A tax increase rather than a reduction in public expenditures is favored on the basis that the foregone expenditures would likely be biased in favor of the advanced sector. Moreover, the persistence of social imbalance led Galbraith to expect that, for the foreseeable future, public expenditures at the margin will be more important to social welfare than the private expenditures foregone as the result of increased progressive, comprehensive taxes.

It follows that Galbraith would increase expenditures rather than decrease taxes when aggregate demand was insufficient. Were structural bias between public and private and between the two private sectors removed, then the effects of expenditure and tax changes would have the basically equivalent effects presently supposed for them in conventional macroeconomic thought.

The comprehensiveness of income taxation is another front in the struggle between the two economic sectors. Tax expenditures and the tax preferences from which they stem are likely to be biased in favor of the advanced sector. The appeal here is the obscure nature of tax expenditures. Less powerful political economic agents tend to have their share of government munificence toted up on the more visible side of expenditures. Hence in general a move to use explicit subsidies rather than tax preferences would at least make the machinations of the powerful more visible.

Galbraith would more or less completely eschew the use of countercyclical monetary policy. As even its most celebrated adherents aver, the short run effects of monetary policy are difficult to estimate as to impact and timing. To combat serious recession, monetary policy is dubious as the conventional metaphor of pushing on a string indicates. Moreover, to counteract inflation, monetary policy achieves its results by lost output and income deprivation which falls most heavily upon the market sector, which lacks the extent of internal finance of the administered sector and the advantages that size confers upon borrowing. This has attendant complications beyond social injustice, since the structure of labor supply and financial solvency of small enterprises is adversely affected. This is conducive neither to the future correspondence of labor supply and demand nor to domestic tranquility.

Galbraith would likely target interest rates at low and stable levels. Indeed one can imagine a rules approach in which the monetary authorities are constrained to maintain the target interest rates. This has the effect of completely subordinating monetary policy to fiscal, and structural, policy considerations. Low interest rates do not imply there is no operant control on borrowing (Galbraith, 1973b, p. 309). The control of aggregate demand operates to limit borrowing for investment purposes per the standard Keynesian investment function. Increased taxes to counteract excess demand would also reduce the after tax income upon which household capacity to borrow is based. Plus, control of inflation, by demand and structural policy, would reduce the tendency for real interest rates to fall to levels that encourage speculative borrowing. Stable long run nominal interest rates and stable inflation rates at low positive levels would go a long way toward stabilizing borrowing.

Galbraith's structural policy proposals, other than the insistent call for wage-price controls, remains an underdeveloped aspect of his thought even with the extended discussion of *Economics and the Public Purpose*. On the matter of controls, he was a persistent advocate from the 1950s, but he became more convinced of their companionship with peacetime high employment policy. By the time of *The New Industrial State*, he concluded that slack was not an operant choice and that controls were inevitable, and would be accepted in practice though not in principle (Galbraith, 1967, ch. 22). At a later date he reversed this sentiment and conceded that controls are politically unfeasible but he does not indicate the revamping he would therefore make in his policy proposals.

Galbraith was from the beginning pessimistic that controls would be based upon the vital distinction made by the dual economy concept. Controls are not necessary nor particularly useful in the market sector. In the administered sector, they are essential and should be focused upon the rate of productivity increase in that sector. Wage increases that exceed productivity advances are inflationary. Galbraith (1973b, p. 314) would hold wage increases to the average gain in productivity in the advanced sector. This would prevent widening wage differentials. Galbraith would vary the application of controls to pursue a narrowing of income differentials in the administered sector as well as between the two sectors. Relatively low wage industries would be allowed wage and therefore price increases above the average.

Galbraith's case for wage compaction seems to have been only that equality is preferred, ceteris paribus, and that income differentials that result from the exercise of the power to administer do not qualify for the familiar line of defense. There may be further basis for wage compaction. A general reduction of differentials may increase solidarity and reduce the stridency of wage bargaining. A national standard for wage increases that includes compaction, should reduce the tendency of trade union leadership to compete with one another in bargaining. The union leadership's fear of looking bad by accepting a package lower than that achieved by other unions would be removed.

No doubt much would turn upon acceptance of the policy by the workers, and no doubt further problems of profit disparities would emerge. The experience in Sweden with the policy of wage-solidarity provides a useful laboratory which should not be dismissed entirely because the Swedes have abandoned it in the face of intensified global competition. In the Galbraithian System, the management of the industrial economies must be coordinated internationally; no policy can work if it runs counter to general practice in ways that would reduce international competitiveness. Hence the failure of policies attempted in isolation cannot be taken to mean that such policies cannot work if adopted in concert and with coordination. This is most especially true in cases in which the policy experiment has been tried in the smaller, more open economies.

Beyond wage compaction in the administered sector, incomes between the two sectors require structural attention. Galbraith would pursue this compaction on several fronts. In the market sector, he would relax anti-trust laws, support the formation of unions, and enact income and price supports similar to the programs long established in agriculture. He would also design international trade policy with the interests of the market sector in mind. An aggressive use of the minimum wage and a guaranteed annual income would also strengthen the market sector by placing a lower bound on exploitation. This would increase prices in the market sector and cause some disemployment. Galbraith (1973b, p. 315) was prepared to accept the continuing upward drift of prices that is implicit in this scenario of narrowing income differentials.

On the matter of displaced employment in the market sector, Galbraith asserted that 'some work and pay are worse than unemployment' (1973b, p. 311). One could add that the sensitivity of our educational system to the hours of work by students is a major social concern that is insufficiently addressed. Much of the disemployment that would result from an increase in the minimum wage would be of adolescents. Society might well prefer them to concentrate on their studies. This is a general question of social value: does society want employment that is not sufficiently productive to earn a decent wage? Would society prefer that those with marginal skills be engaged in upgrading their skills?

In this regard it would be best to pay more attention to the need for active labor market policies than to the issue of minimum wages. Especially in concert with a guaranteed annual income, the presence of substantial programs to retrain and relocate workers would go far to reduce the significance of minimum wages (but not the issue of part time employment for students). Again Sweden provides an example, and its labor market polices are widely perceived to be quite successful. The possibility of tying the guaranteed annual income to the participation in a retraining program should also be considered.

The active labor market polices should have a further advantage in reducing worker resistance to technological change. The present policy whereby workers pay taxes to support R&D that leads to results that they may oppose in practice is indicative of the technostructure's untoward influence in the public sector.

Clarification of the process of capital formation is also provided. Without policies to better match the supply of labor to the demand for it, the hand wringing over capital formation is apologism for inequality. Prima facie, if structural unemployment exists, this means that at macroeconomic balance employers have plant and equipment in place for which they believe they can profitably employ laborers. This means that not physical but so-called human capital is in shortage. An increase in saving and physical capital formation would not lead to enhanced capacity to produce unless matched by increased technically qualified labor (Ranson, 1987; North, 1990).

However the increase in technically qualified labor without any increase in physical capital would increase the capacity to produce. This suggests that much more thought needs to be applied to the strategy of macroeconomic policy. The bias toward enhancing investment should perhaps be replaced with a direct focus on employment (Minsky, 1986). Of course, the interest of the technostructure is served by the preoccupation with investment, so clearly the emancipation of belief must include the emancipation of macroeconomic policy and investment policy.

This reconceptualization should place social policy on par with, and as a companion to, investment policy. The litany of capital shortage and crowding out by public spending leads to policies to increase corporate cash flow and the income of the rich. Such polices damage the ability of many families to sustain the human capital formation of their children, both in terms of formal education and nurturance in the home. In the last twenty-five years America has fomented a disaster in the making that will erode economic performance and the quality of life for a long time to come. Responding to the *nurturance gap* is the most pressing social problem America faces (Stanfield, 1994; Stanfield and Stanfield, 1995).

The transnational system also requires stabilization. That uneven development will occur is to some extent inevitable, though more enlightened policy would do much to close such gaps in the interest of all. The administered sector responds to cost differentials by shifting production to countries which currently enjoy favorable cost trends. This will open up currency crises which lead to demands for austerity in the disadvantaged areas.

The Galbraithian System indicates that the problem is the result of complex planning and coordination problems that austerity will only worsen. Inevitably, state competitiveness policy will arise, but if it does so in the context of economic warfare the only winners will be the technostructure. The needed planning and coordination must be concerted by the industrial countries if it is to be effective in countervailing the technostructure and accomplishing the stabilization that it seeks.

Galbraith emphasized the need for empirical information on the development problem. In his consideration of the purpose of development, he warned against the common tendencies toward a copy-the-West syndrome, toward emphasis on symbolic development of the icons of state, and even toward a focus on maximum growth (Galbraith, 1971a, ch. 3). Clearly the task is to engineer selective development, but questions such as placing the emphasis on agricultural or industrial development remain.

Galbraith asserted the need to emphasize the standard of living of the average citizen, which accords well with the institutionalist emphasis on participation and economic development. 'Until people have a part in economic progress, there will be no economic progress' (Galbraith, 1964a, p. 22).

In discussing the obstacles to development, Galbraith (1971a, ch. 5) again asserted the need for empirical detail so as not to force the variegated problems of underdevelopment into one monolithic category. Indeed, he offers three models, including the absence of an adequate cultural base. In this, the first model, the barrier to advance stems in large part from the legacy of colonialism, under which the skills necessary for leadership and intellectual activity were in the hands of external governors rather than indigenous people. Emergence from colonial suppression inevitably creates a leadership vacuum. In the second model, the evident barrier to development is a highly unequal social structure and the disincentives of extreme inequality. The third model displays the effects of severe disproportions in the factors of production, essentially excess population and capital shortage.

The third model of course is the conventional wisdom's explanation of third world poverty in general. Galbraith (1971a, ch. 6) argued that much error can follow from excess generalization and offers differential prescriptions for the three models. For the first model, the task is to expand human capital formation. Capital transfers are not critical and could well be wasted since the human factor to administer them is lacking. Nor is social reform or resort to publicly planned investment desirable: this would draw upon scarce talent by adding to the tasks of governments which are unable to competently exercise their basic functions. Finance alone would not enable the purchase of the talent necessary. Programs to educate the population, probably in the educational organizations of other nations, are needed.

For the countries that comprise the second model of underdevelopment, neither education nor capital nor finance are the key. In these societies, the need is for structural change to widen popular participation. Galbraith was not optimistic that change in these nations can be accomplished by reform. He did not advocate that American policy support revolution, but he did assert the need for the USA to stop trying to suppress it. Hence he advocated that American moral and material support be withdrawn from such repressive regimes.

For the third model countries, the problem is not one of advancing in a major way the cultural base. Educational and scientific advance are always welcome and may be needed in a few sectors but the general problem is not the absence of the cultural factor. Nor is it a need for basic social change in terms of the political and economic elite. Rather the need is for infusions of funds to finance investment and consumption of the indigent. So also must population control be a focal point.

Hence Galbraith in large part stated the structuralist perspective on the development problem (Street, 1987). The need is to have concrete studies to identify the concrete barriers to development in particular cases. As noted in Chapter 6, there is an transnational context to the development problem, the political economic technostructures of the global economy foment uneven development generally. But beyond application of the public cognizance to the activities of the technostructure in general, these particular structural barriers to development remain and would require attention in any strategy to reduce uneven development in the global economy.

Galbraith concluded *Economics and the Public Purpose* with the assertion that the next step in economic evolution is the development of public planning bodies and programs to impose overall planning on the administered sector. He considered this an all but foregone conclusion (1973b, pp. 318–19). The real question in his view is whether or not the public cognizance will be applied to the design and operation of this planning system. Application of the public cognizance would involve considerations beyond macroeconomic stabilization.

The principal concern is not a stable economy as such but an economy that is directed by the pursuit of a *better society*. Within the context of progressive social reform, the affirmation of humanism is a companion concern to stabilization policy in the resolution of the social predicament.

THE AFFIRMATION OF HUMANNESS

Beyond the requisites of stability in material reproduction, in Galbraith's view, political economy should also aim to affirm and advance the quality of human life. One concern in this affirmation is the 'equitable household'. The neoclassical synthesis here again obscures the reality of power and socially-structured inequality (Galbraith, 1973b, p. 232). Household production for direct use is not generally considered because the emphasis is upon the exchange economy. Time not spent in the paid labor force is generally regarded as time spent in leisure, and there is little examination of what people do with their 'time off'. The decision-making unit of choice is the household which buries any possible issue with regard to the relative status of the genders.

Galbraith proposed several reforms to emancipate women from their 'crypto-servant' role as managers of the family's consumption by facilitating their participation in the paid labor force. These include antidiscrimination laws in employment, state mandates and support to ensure the professional care of children, greater flexibility in work scheduling, and affirmative action to improve access of women to educational opportunities and positions in the technostructure.

These reforms in his view would either give women the upper hand in household decision-making or increase the sharing of household labor where decisions are conjoint. He foresaw this to likely result in 'a drastic change in present consumption patterns' (Galbraith, 1973b, p. 234). Here Galbraith's prescience is evident once again. The dramatic shift toward convenience items, household and restaurant services, catalog buying, and so on are now commonplace.

Galbraith seemed to lean toward the Leninist view that given the ingress of women into the paid labor force all else would change. He quoted Lenin to this effect in the epigraph to the chapter. In a later book, Galbraith (1983, ch. 3) placed far more emphasis upon culture and the effects of emotional conditioning with regard to the propriety of behaviors for the genders. This seems to bring him much closer to an institutionalist explanation of gender inequality, which, in the wake of Veblen, is rather less sanguine about the immediate prospect for undermining the patriarchal culture. It now seems clear that Veblen was right and that the matter of patriarchal culture is more complex and therefore requires examination as a distinct pattern of socially-structured inequality (Wheatley-Mann, 1986).

Nor is there much in the trend toward increased paid labor force participation of women and the related restructuring of output that indicates an assault upon the power of the technostructure and its pre-emptive indoctrination of the ideology of consumption. To the contrary, evidence points to a renewed dedication to the commodity nexus, to the neglect of the personal realm of caring and nurturing each other (Schor, 1991; Stanfield, 1994; and Stanfield and Stanfield, 1995).

The affirmation of humanism requires that the market sector in general be supported by public policy, and that particular attention be given to artistic and cultural activities. The policies for supporting the market sector would be aimed at overcoming or countervailing the basic tendency to uneven development that gave rise to the dual economic structure. There is nothing less important about the commodities which fall to the market sector, they simply resist the degree of organization characteristic of the advanced sector.

Improved social balance thus requires government action to protect and affirm the development of the market sector (Galbraith, 1973b, ch. 25). To this end, as noted above, Galbraith proposed price and income supports for market sector firms and that they be granted a general exemption from antitrust rules to enable them to coordinate prices and output levels. He also advocated a cautious application of tariffs and revision of international trade compacts to stabilize the prices and production experienced by the market sector enterprises, which lack the power and hedging ability routinely practiced by large firms in the advanced sector.

Galbraith would enhance the position of market sector labor by state-mandated effort for unionization and a major increase in the minimum wage. Indeed he would wield the wage minimum aggressively in an effort to eliminate the wage differential between the two sectors. He would also enact a guaranteed income for those that cannot find employment. This too is part of a general effort to dramatically shift the pattern of income distribution toward greater equality.

The market sector should further be affirmed by a major increase in government support of its 'educational, capital, and technological needs' (Galbraith, 1973b, p. 260). This includes government sponsorship of the arts which do not benefit from the resolute lobbying efforts of the technostructure for government funds in support of scientific and technical education and research. This is a matter of power not social economic precept. Indeed the greatest limit on human development in the American century has been not so much the lack of commodities as the one-sided development of the capacity to produce them at the expense of the capacity to select and enjoy them. This was a central theme of Dewey's *Reconstruction in Philosophy*, a series of lectures given after the First World War.

The market sector contains three industries of fundamental importance to the material welfare of the population. For a variety of reasons, health care, housing, and local transportation are not amenable to the organization that is characteristic of the administered sector. Galbraith saw no alternative to their being converted to 'full organization under public ownership' (Galbraith, 1973b, p. 279). Although his case for the uneven development of these industries and for government mitigation in the form of induced countervailing power is clear enough, Galbraith did not explicate the case for public production as opposed to public funding of output produced privately.

Moreover, much of the uneven development problem is not limited to these industries. The power of the administered sector distorts the pattern of long distance transportation, where the dependence on the automobile also appears to be excessive from the view of the public purpose. In terms of energy, solar power and conservation have not been pursued as important alternatives.

Ultimately, the 'revised economics of technical innovation' (Galbraith, 1973b, ch. 15) will have to be stretched to recognize the distortion of the allocation of the resources by which we imagine and design our future. Society allocates a portion of its output to activities such as R&D and investment in tools and skills that shape its future development (Stanfield, 1992). The power to allocate this 'fund for social change' is critical to the effort to overcome the deficiencies related to uneven development. Reform in this regard might well correct much of the inadequacies in the health, housing, and local transportation industries without the need for anything so drastic as overt nationalization.

The market sector also houses the cultural and artistic endeavors that are so important to a life worth living. The administered sector asserts the importance of its output through various channels of persuasion. Failure to assert a public effort to fund the arts will generate a greatly imbalanced society that is wealthy but impoverished by the lack of aesthetic principle in its wealth generation. Galbraith offered no explicit programs but no doubt would favor a major increase in the commitment of funds to the models already available to provide non-commercial programming in various media. Independent public corporations allocating funds on the basis of peer review is an established model in science and the arts.

CONCLUSION

To summarize, Galbraith's policy framework proceeds in two immediate steps that then provide the path to an eventual third step. The first two steps are to change the paradigm of economics, so to emancipate belief, so to emancipate the state. The basic change in economics is to recognize the dual economy and to drop the positivist pretense in favor of an economics that is explicit in regard to the social values it advocates in the process of reform. Escape from the imagery of choice and application of the test of anxiety should enable economists to clarify the economic process and indicate the discretion that society necessarily exercises in the values it upholds and the knowledge and skill it develops and deploys (Tool, 1979). Institutions matter (North, 1990) and an economics that is committed to institutional analysis of power and culture in relation to the economic process is essential.

Emancipation of belief and the state requires the political lead from the educational and scientific estate and a politics dedicated to explication of the public interest as distinct and superior to the interest of the administered sector and its ruling technocracy. This understanding of the political economic culture, the public cognizance, is required to effectively program social change and to deflect the stream of tendencies that comprises the political economic process in the direction of the public purpose.

After the bias of policy has been turned against the administered sector, the third and long run step in the Galbraithian agenda for reform may unfold. It is then the task of the population, empowered by emancipation from the grasp of the administered sector, to refashion their habitual ways and means from the commodity fetishistic, 'high intensity market setting' (Leiss, 1976) to a more satisfying pattern of living. Critical theory has no intent to define the good life, only to illumine the obstacles that now stand in the way of self-authentic choice. Still one may strongly suspect and fervently hope that the unleashed proclivities toward creative craft and thought would generate very different patterns of interaction and allocation of time.

Part of the necessary political lead may well come from the economics profession. Galbraith closes *Economics and the Public Purpose* with a call for the public cognizance to be obtained in the design and operation of the inevitable public planning apparatus. In this endeavor he sees the potential for economists to revivify their discipline and reassert its relevance by expanding their analytic scope to include 'in all its diverse manifestations, the power they now disguise' (1973b, p. 324). Were it to be so, *economics would become political economy and examine power and culture in relation to the economic process.*

8 Galbraith and Intellectual History

> When the liberation of capacity no longer seems a menace to organization and established institutions ... when the liberating of human capacity operates as a socially creative force, art will not be a luxury, a stranger to the daily occupations of making a living. Making a living economically speaking, will be at one with making a life that is worth living.
>
> (J. Dewey, 1948)

> We must confront explicitly the ideology of insatiable want and the social practice that sustains it.
>
> (W. Leiss, 1976)

The present chapter attempts to place Galbraith in intellectual history. From the foregoing it is no doubt evident to the reader that the major contention here is that Galbraith is properly considered to represent the tradition of American institutionalism. This chapter maintains the argument. But there are some surrounding issues in this regard, which in some respects Galbraith shares with other institutionalists, the relation to Keynes, to modern liberalism, to more radical traditions, even to the nascent green intellectual tradition. These issues are also considered in the chapter.

GALBRAITH THE INSTITUTIONALIST

The firmest conclusion to be drawn with regard to his work is that Galbraith fits squarely in the American or 'old' institutionalist (OIE) tradition. There is insight into the core features of institutionalism resident in his mandatory attention to the *social predicament*. The pragmatic bent of the institutionalists is a paradigm – disciplinary device of considerable force that has been egregiously overlooked by those who all too frequently lament the school's lack of a central organizing principle.

The economy as a concrete entity is no mean master for those who will submit to the requirement of direct, demonstrable relevance. Though clearly Veblen founded the school, its nature owes much to several others, notably Walton Hamilton, whose classic article (1919) mandated relevance even as it named the school institutional economics, and John Commons, who exemplified the unity between cogitation and application of an institutionalist understanding of the role of institutions in the social economy. In the article to which allusion was just made, Hamilton insisted that this pragmatic mandate qualified institutional economics to the title of economic theory because 'economic theory must be relevant to the modern problem of control' (Hamilton, 1919, p. 312). This relevance, he continued, could only be achieved if the theory in question relates its central concepts 'to the changeable elements of life and the agencies through which they are to be directed' (Hamilton, 1919, p. 314). Hamilton's genetic economic theory would be dedicated to a treatment of the economic system as a 'stream of tendencies' (Hamilton, 1919, p. 316) by which society carries along the knowledge and authority necessary to reproduce and, hopefully, develop the life-process (Hamilton, 1919).

This pragmatic bent is celebrated in the title of the major journal dedicated to the publication of institutional theory in the post-war period, the *Journal of Economic Issues*, published by the Association for Evolutionary Economics. In this view, the issues over which society is, or should be and will be, disturbed and which threaten to obstruct the reasonable conduct of the life process must be prominent among the theoretical variables of economic studies. Galbraith is a forceful example in this regard, both by his policy advocacy and his elegant statement of the principle in his *test of anxiety*.

Close students of Dewey will find the test of anxiety to be reminiscent of the instrumentalist philosopher.

> If ideas, meanings, conceptions, notions, theories, systems are instrumental to an active reorganization of the given environment, to a removal of some specific trouble and perplexity, then the test of their validity and value lies in accomplishing this work . . . If they fail to clear up confusion, to eliminate defects, if they increase confusion, uncertainty and evil when they are acted upon, then they are false. (Dewey, 1948, p. 156)

Galbraith's basic conception of the economy as a technological process controlled by institutions that, although malleable, are supported by human tendencies that resist change, is decidedly institutionalist. In this view, the economy is not reduced to the problem of choice induced by scarcity and exercized in the exchange process. Exchange is one form of instituting the economic division of labor in society which, first, may or may not be predominant in a given society in a specific time and place.

Second, in any case, exchange operates in conjunction with other integrative mechanisms and this interaction must be understood in order to understand the operation of exchange in a particular setting. This is a fundamental insight of comparative institutional analysis, namely, that social institutions must be understood holistically because the operation of a given process in the context of one overall social pattern will differ in another context. Nor is the psychology of economic life reduced to rationalistic psychology by Galbraith and the institutionalists. Functional or behavioristic psychology is necessary to apprise the empirical social character that is common in given historical situations. Moreover, humanistic psychology is necessary to understand the quality of life experience for human beings in these concrete historical situations. Galbraith's concern for the unnecessary agony of toil in *The New Industrial State* and for the anti-liberal consequences of consumer manipulation illustrate the institutionalist insistence that power and therefore feelings or preferences must be treated as variables to be explained in economic analysis and not taken as datum as the first step of a rationalistic psychology of choice.

Veblen of course emphasized the importance of habitual outlook in the explication of human behavior. Ayres explained that feelings, taken as basic data, are illusory because they are but the habitual conditioning of emotional response to particular stimuli (Ayres, 1961). This is similar to Galbraith's (1983) concept of *conditioned power*. His frequent discussion of the motivation of the corporate technostructure is another example of his agreement with OIE on the matter of the psychology of economic life. Not that self-interest is set aside, rather it is placed in a concrete setting and interwoven with relational sentiments and affinities.

Despite his apparent demur in this regard, Galbraith (1979c p. 144) also shared the famous Veblenian dichotomy inherent in viewing the economy as an evolving set of technological relationships and a power structure that regulates this technological process. Commerce is merely a very visible aspect of the economy; it is not the basic ingredient of economic life. Galbraith and the institutionalists insist that this basic element is the force of technology. Technological change generates new problems and conflicts that law and morality have not yet faced; this implies the need for adaptation of law and morality to the changed situations brought on by technological change.

However, institutions, though malleable, possess inertial tendencies and do not adjust or evolve under the exigencies of technological change without the expenditure of social energy in achieving this adaptation. This expenditure of energy is necessary to achieve the intellectual reconstruction of social life in novel settings. Galbraith captured this inertial tendency with remarkable cogency in his concept of conventional wisdom, and his discussion thereof is very reminiscent of Veblen. This inertial tendency means that institutional or cultural lag will exist, that is, that at any given time there will be lacunae in social understanding and resolution of conflicts and problems. Galbraith's (1960, pp. 105–17) discussion of 'the nature of social nostalgia' in the face of social change is a very adept essay on the problem of cultural lag.

It follows that the economic problem in the institutionalist view is not the rational allocation of given resources to meet given ends in order to maximize real income. Rather the fundamental economic problem is the continuous reinstitutionalization of economic life in society. This means the continuous reform of economic institutions to deal with the changing exigencies brought on by technological change. In short, *the* economic problem is institutional adjustment, the redistribution of power to correspond more closely to the concrete economic problems of the day.

The shared insistence that technology and preferences are variables gives Galbraith and the institutionalists a common long run and dynamic focus on the economy. As technology changes, it redefines the available resources to be deployed toward generating real income. Petroleum was transformed from a nuisance byproduct of the search for water to a highly-prized economic resource by the invention of the internal combustion engine. Resources can no more be taken as given than technology in anything but the briefest period of economic analysis. Real time analysis needs to stay abreast of the continuous redefinition of resources by technologic change.

Nor are tastes and preferences fixed in any but the shortest real time period. People are continuously learning and expanding their horizons, partly from the necessity to adapt to altered circumstance and partly from the force of their curious intellects. As they do so, they inevitably revise assessments of their wants and aspirations and the ways and means by which to improve their life process.

Of particular importance in this regard is the understanding of the changing basis of human valuations in the industrial societies of the twentieth century. Veblen (n.d.) referred to the 'cultural incidence of the machine process' to emphasize this dramatic shift of popular allegiance and commitment. Society is still in the process of sorting out the consequences of this cultural change, especially in regard to the potential disorder that is possible as metaphysically induced 'spontaneous conformity' is undermined without a secular replacement (Baran and Sweezy, 1966, ch. 11; Lowe, 1988).

In contrast to the approach of orthodox theory, Galbraith and the institutionalists take not only the flow of real income to be an analytic variable but also the resources and ends to be served by their deployment. Since the direction of technological change and the drift of human sentiment is an evolutionary tendency of the social process, the institutionalists insist upon the necessity of including power in the analysis. Conversely, to take resources, therefore technology, and preferences as datum, is to take the existing power structure as given and render nugatory any conclusion involving the redistribution of power in economic and social life.

This is the basis of the claim that orthodoxy embeds the existing value sentiments and structure of power in its axiomatic presumptions, a claim that extends to the argument that the claim of scientific neutrality made by orthodoxy is chimerical. Galbraith expresses this with the concept of the *convenient social virtue* of the economics profession and the telling phrase, the *imagery of choice*.

Galbraith's definition of the technological aspect as the 'systematic application of scientific or other organized knowledge to practical tasks' (Galbraith, 1967, p. 24) is also similar to that employed by the institutionalists, who following Veblen, emphasize the mental aspects of the technologic process. The deadening tendency to identify machines as technology is avoided by the insistence that the principal ingredient is human knowledge and skill, both to produce the machine tool and to operate it.

This view of technology leads Galbraith and the institutionalists away from the savings-centered theory of economic progress that persists in orthodox economic thought. Of course, construction of new physical capital must be financed in a commercial economy, but institutionalists insist that this does not mean reliance on private saving nor upon the effectiveness of capital markets (Galbraith, 1971a, p. 216).

Moreover, if capital formation is taken to mean an increase in productive capacity, it is not primarily or even necessarily an increase in the physical means of production. An additional tool adds to productive capacity only if the skilled labor exists to operate it. Capital formation can occur by an increase in the machines *and* the labor to operate the machines but it does not occur without this accommodation of the labor supply. Moreover, capital formation can occur without an increase in the machines if more people are provided the systematic knowledge required to operate the machinery that already exists (Ranson, 1987).

The emphasis on saving and investment in physical capital may be misplaced if the requisite human capital is not forthcoming. Since much of this accommodation is by public sector funding of education and retraining, the concept of *social balance* comes into play in the process of capital formation. Increasing private investment in the physical means of production adds to the social capacity to produce only if balanced by the public sector's accommodation of the labor supply. Galbraith's (1967) analysis of the imperatives of technological change and the concomitant growth in the public provision of education is similarly instructive. So also is the general emphasis he placed upon economic structure and the need to formulate economic theory and policy in the context of realistic assumptions.

As noted in Chapter 7, this emphasis on the problems posed by the dynamic empirical economy has been referred to as *evolutionary positivism*. Galbraith well exemplifies this emphasis with his contrast of the conventional wisdom to the changing technological and organizational circumstances of life and by his frequent insistence that habits of thought yield not to improved theory so much as to the force of circumstance. Galbraith and the institutionalists share an emphasis on anticipating the trajectory of technological and social change in order to anticipate social problems for analysis and policy response.

Institutionalists, like the historicists before them, have emphasized the historical relativity of economic precepts generally and in particular the need to comprehend the positive state and its altered role in relation to the modern industrial economy (Polanyi, 1944; Gruchy, 1967; Hamilton, 1957; Stanfield, 1986). In traditional discussions of its expanding scope, the state has been treated negatively in terms of what it does *not* signify. For socialists, the expanded state does *not* result in socialism because the mode of production has not been changed, hence alienation of workers and class inequality is still strongly manifest. For classical liberals, the result of the expanding role of the state is *not* capitalism, there is too much government interference with the rights of private property and the exercise of enterprise.

Even the compromise concept of a *mixed economy* that modern liberals offer is more a refusal to conceptualize a new reality than an attempt to do so; that the system is neither capitalist nor socialist but some of both does not tell us what it is, only two things that it is not exactly. With the expression the *new industrial state*, Galbraith sought to convey this sense that a new system exists that must be understood on its own terms not upon the ideological expressions of the nineteenth century. That this new system entails substantial private planning and administration is a point emphasized by Galbraith that has long been a major thrust of institutionalism (Hamilton, 1957; Polanyi, 1944; Stanfield, 1986).

Galbraith implicitly employed the instrumental value premises of institutionalism. In this view the task of social science is to analyze the institutional practices of society with respect to their relation to the fundamental human values of excellence, security, freedom, solidarity, democracy, abundance, and equality. Galbraith's emphasis upon environmental preservation, the distribution of life chances, and the quality of human life, including the aesthetic dimension, is ample evidence of his commitment to this scheme of valuation. So also his pragmatic bent, as noted, exemplified by his *test of anxiety.*

For Galbraith as for other institutionalists, Rick Tilman's (1987) observation that the social scientist merges with the social reformer is entirely apt. Galbraith's imploring the scientific and intellectual estate to take the *political lead* comes to mind as well as his partisan involvement in the political process. As has been noted in these pages, Galbraith's analysis may have been improved at important junctures had he been more explicit about the instrumentalist value premises underlying his work.

Galbraith's view of the structural aspects of the American economy built upon the institutionalist tradition. The institutionalist concern with economic balance was evident in many of his concerns, especially, as explained in Chapter 2, in his explanation of the Great Crash and the Great Depression. Galbraith's emphasis on the dual economy model exemplifies the concern for the issue of balance. The problem of price control was placed in the context of dual economic sectors and the theory of countervailing power was aimed at overcoming imbalances in power and revenue. The question of social balance both as originally expressed and in its more mature expression is essentially a concern for balance in the dual economy.

Galbraith's frequent theme of the contrast between growing affluence and the use that is made of it can be traced back to the likes of Veblen and Patten (1968) and is echoed in the work of Ayres (1962). Here again Galbraith exemplifies the Veblenian contrast between making goods and making money in an economy which is no longer consistently small-scale and competitive in structure. The contrast between corporate purpose and the pubic interest was strikingly made by Galbraith and echoed the indictment made by Veblen at the turn of the century.

That income distribution is to be explained more by habitual status differentiations and administrative power than by the doctrine of necessary supply price of industrial serviceability is very Veblenian. Galbraith (1967, p. 257) apparently subscribed to Veblen's theory that income distribution is in large part a matter of legitimate extortion in which one's income is a function of the mayhem one can cause by refusing to cooperate.

The Veblenian dichotomy was also evident in Galbraith's discussion of the problem of economic development. As noted, his approach is very near that of other institutionalist development economists in its emphasis on the need for concrete case studies to identify the structural barriers to development. The problem is clearly one of institutional adjustment. 'In fact, institutions do chain economies to the past, and the breaking of these chains is essential for progress' (Galbraith, 1964a, p. 32). Galbraith did not therefore downplay the significance of democracy because 'a widespread yearning for the dignity of democratic and constitutional government' is very common, even among those who evidently lack the rudiments of economic well-being (Galbraith, 1964a, p. 33). For institutionalists, democratic participation is no luxury to be purchased by economic development, it is a major instrument to that goal because popular participation in the process and rewards of development is the core component of the strategy for progress (Ayres, 1962). 'There can be no effective advance if the masses do not participate . . . As literacy is economically efficient, so is social justice' (Galbraith, 1964a, p. 46). This echoed the institutionalist insistence that 'social justice' is not simply a value judgement about equality but an essential ingredient of economic effectiveness.

THE RADICAL AND LIBERAL GALBRAITH

Galbraith shares with other institutionalists an affinity for the ideas of Keynes and a faith in the capacity of common people for effective participation in democratic self-government. Clearly institutionalists are modern liberals. But there is a radical undertone to all institutionalist literature, an inclination that may find expression in red or green political rhetoric.

Galbraith the Keynesian

Galbraith has often spoken of the importance of Keynes in the development of his ideas and has been known to refer to himself as an 'American Keynesian' whose system took its point of departure form the Keynesian Revolution (Galbraith, 1971a, pp. ix and 266). In his rendition of the coming of Keynes to America, Galbraith (1971a, ch. 4; 1981, chs. 5, 6) did not indicate any significant role to institutionalists. Nonetheless, other institutionalists of his generation, such as Clarence Ayres (1946) and Allan Gruchy (1949), were also quick to align themselves with the basic message of John Maynard Keynes. No doubt much of this appeal resided in the fact that Keynesian macroeconomics was meant to be relevant to the problem of control, specifically to the social problem of macroeconomic instability. This pragmatic thrust of Keynesian macroeconomics is probably what Ayres had in mind in his observation that macroeconomics is Veblenian economics (Ayres, 1964).

There is also historicity in Keynes's views. The idea that a mature economy is more likely to be plagued by an excess rather than a shortage of saving would have appeal to institutionalists well beyond the policy conclusions of deficit spending to overcome economic stagnation. It embodies recognition that the economy evolves as it grows and that its mature operation, in the context of current technology, is very different from its performance in the competitive era with its context of much simpler and smaller scale technology.

This was an important thrust of Veblen's *Theory of Business Enterprise*, which emphasized that modern industrial crises are fundamentally different from the financial panics of early capitalism in that modern crises are the result of a fundamental tendency toward overproduction induced by the advance of the technological arts and sciences. This emphasis on changing economic structure with the advent of maturity seems to be bound up with the Keynesian explanation of the Great Depression. The initial Keynesian thrust seemed tied into the reduced automaticity of the market economy because of the growth of economic concentration. This is very close to the economic imbalance theme of the institutionalists (see Chapter 2 above).

The paradox of thrift appealed not only to the institutionalists' sense of historical change but also to their dissent from the saving-centered theory of economic progress, which they habitually regard as ceremonial mythology. Ayres (1967, p. 4), commenting on the notion of bonds earning interest, noted that 'we are invited to picture the bonds in the locked steel drawer of some bank vault, sweating profusely as they heave and writhe in their efforts'. Or again, that 'no one secretes steel rails by going without lunch' (Ayres, 1962, p. 49). Keynes' paradox of thrift and the euthanasia of the rentier undermined the saving-centered theory of economic progress with its insistent litany of delayed abstinence and gratification as the key to the capital formation from whence economic growth must spring.

This cynicism about the role of personal saving and the companion case made by Keynes for increasing aggregate demand by income redistribution would also have been welcome to the institutionalists. They are egalitarian in spirit, and prone to emphasize distribution to secure maximum participation.

Finally, Keynes' reference in *The General Theory* to a 'somewhat comprehensive socialization of investment' seems to point toward the mild form of economic planning or industrial policy that institutionalists generally advocate. Indeed, this sort of structural policy was a large part of the institutionalist oriented brain trust of the New Deal, well in advance of Keynes.

If this be what Keynes had in mind by the somewhat comprehensive socialization, it is safe to say that the point was lost on his neo-Keynesian disciples of the neoclassical synthesis. Not surprisingly, Galbraith, and other institutionalists such as Allan Gruchy and Ben Seligman, were among the earliest and most insistent critics of the neoclassical synthesis for its neglect of economic structure in the consideration of price and employment performance. The prominent dissent from the neoclassical synthesis of so-called post-Keynesian economics is similar in some respects to the institutionalists. Of late there is a trend in the institutionalist direction in so-called New Keynesian economics as well (Ferguson, 1993).

Galbraith the Modern Liberal

The Keynesian movement is part of a wider shift in political economic philosophy toward *modern liberalism*. Galbraith certainly continues and in some ways even epitomizes the drift begun by J.S. Mill, if not Thomas Paine before him. In contrast to the highly specific and restrictive view of the state's role that characterized the classical economics of his father and Ricardo, the younger Mill espoused the convenience principle in setting the role of the state. Upon reviewing the many activities already undertaken by the state, which apparently brook at most inconsequential dissent, Mill observed that no reasonably concise set of general principles could encompass them all, except for the intentionally broad principle of convenience (1985). The convenience principle enlarges upon Smith's somewhat elastic principle that the state should undertake such projects that are in the interest of a great society but which do not repay a small set of individuals to undertake.

Mill also set the theme of the social reformer's task of improving the lot of the common human within capitalism. His famous distinction between the laws that govern productive efficiency and those that govern distribution are the basis not only of modern liberalism's penchant for redistributive policies but also for the equality versus efficiency posture of conventional economics. The natural laws that governed production were fundamentally the natural human desires to consume but to avoid work. By retaining private property and market competition, Mill hoped to have the efficiency of capitalism but to ameliorate its maldistribution

through institutional reform. In short, he embraced the goals of the socialists but not their means.

Modern liberalism has been slower to embrace Mill's later pronounce-
ments on these and related questions. Perhaps under the influence of
Harriet Taylor, he seemed to have cast aside much of his reluctance to the
means of socialism, as when he observed that humanity would work in the
service of a wide range of motivations (Mill, 1924, p. 163). This implies
that he had recanted the notion of a 'natural indolence' of humanity (Mill,
1985, p. 142). This seems to negate the idea that efficiency can be gained
only by the competitive resort to the individual's spontaneous calcula-
tion of self-interest.

Even in the *Principles*, Mill introduced a concern for the environment
and for the quality of life, as opposed to the quantity of commodities,
which has not been emphasized by modern liberalism in general. He noted
that he did not regard the stationary state with the undiluted aversion so
often attached to it by the other classicists. Indeed, he questioned the need
for eternal economic growth and injected the notion of invidious self-
seeking into the discussion (Mill, 1985, Bk. IV, pp. 113–4). He clearly
lamented the destruction of the rest of nature and of the opportunity for
the human being to seek the solitude and communion to be found there.

The Cambridge School followed up on much of Mill's reformist bent.
The 'social enthusiasm' of the school was early on focused on poverty
and industrial disputes (Hutchison, 1981, ch. 3). As noted above, Keynes
advanced this reformist bent by mandating concern for macroeconomic
instability. In the wake of Keynes, it was to be ever after quite difficult
to maintain that unemployment and the deprivation that it induced were
the result of some moral failure of the individual. Keynes also returned
to Mill's theme of eventual resolution of the economic problem and for
the need to separate invidiously based wants from those based on primary
or absolute utility (Keynes, 1963, pp. 358–73). Of course, the masterful
statement in this regard remains Veblen's (1953) concept of conspicuously
and invidiously deployed ability to pay.

There is also a more narrowly political aspect of modern liberalism. In
Mill's wake, English 'new liberalism' provided a reinterpretation of the
state in relation to the citizen and hence of the role of the state. Classical
liberalism conceived the state as a super agency over and above the individual citizens. The prototypes of this view of the state are the dynastic
absolutist states of early modern Europe and elsewhere. New liberals such
as L.T. Hobhouse and Thomas Green argued that, with the extension of
the franchise, the relation of the state to the populace had changed for the

better. The state was now properly viewed not as the ruler of subjects but as the expression of the popular will. As such, its activities required far less delimitation in principle because the democratic process promised to restrain the state's reach. Such a view would seem to be implicit in Mill's convenience principle. The Fabians, evolutionary socialists, some aspects of the historicists, and the institutionalist movement in the USA were intertwined with the growth of modern liberalism.

Galbraith the Radical

Very often modern liberalism displays a somewhat schizoid tendency. It seeks to uphold the liberal sphere but at the same time it asserts something like a doctrine of false consciousness. As part of the liberal sphere it upholds the sanctity of private property but it also espouses rather extensive abrogation of private property to promote social justice in distribution and industrial relations or to enforce social regulation in the workplace, consumer protection, or environmental areas.

Modern liberalism also makes frequent resort to the role model aspect of affirmative action, which obviously cannot come into play if the abstract individual of methodological individualism is postulated. Role models can only be a factor if the abstract individual is abandoned in favor of a methodological collectivist view that examines the process of character formation.

Much of this seeming confusion stems from lack of clarity with respect to methodological collectivism and the nature of the state. Too often the state is treated as a deus ex machina, invoked to intervene to correct one or another market failure. No analysis is offered as to the nature of the state and whether or not its habitual tendencies are likely to enable effective intervention in the area in question.

Galbraith's (1987, pp. 266–7) recognition of the political asymmetry of Keynesian fiscal policy points to one instance of this failure. A rudimentary understanding of politics reveals that the palliatives for treating unemployment are likely to be more palatable politically than those for reducing inflation. The advocacy of an enhanced role of the state in macroeconomic coordination without confronting the values that should guide the state's influence on the structure of output is another (Robinson, 1972). In general, many of the policies of the modern liberal trend display interventionist drift (Stanfield, 1979, ch. 5) that undermine the structural limits of the liberal state form without providing any clear rubric to replace the strictures of classical liberalism (Clarke, 1989). As noted above, critical junctures are thus perceived as crises of the pattern of intervention (Heilbroner, 1985; Stanfield, 1995a, ch. 9).

The matter becomes even more complicated when methodological collectivism is invoked to challenge the attitudes and propensities monitored by the market and political processes. The classical liberal procedure is to take the abstract individual as given and to take social value as but the sum of individual welfare. The modern liberals are inclined to bring socialization and behavioral issues into the argument, but in doing so they generate issues that the formal theory of choice in politics and markets is ill equipped to manage.

Institutionalists have a diverse record in these regards. Although socialization is always an element in the analysis, the advocacy of democracy as a process is often not examined in light of the operation of power in the formation of individual outlooks and preferences. This was not so of Veblen, who had a basically Marxist disdain for the capitalist state. And Galbraith and other radical institutionalists have taken up Veblen's suspicion toward the operation of democracy in a business culture (Stanfield, 1979 and 1995a; Tilman, 1987; Dugger, 1989, 1992a, 1992b; Dugger (ed.), 1989; Dugger and Waller (eds), 1992). Building upon Veblen, Galbraith, and Marx, these institutionalists have taken modern liberalism in fundamentally critical directions.

From what has been said above, it should occasion no surprise that these institutionalists were able to take Galbraith to a radical turn. The critical examination of the role of power in culture necessarily leads to a fundamental questioning of the prevalent institutional pattern and a willingness to see its results as the result of the self-serving machinations of powerful vested interests. Galbraith's *imagery of choice* is a veritable call to arms to young institutionalists to engage in resolute struggle against corporate cultural hegemony and the complacent duplicity of the elegant conventional economic models that shroud it.

There are parallels to Marx in Galbraith's work, as in institutionalism generally, that often go unnoticed. He does not explicitly confront the perennial Marxian problem of alienated labor but his consideration of toil was not without Marxist overtones. Galbraith (1958, ch. 24) advocated improving the quality of work life and reducing the customary hours of work; he even foresaw the need 'to eliminate toil as a required economic institution'.

Later, Galbraith (1967, ch. 32) amended this discussion somewhat by noting that there is no obvious reason for leisure to be more pleasant than work, and that the key in any event is to free people from the management of their wants. Without raising the issue of coerced labor in so many words, he did indict the self-commodification necessary to replenish the technostructure (Galbraith, 1967, p. 374). Then too, Galbraith's persistent advocacy of a guaranteed annual income accords well with the Marxist dictum that distribution should be determined according to need.

Galbraith's overall concern with the vacuous nature of mass leisure administered in the interest of the corporate elite has a Marxian ring to it: it clearly invokes the image of an alien power controlling the material process on the basis of criteria that are alien to the actualization of some fundamental human potential. To repeat, Galbraith could very well have improved his argument had he connected with the explicit traditions available on alienation and instrumental reasoning (Stanfield, 1995a, ch. 10). Indeed a general advance could have been made if the essential thematic similarity of alienation and commodity fetishism, conspicuous consumption and invidious distinction, revised sequence and the imagery of choice, had been recognized.

False consciousness is the major chord in each case and false consciousness can only be postulated in light of some true consciousness, some obdurate standard of human value, dignity, and development. This obdurate standard supplies a 'higher efficiency' than the market standard for evaluating economic performance (Klein, 1987, p. 1369), and there is remarkable similarity in the standard of evaluation applied in the work of Marx, Veblen, and Galbraith (Stanfield, 1995a, chs 12 and 13).

In general outline Galbraith's model of capitalist evolution is also reminiscent of Marx on the socialization of labor and capital. The idea that new technological forces and the related reorganization of the labor process induces changes in practice that militate toward changes in consciousness is common to Marx, Veblen, and Galbraith. The separation of ownership and control which is central to Galbraith was explicitly anticipated by Marx. Indeed Marx seemed to view this signal change as the key transitional element between capitalism and socialism (Marx, vol. III, 1967).

Moreover, Galbraith seemed to employ Marx's concept of internal contradiction in citing the operant antagonism between the technostructure and the educational and scientific estate, though admittedly he stopped short of referring to the technostructure as its own gravedigger. Marx identified the universal proletariat class as the element in society that would both recognize the need to fundamentally alter the system and possess the potential power in the material process to effect this transformation. Lenin added the notion of a vanguard that would contemplate the revolutionary prospect from the proletarian perspective and supply theoretical and organization leadership. Is it far-fetched to examine in these terms Galbraith's call for the political lead to be exercized by the academic intelligentsia?

It is thus not altogether surprising that the distance between Galbraith and American radicals has narrowed considerably. Galbraith has become more stridently critical of the power and inequality in late capitalism and of the resultant failure to realize the quality of life that is potentially available. The radicals have shifted as well. The criticism of bourgeios democracy as fundamentally flawed by the economic structure of capitalism has been, if not muted, shifted to another plane. The emphasis in the last two decades has been upon invigorating the democratic process so to utilize the capitalist state in the pursuit of social reform. The seminal statement of Bowles, Gordon, and Weisskopf (1983) may be considered in this regard.

Galbraith the Green

The radical discourse has veered to a new left which is perhaps more green than red. So also does Galbraith take institutionalism in this direction. He is early on and persistently concerned with environmental protection. And he has persistently associated the ecological problematic with education and aesthetic development. Social imbalance is invariably associated with various forms of pollution and the aesthetic ruin of commercial artifice in general. In the closing paragraphs of the first leg of his trilogy, he noted that the problems of the future cannot be known with certainty but whether the issue be

> that of a burgeoning population and of space to live with peace and grace, or whether it be the depletion of the materials which nature has stocked in the earth's crust and which we have drawn upon more heavily in this century than in all previous time together, or whether it be the that of preoccupying minds no longer committed to the stockpiling of consumer goods, the basic demand on America will be on its resources of ability, intelligence, and education. (Galbraith, 1958, p. 355)

In 1960, Galbraith explicitly raised the question of whether or not more economic output is a valid goal for American society and warned that increased automobile production would bring 'appalling problems of storage and driving space', including 'the ghastly surgery of the superhighway' (Galbraith, 1960, p. 20). The theme of environmental destruction in the interest of producing goods of dubious import under the sway of powerful vested interests runs through *The New Industrial State* as well, though one may in hindsight opine that more explicit attention might have been given. In *Economics and the Public Purpose*, the attention afforded environmental issues is more extended. Galbraith rejected the internalization strategy of conventional economists as unpractical and the eventual limits to growth alternative as too distant, and argued that the only immediate alternative is continued growth constrained by legislative mandates (Galbraith, 1973b, pp. 287–9). In the course of setting out the now familiar requirements of environmental regulation, Galbraith (1973b, p. 290) included 'visual pollution' and noted that aesthetic considerations are part of the environmental problem. He had earlier referred to the suppression of the claims of 'environment and amenity' under the preoccupation with economic growth (Galbraith, 1973b, p. 207).

Similarly, in assessing President Nixon's environmental policy proposals in a 1970 essay in *Life*, Galbraith (1971a, pp. 284–7) asserted that serious environmental policy would require increased taxes, direct regulation of private enterprise and land use, and a reduction in the production and consumption of some goods, notably the automobile. Although Galbraith scoffed at the radical notion of fundamentally altering the system in some unspecified way, this should not be taken to mean that he opposed to fundamental change. Only a moment's reflection is necessary to conclude that the measures just noted would involve a dramatic revision of the habitual ways and means of American capitalism. Moreover, Galbraith had questioned the remaining content of the liberal social reform tradition in the first two installments of his trilogy. It would seem to be the lack of specificity in some radical protestations rather than the extent of the change that Galbraith criticized.

In this discussion as well it is interesting to note that Galbraith moved smoothly to include the built environment and the aesthetic dimension in his discussion of environmental problems. This connection of environmental and aesthetic concerns is not serendipitous. It seems quite clear that Galbraith long ago foresaw that ultimately environmental problems would be resolved, if at all, by alteration of the culture of consumerism. In *The New Industrial State* he devoted a chapter (ch. 30) to the aesthetic dimension of the social predicament. The aesthetic experience is of little interest to the administered sector; indeed in large part aesthetic achievement is contradictory to its interest because it mandates interference with many aspects of the technostructure's decision-making and renders the task of consumer manipulation more difficult.

In advancing the case for application of the test of aesthetic achievement, Galbraith commingled environmental preservation with aesthetic concern and argued for the superiority of such considerations over industrial efficiency as endorsed by the technostructure. Later in the book (1967, p. 387), in identifying the necessary 'political lead', he emphasized its importance in securing not only a secure but an 'aesthetically progressive society'.

Hence the most apt label of all for Galbraith might be *green*. The insistence that environmental preservation need not come at the expense of the quality of life, but indeed would likely augment that standard, dates back at least to J.S. Mill who, along with Veblen, identified insatiable consumer demand with invidious distinction. And it is supported generally by the institutionalist emphasis on the substantive economy and the need for stability and continuity in the provisioning function. Galbraith's stolid dissent from the persuasion of the military complex is another case in point.

Charles Reich's *The Greening of America* (1970) clearly displayed the imprint of Galbraith's ideas. Galbraith's (1971b) criticism of the now almost forgotten bible of the counterculture was artfully sympathetic. He clearly endorsed the main lines of the cultural criticism Reich levelled. Nor should we expect otherwise, given his emphasis on cultural resistance to emancipating belief, to form the public cognizance, and to challenge the autonomy of the advanced sector and the insipid and dangerously neurotic character of the present pattern of living.

Galbraith's thrust is very similar to that William Leiss (1976) who concluded that nothing less will suffice than a direct confrontation with the 'high-intensity market setting' that presently structures the articulation of human wants. For Galbraith, for Leiss, as for all greens, the task ahead is to connect human liberation and human betterment, to imagine and institute a pattern of living that unites self-authentic human development with enjoyment both of human technical artistry and the rest of nature.

Galbraith's greenness is neither pious nor euphoric; he does not condemn all that is pleasant and comfortable but he does not accept arrogant and myopic pillage. He recognizes that social change to solve real problems would require serious discourse and concerted effort, but he does not scoff at the notion of fundamental change nor the vision necessary to achieve it.

So Galbraith, like many institutionalists, occupies an uneasy space between modern liberalism and radicalism. The commitment to progressive social change is fervid but impatience with the pace of progress is not allowed to overshadow the need to proceed within the confines of cultural continuity, governed by the democratic process. The terrain occupied is rather like that claimed by the late Michael Harrington, 'the left wing of the possible'.

THE GALBRAITHIAN CHALLENGE

The Galbraithian System is open-ended. It leaves a research and policy agenda that must necessarily be revised in the wake of changing circumstance. The pulse of the public must be routinely taken to satisfy the strictures of the test of anxiety. The spectacular expansion of merger and takeover activities adds new questions to the issues of corporate governance that Galbraith raised. Nor did he put to rest lingering questions about financial versus managerial control (Kotz, 1978; Balogh, 1982, p. 241; Munkirs, 1985), the relation between corporate size and innovation, or the distinction between real and pecuniary economies of scale in relation to the increase in corporate size (Adams, 1953 and 1967).

The critical examination of advertising requires considerably more work with regard to the specifics of the effects of advertizing on public sentiment (Schudson, 1984). Galbraith (1983, pp. 29–30) continued to slide too readily from the visibility of advertizing to its effectiveness even in the promotion of particular brands. His case would perhaps be stronger if he had stuck to the aggregate effect of advertizing in promoting the ideology of consumption. But even so, some examination of the role of transactions costs in shaping the development of advertising would still be needed (Ekelund and Saurman, 1988; North, 1990).

Continuing work is necessary on the problem of economic structure in relation to unemployment and inflation. Galbraith's abandoning wage and price controls as politically inexpedient left a chasm in his macroeconomic policy scenario. Moreover the results of such countries as Sweden which attempted to combine aggressive social democracy and active labor market policies with capitalist economic structure are less than encouraging in their implications for the Galbraithian Prospect. Of course, the strictures of the global economy come into play at this point. Intensifying international competition and the emergence of new economies raise many nuances that were neglected by Galbraith; indeed, his treatment of the international dimensions of his system was sketchy at best. In any case the details of international trade management regimes require a strong dose of the public cognizance (McClintock, 1990).

The Galbraithian Challenge is that laid down by the tradition of social or institutional economics – lives and livelihood. To examine economy and society is to examine the instituted process by which a living is made in the context of its effects on the pattern of living. It is a critical concern for the organization of work, the stability and the distribution of the flow of real income, the continuity of cultural context, the preservation of the rest of nature, the widening of participation in social process, and the liberation of the human spirit. It is a commitment to reform based upon identification of particular problems and the institutional adjustment necessary to empower people to solve them. The Galbraithian Challenge is to resolutely apply the public cognizance to all issues of public policy. In so doing, the critical scrutiny of the present order must proceed on the two levels raised as well by other institutionalists. One level is concerned simply with the accuracy of relative prices in reflecting current individual preferences. The issues here have to do with the ability of powerful agents to administer prices and shape political decisions.

But there is a second and more fundamental level. The critical examination of power does not stop with the contexts of choice. It extends beyond this to include grave questions about the formation of the preferences which operate within the contexts of relative prices and political advocacy. Critical theory in this regard challenges the validity and authenticity of preferences shaped by the exercise of concentrated power (Stanfield, 1995a and 1995b). Here, as noted above on more than one instance, Galbraith's analysis needs to be linked explicitly to a higher standard of efficiency.

The issues raised by the Galbraithian System are as daunting as they are compelling. The challenge posed is to reconstruct the complex of liberal values upon firmer foundations than the litany of natural rights and atomistic individualism. The promise of the Galbraithian Prospect is that humanity will consciously accept collective responsibility for its social economy and hence for the volume of individual freedom and self-actualization that its institutions permit, indeed *mandate*. So also with respect to security, equality, abundance, achievement, and solidarity. So also with respect to the democratic process, for in the end the Galbraithian Challenge is the democratic challenge of fostering the widest possible participation in the reasonable discourse and inquiry that is democracy.

The Galbraithian Prospect, as that of the other institutionalists and the Marxists and existentialists, remains open. This openness is a basic feature of the evolutionary paradigm. Recognition that human life is an unfolding stream of tendencies and that human discretion configures this incessant change promises to be a liberating albeit intimidating awakening.

If the Galbraithian Challenge seems to promote radical change it is because the present institutional pattern so wildly violates the values of liberal culture. But it is not revolutionary in the sense of advocacy of a sharp disjuncture and reconstruction. The institutional complex is steadily evolving and the trajectory of this change can be deflected in a more sustainable and serviceable direction.

One could say that Galbraith is liberal and conservative in the same paradoxical sense that he attributed to Keynes (Galbraith, 1987, pp. 235–6). He challenges fundamental conceptions as to how the present social economic system operates but he does so in the interest of improving upon its performance in particular problem areas and not to make the case for its eradication in the interest of wholesale reconstruction.

The Galbraithian Challenge concerns the critical examination and conscious adjustment of the institutions that pattern social life. The Galbraithian Challenge is part of a much larger project to unify social inquiry. The task is to connect examination of the economic process with the psychological and cultural examination of the quality of human life. Nothing less than an understanding of the human individual and the joy to be derived from the self-authentic conduct of everyday life will suffice.

References

Adams, W. (1953) 'Competition, Monopoly, and Countervailing Power', *Quarterly Journal of Economics*, 67 (November), pp. 469–92.
Adams, W. (1967) 'A Blueprint for Technocracy', *Science* (August), pp. 532–3.
Adams, W. and J.W. Brock (1986) *The Bigness Complex* (New York: Pantheon).
Adelman, M. (1954) 'Fundamentals of the American Economy: Discussion', *American Economic Review*, 44 (May), pp. 26–34.
Appleby, J.O. (1978) *Economic Thought and Ideology in Seventeenth-Century England* (Princeton, NJ: Princeton University Press).
Ayres, C.E. (1946) *The Divine Right of Capital* (Boston: Houghton Mifflin).
Ayres, C.E. (1961) *Toward a Reasonable Society* (Austin: University of Texas Press).
Ayres, C.E. (1962) *The Theory of Economic Progress* (New York: Schocken).
Ayres, C.E. (1964) 'The Legacy of Thorstein Veblen', in *Institutional Economics: Veblen, Commons, and Mitchell Reconsidered* (Berkeley: University of California Press) pp. 45–62.
Ayres, C.E. (1967) 'Ideological Responsibility', *Journal of Economic Issues*, 1 (June), pp. 3–11.
Balogh, T. (1982) *The Irrelevance of Conventional Economics* (New York: Liveright).
Baran, P.A. and P.M. Sweezy (1966) *Monopoly Capital* (New York: Monthly Review Press).
Barkin, S. (1964) 'The Decine of the Labor Movement', in A. Hacker, *The Corporation Take-Over* (New York: Harper and Row) pp. 216–38.
Bell, D. (1976) *The Cultural Contradictions of Capitalism* (New York: Basic Books).
Berle, A.A. and G.C. Means (1932) *The Modern Corporation and Private Property* (New York: Macmillan).
Bowles, S., D. Gordon and T. Weisskopf (1983) *Beyond the Waste Land* (Garden City, NY: Anchor Press).
Brown, D.M. (1985) 'Institutionalism, Critical Theory, and the Administered Society', *Journal of Economic Issues*, 19 (June), pp. 559–66.
Brown, D.M. (1988) *Towards a Radical Democracy* (London: Unwin Hyman).
Carson, R. (1962) *Silent Spring* (Boston: Houghton Mifflin).
Clark, J.M. (1940) 'Toward a Concept of Workable Competition', *American Economic Review*, 30 (June), pp. 241–56.
Clarke, S. (1989) *Keynesianism, Monetarism and the Crisis of the State* (Brookfield, VT: Gower).
Commons, J.R. (1934) *Institutional Economics* (New York: Macmillan).
Dewey, J. (1948) *Reconstruction in Philosophy* (Boston: Beacon) enlarged edn.
Dewey, J. (1960) *The Quest for Certainty* (New York: Capricorn Press).
Dewey, J. (1963) *Liberalism and Social Action* (New York: Capricorn Press).
Dillard. D. (1987) 'Money as an Institution of Capitalism', *Journal of Economic Issues*, 21 (December), pp. 1623–47.
Dugger, W.M. (1989) *Corporate Hegemony* (New York: Greenwood Press).

Dugger, W.M. (1992a) *Underground Economics: A Decade of Institutionalist Dissent* (Armonk, NY: M.E. Sharpe).

Dugger, W.M. (1992b) 'The Great Retrenchment and the New Industrial State', *Review of Social Economy*, 50 (December), pp. 453–71.

Dugger, W.M. (ed.) (1989) *Radical Institutionalism* (New York: Greenwood Press).

Dugger, W.M. and W.T. Waller, Jr (eds) (1992) *The Stratified State* (Armonk, NY: M.E. Sharpe).

Edsall, T.B. (1984) *The New Politics of Inequality* (New York: Norton).

Eichner, A.S. (1983) 'Why Economics is not Yet a Science', in A.S. Eichner (ed.), *Why Economics is not Yet a Science* (Armonk, NY: M.E. Sharpe) pp. 205–40.

Ekelund, R.B., Jr, and D.S. Saurman (1988) *Advertising and the Market Process* (San Francisco: Pacific Research Institute for Public Policy).

Ferguson, D. (1993) 'New Keynesian Theories of Unemployment: Toward a New Consensus on Stabilization Policy', M.A. Technical Paper, Colorado State University.

Galbraith, J.K. (1946) 'Reflections on Price Control', *Quarterly Journal of Economics*, 60 (August), pp. 475–89.

Galbraith, J.K. (1947) 'The Disequilibrium System', *American Economic Review*, 37 (June), pp. 287–302.

Galbraith, J.K. (1951) 'The Strategy of Direct Control in Economic Mobilization', *Review of Economics and Statistics*, 33 (February), pp. 12–17.

Galbraith, J.K. (1952a) *A Theory of Price Control* (Cambridge, MA: Harvard University Press).

Galbraith, J.K. (1952b) *American Capitalism: The Concept of Countervailing Power* (Boston: Houghton Mifflin) (Sentry edn. 1956).

Galbraith, J.K. (1954a) *The Great Crash* (Boston: Houghton Mifflin).

Galbraith, J.K. (1954b) 'Countervailing Power', *American Economic Review*, 44 (May), pp. 1–6.

Galbraith, J.K. (1955) *Economics and the Art of Controversy* (Rutgers, NJ: Rutgers University Press).

Galbraith, J.K. (1957) 'Market Structure and Stabilization Policy', *Review of Economics and Statistics*, 39 (May), pp. 124–33.

Galbraith, J.K. (1958) *The Affluent Society* (Boston: Houghton Mifflin).

Galbraith, J.K. (1960) *The Liberal Hour* (Boston: Houghton Mifflin).

Galbraith, J.K. (1961) 'Economic Power and the Survival of Capitalism', in S. Tsuru (ed.), *Has Capitalism Changed?* (Tokyo: Iwanami Shoten) pp. 167–81.

Galbraith, J.K. (1964a) *Economic Development* (Boston: Houghton Mifflin).

Galbraith, J.K. (1964b) *The Scotch* (Boston: Houghton Mifflin).

Galbraith, J.K. (1967) *The New Industrial State* (Boston: Houghton Mifflin) (Subsequent edns in 1971, 1978, and 1985).

Galbraith, J.K. (1969) *How to Control the Military* (New York: New American Library).

Galbraith, J.K. (1970a) 'Economics as a System of Belief', *American Economic Review*, 60 (May).

Galbraith, J.K. (1970b) 'Who's Minding the Store?', in P. Nobile (ed.), *The Con III Controversy* (New York: Pocket Books) pp. 18–20.

Galbraith, J.K. (1971a) *Economics, Peace and Laughter* (Boston: Houghton Mifflin).

Galbraith, J.K. (1971b) 'Who's Minding the Store?', in P. Nobile (ed.), *The Con III Controversy: The Critics Look at the Greening of America* (New York: Pocket Books) pp. 18–20.

Galbraith, J.K. (1973a) 'Power and the Useful Economist', *American Economic Review*, 63 (March), pp. 1–11.

Galbraith, J.K. (1973b) *Economics and the Public Purpose* (Boston: Houghton Mifflin).

Galbraith, J.K. (1973c) *A China Passage* (Boston: Houghton Mifflin).

Galbraith, J.K. (1975) *Money* (Boston: Houghton Mifflin).

Galbraith, J.K. (1977) *The Age of Uncertainty* (Boston: Houghton Mifflin).

Galbraith, J.K. (1979a) 'Social Balance and the Tax Revolt', Southwest Social Science Association meeting, March.

Galbraith, J.K. (1979b) 'How to Get Ahead', *The New York Review*, 26 (July 19), pp. 4–6.

Galbraith, J.K. (1979c) *Annals of an Abiding Liberal* (Boston: Houghton Mifflin).

Galbraith, J.K. (1981) *A Life in Our Time* (Boston: Houghton Mifflin).

Galbraith, J.K. (1983) *The Anatomy of Power* (Boston: Houghton Mifflin).

Galbraith, J.K. (1984) *The Affluent Society*, 4th edn (Boston: Houghton Mifflin).

Galbraith, J.K. (1985) *The New Industrial State*, 4th edn (Boston: Houghton Mifflin).

Galbraith, J.K. (1986) *A View from the Stands* (Boston: Houghton Mifflin).

Galbraith, J.K. (1987) *Economics in Perspective* (Boston: Houghton Mifflin).

Galbraith, J.K. (1992) *The Culture of Contentment* (Boston: Houghton Mifflin).

Galbraith, J.K. (1993) *A Short History of Financial Euphoria* (New York: Penguin).

Galbraith, J.K. (1994) *A Journey Through Economic Time: A Firsthand View* (Boston: Houghton Mifflin).

Galbraith, J.K., and N. Salinger (1978) *Almost Everyone's Guide To Economics* (Boston: Houghton Mifflin).

Gambs, John S. (1975) *John Kenneth Galbraith* (Boston: Twayne Publishers).

Gruchy, A.G. (1949) 'J.M. Keynes' Concept of Economic Science', *Southern Economic Journal*, 15 (January), pp. 249–66.

Gruchy, A.G. (1967) *Modern Economic Thought* (New York: A.M. Kelley).

Gruchy, A.G. (1972) *Contemporary Economic Thought* (New York: A.M. Kelley) ch. 4 on JKG.

Hamilton, W.H. (1919) 'The Institutional Approach to Economic Theory', *American Economic Review*, 9 (March), pp. 309–18.

Hamilton, W.H. (1957) *The Politics of Industry* (New York: A.A. Knopf).

Harrington, M. (1962) *The Other America* (New York: Macmillan).

Harrington, M. (1966) *The Accidental Century* (Baltimore, MD: Penguin).

Hayek, F.A. (1944) *The Road To Serfdom* (Chicago: University of Chicago).

Heilbroner, R.L. (1970) *Between Capitalsim and Socialism* (New York: Random House).

Heilbroner, R.L. (1974) *An Inquiry into the Human Prospect* (New York: Norton).

Heilbroner, R.L. (1981) *Marxism: For and Against* (New York: Norton).

Heilbroner, R.L. (1985) *The Nature and Logic of Capitalism* (New York: Norton).

Heilbroner, R.L. (1986) *The Worldly Philosophers* (New York: Simon and Schuster).

Heilbroner, R.L. (1992) 'Is a Worldly Philosophy Still Possible?: Adolph Lowe as Analyst and Visionary', *Review of Social Economy*, 50 (Winter), pp. 374–82.

Hession, C.H. (1972) *John Kenneth Galbraith and His Critics* (New York: New American Library).

Hirsch, F. (1976) *The Social Limits to Growth* (Cambridge, MA: Harvard University Press).

Hutchison, T.W. (1981) *The Politics and Philosophy of Economics* (New York: New York University Press) ch. 3 on Camb.

Kash, D.E. (1989) *Perpetual Innovation* (New York: Basic Books).

Kern, W.S. (1982) 'The Implications of Limited Knowledge: The Economic and Social Philosophy of Friedrich A. Hayek', Ph.D. dissertation, Colorado State University, Fort Collins, Colorado.

Keynes, J.M. (1963) *Essays in Persuasion* (New York: W.W. Norton).

Kindleberger, C. (1978) *Manias, Panics, and Crashes* (New York: Basic Books).

King, P.G. and Woodyard, D.O. (1982) *The Journey Toward Freedom* (London: Associated University Presses).

Klein, P.A. (1987) 'Power and Economic Performance: The Institutionalist View', *Journal of Economic Issues*, 21 (September), pp. 1341–77.

Kornai, J. (1992) *The Socialist System* (Princeton, NJ: Princeton University Press).

Kottke, F.J. (1954) 'Fundamentals of the American Economy: Discussion', *American Economic Review*, 44 (May), pp. 26–34.

Kotz, D.M. (1978) *Bank Control of Large Corporations in the United States* (Berkeley: University of California Press).

Kristol, I. (1967) 'Professor Galbraith's New Industrial State', *Fortune* (July), pp. 190–5.

Kuhn, T.S. (1970) *The Structure of Scientific Revolutions*, 2nd edn (Chicago: University of Chicago Press).

Kuttner, R. (1987) *The Life of the Party* (New York: Penguin).

Lamson, P. (1991) *Speaking of Galbraith* (Boston: Houghton Mifflin).

Leiss, W. (1976) *The Limits to Satisfaction* (Toronto: University of Toronto Press).

Lowe, A. (1966) *On Economic Knowledge: Toward a Science of Political Economics* (New York: Harper & Row). Second enlarged edn, 1983 (Armonk, NY: M.E. Sharpe).

Lowe, A. (1988) *Has Freedom a Future?* (New York: Praeger).

McClintock, B.T. (1990) 'International Economic Policy and the Welfare State', Ph.D. dissertation, Colorado State University, Fort Collins, Colorado.

Maccoby, M. (1976) *The Gamesman* (New York: Simon & Schuster).

Markowitz, N.D. (1973) *The Rise and Fall of the People's Century* (New York: Free Press).

Marx, K. (1967) *Capital*, vols V. I, II, III (New York: International Publishers).

Mill, J.S. (1924) *Autobiography of John Stuart Mill* (New York: Columbia University Press).

Mill, J.S. (1985) *Principles of Political Economy* (New York: Penguin).

Miller, J.P. (1954) 'Competition and Countervailing Power: Their Roles in the American Economy', *American Economic Review*, 44 (May), pp. 15–25.

Minsky, H.P. (1986) *Stabilizing an Unstable Economy* (New Haven: Yale University Press).

Munkirs, J.R. (1985) *The Transformation of American Capitalism* (Armonk, NY: M.E. Sharpe).

Munro, C.L. (1977) *The Galbraithian Vision: The Cultural Criticism of John Kenneth Galbraith* (Washington, DC: University Press of America).

North, D.C. (1977) 'Markets and Other Allocation Systems in History: The Challenge of Karl Polanyi', *Journal of European Economic History*, 6 (Winter), pp. 703–16.

North, D.C. (1990) *Institutions, Institutional Change and Economic Performance* (New York: Cambridge University Press).

O'Connor, J. (1973) *The Fiscal Crisis of the State* (New York: St. Martin's Press).

Okun, A. (1975) *Equality and Efficiency: The Big Tradeoff* (Washington, DC: Brookings).

Papandreou, A. (1972) *Paternalistic Capitalism* (Minneapolis: University of Minnesota Press).

Patten, S.N. (1968) *The New Basis of Civilization* (Cambridge, MA: Harvard University Press).

Peach, J.T. (1987) 'Distribution and Economic Progress', *Journal of Economic Issues*, 21 (December), pp. 1495–529.

Phelps, E.S. (ed.) (1965) *Private Wants and Public Needs: An Introduction to a Current Issue of Public Policy*, rev. edn (New York: W.W. Norton and Co.).

Phillips, R.J. (1988) 'Veblen and Simons on Credit and Monetary Reform', *Southern Economic Journal*, 55 (July), pp. 171–81.

Polanyi, K. (1944) *The Great Transformation* (New York: Rinehart). Pb. edn (1957) (Boston: Beacon).

Polanyi, K. (1968) *Primitive, Archaic, and Modern Economies*. Ed. by G. Dalton (Garden City, NY: Doubleday).

Potter, D.M. (1954) *People of Plenty* (Chicago: University of Chicago Press).

Ranson, B. (1987) 'The Institutionalist Theory of Capital Formation', *Journal of Economic Issues*, 21 (September), pp. 1265–78.

Reich, Charles (1970) *The Greening of America* (New York: Random House).

Reisman, D. (1980) *Galbraith and Market Capitalism* (New York: New York University Press).

Reisman, D.A. (1990) 'Galbraith on Ideas and Events', *Journal of Economic Issues*, 24 (September), pp. 733–60.

Robson, W.A. (1976) *Welfare State and Welfare Society* (London: George Allen & Unwin).

Robinson, J. (1972) 'The Second Crisis of Economic Theory', *American Economic Review*, 62 (May), pp. 1–10.

Samuelson, P.A. (1964) *Economics: An Introductory Analysis*, 6th edn (New York: McGraw-Hill).

Schor, J.B. (1991) *The Overworked American: The Unexpected Decline of Leisure* (New York: Basic Books).

Schudson, M. (1984) *Advertising, the Uneasy Persuasion* (New York: Basic Books).

Schumpeter, J.A. (1950) *History of Economic Analysis* (New York: Oxford University Press).

Schumpeter, J.A. (1962) *Capitalism, Socialism, and Democracy*, 3rd edn (New York: Harper & Row).

Schweitzer, A. (1954) 'A Critique of Countervailing Power', *Social Research*, 21 (October), pp. 353–85.

Sharpe, M.E. (1972) *John Kenneth Galbraith and the Lower Economics* (White Plains, NY: International Arts and Sciences Press).

Shulman, S.J. (1987) 'Discrimination, Human Capital and Black–White Unemployment: Evidence from Cities', *Journal of Human Resources*, 22 (Summer).

Solow, R.M. (1967) 'The New Industrial State or Son of Affluence', *The Public Interest*, (Fall), pp. 100–8.

Sraffa, P. (1926) 'The Laws of Returns Under Competitive Conditions', *Economic Journal*, 36, pp. 535–50.

Stanfield, J.R. (1979) *Economic Thought and Social Change* (Carbondale, IL: Southern Illinois University Press).

Stanfield, J.R. (1981) 'The Instructive Vision of John Maurice Clark', *Review of Social Economy*, 39 (December), pp. 279–87.

Stanfield, J.R. (1986) *The Economic Thought of Karl Polanyi* (London: Macmillan Press and New York: St. Martin's Press).

Stanfield, J.R. (1990) 'Keynesianism, Monetarism, and the Crisis of the State: A Review Article', *Journal of Economic Issues*, 24 (December), pp. 1139–46.

Stanfield, J.R. (1992) 'The Fund for Social Change', in J. Davis (ed.), *The Economic Surplus in Advanced Economies* (Brookfield, VT: Edward Elgar) pp. 130–48.

Stanfield, J.R. (1994) 'Learning from Japan about the Nurturance Gap in America', *Review of Social Economy*, 52 (Spring), pp. 2–19.

Stanfield, J.R. (1995a) *Economics, Power, and Culture* (London: Macmillan and New York: St. Martin's).

Stanfield, J.R. (1995b) 'Institutions and the Significance of Relative Prices', *Journal of Economic Issues*, 14 (June).

Stanfield, J.R. and R.J. Phillips (1991) 'Economic Power, Financial Instability, and the Cuomo Report', *Journal of Economic Issues*, 25 (June), pp. 347–54.

Stanfield, J.R. and J.B. Stanfield (1980) 'Consumption in Contemporary Capitalism: The Backward Art of Living', *Journal of Economic Issues*, 14 (June), pp. 437–50.

Stanfield, J.R. and J.B. Stanfield (1995) 'Where Has Love Gone? Reciprocity and the Nurturance Gap', International Association for Feminist Economics, Washington, DC.

Sternsher, B. (1964) *Rexford Tugwell and the New Deal* (New Brunswick, NJ: Rutgers University Press).

Stigler, G.J. (1954) 'The Economist Plays with Blocs', *American Economic Review*, 44 (May), pp. 7–14.

Stone, E.D. (1959) 'The Case Against the Tailfin Age', *New York Times* (October 18).

Street, J.H. (1987) 'The Institutionalist Theory of Economic Development', *Journal of Economic Issues*, 21 (December), pp. 1861–87.

Sweezy, P.M. (1972) 'Comment', *Quarterly Journal of Economics*, 86 (November), p. 661.

Tabb, W.K. (1980) 'Playing "Productivity" Politics', *The Nation*, 230 (January 5–12), pp. 1, 15–19.

Thurow, L. (1992) *Head to Head* (New York: William Morrow).

Tilman, R. (1987) 'The Neoinstrumental Theory of Democracy', *Journal of Economic Issues*, 21 (September), pp. 1379–401.

Tool, M.R. (1979) *The Discretionary Economy* (Santa Monica, CA: Goodyear Press).

Veblen, T.B. (n.d.) *The Theory of Business Enterprise* (New York: New American Library).

Veblen, T.B. (1948) 'Why is Economics Not an Evolutionary Science?', in M. Lerner (ed.), *The Portable Veblen* (New York: The Viking Press).

Veblen, T.B. (1953) *The Theory of the Leisure Class* (New York: New American Library).

Veblen, T.B. (1963) *The Engineers and the Price System* (New York: Harcourt, Brace, & World).

Ward, B. (1972) *What's Wrong with Economics?* (New York: Basic Books).

Ward, B. (1979) *The Liberal Economic World View* (New York: Basic Books).

Wheatley-Mann, K. (1986) 'Engels and Veblen on the Oppression of Women', M.A. Technical Paper, Colorado State University.

Wilber, C.K. and R.S. Harrison (1978) 'The Methodological Basis of Institutional Economics: Pattern Model, Storytelling, and Holism', *Journal of Economic Issues*, 12 (March), pp. 61–89.

Wray, L.R. (1990) *Money and Credit in Capitalist Economies* (Brookfield, VT: Edward Elgar).

Wright, D.M. (1954) 'Discussion', *American Economic Review*, 44 (May), pp. 26–34.

Zebot, C.A. (1959) 'Economics of Affluence', *Review of Social Economy*, 17 (September), pp. 112–25.

Index

active labor market policies, 93,
144–5, 170
see also structural policy
Adams, W., 37, 113, 170
administered prices, 23, 27, 34, 64,
70, 74, 76, 94, 138, 140, 141,
171
administered sector, 6–7, 28, 38, 66,
69–85, 90, 91, 93–6, 99–103,
107–13, 118, 121, 123, 124, 126,
127–30, 135–9, 142–4, 146, 147,
150, 151, 169
administered economy, *see*
administered society
administered society, 14, 32, 51,
61–85, 87, 91, 97, 102, 105,
115, 120–4, 143, 166, 171
adverse selection, 21, 99
advertising, 5, 6, 7, 27, 30, 38, 45–8,
49, 64, 68, 73, 76, 79, 81, 83,
109, 112, 169–70
see also dependence effect; revised
sequence; want formation
affirmation of humanness, 20, 147–50
affirmative action, 79, 148, 164
Affluent Society, The, 1, 3–6, 15, 17,
19, 38, 41–3, 45, 46, 48–54,
56–9, 61, 84, 96, 116, 118
Age of Uncertainty, The, 3, 16
alienation, 20, 47, 66, 158, 165–6
ambiguity of costs, 27, 64
see also administered society
ambiguity of wants, 20, 38–9, 43–8, 125
see also want formation; Leiss;
revised sequence; administered
society
American Capitalism, 2, 5, 15, 19,
25–39, 52, 57
Anatomy of Power, The, 8
antitrust policy, 14, 26, 35, 68, 83,
122, 144, 149
Averitt, R., 129
Ayres, C.E., 5, 36, 47, 58, 102, 103,
131, 134, 155, 159, 160–1

Balogh, T., 170
Baran, P.A., 5, 7, 13, 20, 23, 51, 62,
81, 131, 156
Barkin, S., 66
Berle, A.A., 75
Bowles, S., 1, 38, 62, 167
Brady, R., 2
Brown, D.M., 42
Buchanan, J., 107
Buckley, W.F., 12
built environment, 96, 168
bureaucratic symbiosis, 116
see also co-opted state
Burns, A.F., 11
Bush, G.H.W., 53, 54

Cambridge School, 29, 64, 163
Carson, R., 53
Carter, J., 11, 33, 54
Clark, J.M., 109
Clarke, S., 38, 165
classical liberalism, 15, 30, 44, 45,
52, 68, 98, 107, 164–5
Clay, L., 16
co-opted state, 115–18
commodity fetishism, 48, 166
see also alienation; want formation
Commons, J.R., 154
constructivism, 98
convenient social virtue, 102, 157
conventional economics, 7–8, 25–33,
56–8, 67, 70–1, 83, 85, 102,
103–7, 111, 113, 115, 117–24,
127, 129–30, 133, 156–7
see also neoclassical synthesis;
conventional wisdom
conventional wisdom, 1, 42–3, 49,
56–9, 64, 111, 129, 130, 146,
155–6
see also institutional lag;
conventional economics;
neoclassical synthesis
countervailing power, 1, 4–5, 19, 25, 31,
33–7, 40, 74, 135, 136, 150, 159

181

McClintock, B.T., 171
McGovern, G., 4
Means, G., 75
mergers and acquisitions, 7, 20–2,
    26–7, 33, 79, 112, 170
methodological collectivism and
    individualism, 164–5
    see also ambiguity of wants; want
    formation
military industry, 9–10, 48, 51, 57–8,
    80–1, 96–7, 101–2, 106, 114–15,
    116
military-industrial complex, *see*
    military industry
Mill, J.S., 41, 42, 162–4, 169
Minsky, H., 20, 23, 24, 37, 49, 75,
    92, 135, 145
modern liberalism, 19, 37–8, 44,
    55–6, 59, 68, 98, 130, 153,
    162–5, 169
monetary policy, *see* economic
    stabilization policy
Money, 8
Monopoly Capital, 5, 7, 30, 34, 58,
    62, 109
    see also Baran; Sweezy
multi-culturalism, 100
Munkirs, J., 170

natural rate of inflation, 140
neo-Keynesian economics, *see*
    neoclassical synthesis
neoclassical synthesis, 5, 14, 24, 28,
    32, 36, 37, 47, 57, 103, 119,
    120, 122, 129, 148, 162
    see also conventional economics
New Deal, 3, 5, 13, 135, 162
New Industrial State, The, 4, 6–7, 19,
    39, 51, 57, 58, 61–102, 103, 111,
    115–16, 125, 143, 155, 158, 168
New Keynesian economics, 89, 162
Nixon, R.M., 10, 11, 168
North, D.C., 64, 99, 105, 124, 141,
    145, 151, 170
Novak, R., 12
nurturance gap, 55, 145

O'Connor, J., 53
Okun, A., 110

oligopoly, 19, 21–3, 30–1, 33–4,
    69–71, 134–5

Paine, T., 162
Papandreou, A., 8, 61, 85
path dependence, *see* cumulative
    causation
Patten, S.N., 42, 159
pattern-modelling method, 68
Phillips, R.J., 20, 23, 48, 64
place of economy in society, 71, 88,
    95, 97, 130, 133, 141
Polanyi, K., 41, 45, 56, 59, 68, 88,
    95, 127, 130–2, 158
political asymmetry, of fiscal policy,
    36, 164
Potter, D., 42
poverty, 39, 41, 50, 53, 147, 163

radical positivism, *see* evolutionary
    positivism
Randall, C., 9
Ranson, B., 30, 141, 145, 157
Reagan, R., 33, 53, 54, 120
Reich, C., 169
revised sequence, 6–7, 27–8, 45,
    47–8, 54–5, 71, 83–5, 126
    see also dependence effect; imagery
    of choice; want formation
Ricardo, D., 162
Robinson, J., 23, 27, 29, 165
Rogin, L., 2
Ruskin, J., 84

Samuelson, P.A., 1, 14, 28, 136
Saurman, D.S., 64, 170
saving-centered theory of economic
    progress, 28–30, 53, 57–8, 145,
    157, 161
Say's Law, 89
Schlesinger, A., 42
Schor, J., 55, 149
Schudson, M., 47, 64, 170
Schumpeter, J.A., 13, 15, 31, 109
Schweitzer, A., 37
scientific and intellectual estate,
    99–102, 159
scientific separatism, 101–2
scientism, 98